The Buried Foundation of the Gilgamesh Epic

Cuneiform Monographs

Edited by
T. Abusch — M. J. Geller
S. M. Maul — F. A. M. Wiggermann

VOLUME 39

The Buried Foundation of the Gilgamesh Epic

The Akkadian Huwawa Narrative

Daniel E. Fleming
Sara J. Milstein

SBL Press
Atlanta

Library of Congress Cataloging-in-Publication Data
Fleming, Daniel E. author.
  The buried foundation of the Gilgamesh Epic : the Akkadian Huwawa narra-
tive by / Daniel E. Fleming and Sara J. Milstein.
    pages cm. — (Cuneiform monographs; Volume 39)
  Includes bibliographical references and index.
  ISBN 978-1-62837-032-4 (paper binding : alk. paper)
1. Gilgamesh. 2. Epic poetry, Assyro-Babylonian—History and criticism. 3.
Assyriology—History. I. Milstein, Sara J. (Sara Jessica), 1978- author. II. Title.
  PJ3771.G6F57 2014
  892'.1—dc23
                        2014036335

"He has seen the path,
he has traveled the road.
[He knows] the entrances to the forest
(and) all the plots of Huwawa."

Yale VI 252–254

CONTENTS

ABBREVIATIONS

AHw   W. von Soden. *Akkadisches Handwörterbuch*. 3 vols. Wiesbaden: Harrassowitz, 1963–1981

AOAT   Alter Orient und Altes Testament

ARM   Archives Royales de Mari

ASJ   *Acta Sumerologica*

AuOr   *Aula Orientalis*

BCSMS   Bulletin. *The Canadian Society for Mesopotamian Studies*

CAD   I.J. Gelb et al. eds. *The Assyrian Dictionary of the Oriental Institute of the University of Chicago*. Chicago: Oriental Institute, 1956–

CRRAI   Compte Rendu de la Rencontre Assyriologique Internationale

CT   Cuneiform Texts from Babylonian Tablets in the British Museum

FM   *Florilegium Marianum*

JANES   *Journal of the Ancient Near Eastern Society of Columbia University*

JAOS   *Journal of the American Oriental Society*

JCS   *Journal of Cuneiform Studies*

KBo   Keilschrifttexte aus Boghazköi

LAPO   Littératures Anciennes du Proche-Orient

MB   Middle Babylonian (Akkadian)

MVAG   Mitteilungen der Vorderasiatisch-Aegyptischen Gesellschaft

N.A.B.U.   *Notes assyriologiques brèves et utilitaires*

OB   Old Babylonian (Akkadian)

OBO   Orbis Biblicus et Orientalis

RA   *Revue d'assyriologie et d'archéologie orientale*

SAK   Studien zur Altägyptischen Kultur

SB   Standard Babylonian (Akkadian)

SBV   Standard Babylonian Version (of the Gilgamesh Epic)

WAW   Writings of the Ancient World

ZA   *Zeitschrift für Assyriologie und Vorderasiatische Archäologie*

TABLE 1

EARLY SECOND-MILLENNIUM GILGAMESH NARRATIVE

Sumerian Compositions[1]

Gilgamesh and Huwawa, version A
Gilgamesh and Huwawa, version B
Gilgamesh and the Bull of Heaven
Gilgamesh and Aga
Gilgamesh, Enkidu, and the Netherworld
The Death of Gilgamesh

Akkadian Texts[2]

Penn	Six-column "Tablet II" of *šūtur eli šarrī* series, 240 lines; found at Larsa?; in University Museum of Philadelphia.
Yale	Six-column tablet, part of same series as Penn, roughly 295 lines; found at Larsa?; in Babylonian Collection of Yale University.
UM	Fragment of multi-column tablet for part of series, roughly 20 lines partly visible; uncertain origin; in University Museum of Philadelphia.
Schøyen-1	Single-column extract, 13 lines partly preserved; uncertain origin; in private collection.
Schøyen-2	Single-column extract, 84 lines mostly visible; uncertain origin; in private collection.
Schøyen-3	Proposed as one tablet from numerous small fragments; single-column extract; uncertain origin; in private collection.
Nippur	Single-column extract, 25 lines mostly visible; from House F at Nippur; in Iraq Museum of Baghdad.
Harmal-1	Single-column extract, all 17 lines preserved; from Shaduppum; in Iraq Museum of Baghdad.

---

[1] Titles match those found in Oxford's on-line Electronic Text Corpus of Sumerian Literature (etcsl.orinst.ox.ac.uk).

[2] The texts are listed according to Andrew George, *The Babylonian Gilgamesh Epic: Introduction, Critical Edition and Cuneiform Texts* (Oxford: Oxford University Press, 2003), in which they follow the narrative sequence.

Harmal-2   Single-column extract, roughly 63 lines, poorly preserved; from
           Shaduppum; in Iraq Museum of Baghdad.
Ishchali   Single-column extract, 45 lines partly preserved; from Nerebtum;
           in Oriental Institute Museum of Chicago.
IM   Single-column extract, roughly 40 lines partly visible; uncertain
           origin; in Iraq Museum of Baghdad.
Sippar   Four-column tablet, originally 180 lines, slightly less than half
           of these visible; found at Sippar?; two fragments joined but left
           separate at British Museum of London and Vorderasiatisches
           Museum of Berlin.

TABLE 2

RECONSTRUCTED RELATIONSHIPS BETWEEN EARLY SECOND-MILLENNIUM GILGAMESH COMPOSITIONS

Stage I. *Sumerian Gilgamesh and Huwawa tale*

All Sumerian and Akkadian evidence for Gilgamesh and Huwawa comes from the early second millennium, so even the existence of a Sumerian story that preceded the attested Akkadian must be hypothetical. The Sumerian version B is shorter than version A and has little in common with the Akkadian, so it appears to reflect a Sumerian tradition without influence from Akkadian Huwawa material.

Stage II. *Reconstructed Akkadian Huwawa narrative*

Prior to composition of the Old Babylonian Gilgamesh Epic, the Sumerian Huwawa tale inspired an Akkadian rendition that radically recast the characters and plot. Ten of twelve early second-millennium Akkadian Gilgamesh tablets treat the Huwawa adventure: Yale, UM, Schøyen-1, Schøyen-2, Schøyen-3, Nippur, Harmal-1, Harmal-2, Ishchali, and IM. These show fluidity of textual form, yet the underlying perspective contrasts consistently with the Gilgamesh tablets before and after the Huwawa narrative. The introduction of the Akkadian Huwawa narrative is lost, supplanted by the longer introduction reflected in Penn, as the whole narrative was replaced by the epic.

Stage IIIa. *Old Babylonian Gilgamesh Epic (partially preserved)*	Stage IIIb. *Revised Sumerian Gilgamesh and Huwawa tale*
A long Gilgamesh Epic with episodes before and after the Huwawa episode is known as a complete narrative from the first millennium and attested with almost all of its parts in Hittite paraphrase from the 14th–13th centuries. Two early second-millennium tablets prove that the epic already existed in this period, one set before Huwawa (Penn) and the other after (Sippar). The Penn and Yale tablets were produced by the same scribe, showing that Yale was copied as part of this OB epic, and most (if not all) of the Akkadian Huwawa texts most likely assume the epic's existence as well. Yale columns I and II represent a rewritten bridge between the new epic introduction and the received Huwawa tale, which was generally left unaltered.	The Sumerian Gilgamesh and Huwawa version A shares traits with the Akkadian Huwawa material that suggest cross-pollination, if not one-way influence. Version A became the standard Sumerian Huwawa tale studied in Nippur scribal schools and elsewhere, as found in copies contemporary with the OB epic. This Sumerian version was recast with knowledge of the Akkadian Huwawa narrative, and no detail demonstrates the impact of material specific to the extended epic.

FOREWORD

This project had its genesis in the fall of 2005 in an Akkadian seminar taught by Daniel Fleming at New York University, in which the following students participated: Sara Milstein, Ian Case, Cory Peacock, and Nathanael Shelley. After reading the Pennsylvania tablet ("Tablet II") of the Old Babylonian Gilgamesh Epic, we moved naturally to the Yale tablet ("Tablet III"), where Gilgamesh and Enkidu set out to confront Huwawa, the fearsome guardian of the Cedar Forest. Given that Yale belongs to the same series as Penn, we expected to find continuity from one tablet to the next, and our task was to search for connections across the texts in terms of content, language, and orthography. What we found, however, was not what we expected. At just those points where Yale appeared to recall events that were described in Penn, the details did not match up. The more we read, the more we came to the realization that Yale did not necessarily assume the storyline of the Penn tablet. But how could this be, given that the two belonged to the same series, and were even copied by the same scribe?

In the spring of 2006, Sara Milstein wrote a paper on the narrative logic of the Yale tablet alone, if read without assuming the contents of Penn, and this project led to the two of us presenting joint papers at the 2007 Meeting of the American Oriental Society in San Antonio, Texas, on the limited issue of how Penn and Yale were related. Without addressing all of the Old Babylonian evidence or the Sumerian Gilgamesh texts, we tentatively proposed that the Gilgamesh Epic had to have been preceded by a previous Akkadian narrative that included at least the expedition to the Cedar Forest. Feedback at the meeting was both enthusiastic and hesitant. The notion that the Old Babylonian Gilgamesh Epic, that brilliant creation of the early second millennium, had a hitherto unnoticed literary precursor was not going to go down easy. We welcomed the questions and challenges, and over the course of the next few months, set out to address them, one by one.

A systematic study would have to account for all of the early second-millennium Gilgamesh evidence, of which there are at present a total of twelve Akkadian tablets and numerous copies of Sumerian tales. In particular, what we call the "Sippar" tablet represents the only Old Babylonian text that follows the trip to combat Huwawa, and it showed striking correlations with the language and perspective of Penn. The remaining Akkadian material for the Huwawa adventure offered a consistent contrast to what preceded and followed, suggesting the possibility of a separate Huwawa-focused narrative. Moreover, the two Sumerian versions of Gilgamesh and Huwawa demonstrated that the Huwawa "episode" could exist on its own as an independent tale. One version of the Sumerian Huwawa tale was the most widely copied Gilgamesh tale, with nearly one hundred copies attested for Babylonia. The Old Babylonian evidence confirmed the priority of the Huwawa adventure in early second-millennium scribal interest in Gilgamesh, with ten of the twelve tablets related to this tale. To our delight, the Sumerian and Akkadian evidence converged. When second-millennium scribes were copying Gilgamesh texts, they were copying the Huwawa story more than anything else, whatever the language. In this broader context, our solution to the problem was beginning to make sense.

For both of us, this was our first full-scale joint project, which posed its own set of advantages and challenges. We started by dividing up sections to write, and then handed these sections over to one another for thorough revision. After several rounds of revision, we swapped responsibilities, so that we were now accountable for those sections that we had not written originally. This was accompanied by numerous conversations about the project, which constantly informed our writing. It was important that we were always on the same page, that our newest discoveries and revelations were incorporated into every section of the book. At each juncture where we disagreed, one had to convince the other that his/her argument was more tenable. What emerged was a truly collaborative project, with every page of the book the product of collective thought.

In order to follow our argument, we felt it was necessary to provide the reader with a fresh translation of all of the second-millennium evidence that related directly to our hypothesis, Sumerian and Akkadian. Andrew George's foundational edition, *The Babylonian Gilgamesh Epic*, remains an invaluable resource, and the reader is directed there for the Akkadian transliterations as well as for extensive and thoughtful discussions of all Akkadian Gilgamesh evidence. It goes unsaid that translation reflects interpretation, and our sense that the Yale tablet and the nine other "Huwawa texts" do not assume the logic of the Penn tablet informed our translations of key sections in the Akkadian Gilgamesh material. With our translations, we hope first and foremost to offer readers access to the Huwawa texts on their own terms, as the first preserved expressions of Gilgamesh in Akkadian.

We are aware that our approach to the Old Babylonian Gilgamesh material involves the postulation of a narrative that cannot yet be proven to exist as a separate text in Akkadian, and this is not common practice in Assyriology. As a rule, Assyriologists base their analyses of literary expansion on hard evidence, namely, multiple copies of the same work deriving from different time periods. The birth of Akkadian literature in the early second millennium, however, presents a particular problem. Many tales in both Sumerian and Akkadian are first attested in this period without adequate evidence to track either their variability or their antecedents. More than any other body of related material, the Gilgamesh texts in both languages allow exploration of these questions through comparing roughly contemporaneous evidence. As we began our work, marked contrasts between the Huwawa-oriented texts on the one hand and the Penn and Sippar tablets on the other compelled us to seek some sort of explanation. We do not presume that we can reconstruct every detail of an "original" Akkadian Huwawa narrative. What we do propose, however, is that we have discovered a new way of looking at this hoary text, a way that illuminates the logic of the Gilgamesh story at an earlier phase of its existence. In coming to the Old Babylonian Gilgamesh material afresh, we found ourselves discovering another voice buried beneath the final form. We only hope that our effort will inspire future readers to revisit the material with open eyes, too, and to discover something new.

This project has benefited from the suggestions and support of several colleagues. Tzvi Abusch offered enthusiastic support from the very beginning, provided helpful feedback on the manuscript at multiple phases, and shepherded the volume through submission and editing for the Cuneiform Monographs series at Brill. Michiel Swormink and Jennifer Pavelko handled this process from the Brill side. Anne Porter and Cory Peacock read the manuscript at an early phase and offered important suggestions for its improvement and clarification. Sarah Graff not only offered reactions but was also instrumental in providing us with the terrific images of Huwawa reprinted in the book. Paul Delnero reviewed our final version of the introduction and offered essential insight into the Sumerian Gilgamesh and Huwawa A and into questions of textual transmission. As always, we are most thankful to and for our wonderful spouses, Aaron and Nancy, who have had to endure numerous conversations about Mesopotamian literary history. Dan cannot think about Gilgamesh without the constant memory of his advisor William Moran, for whom this text was an abiding delight. And I, Sara, would also like to acknowledge my beloved daughter Aviva, whose birth coincided with the first draft of the manuscript, and whose current pronunciation of her name, "A-wa-wa," sounds uncannily like the central figure of this book.

CHAPTER ONE

INTRODUCTION

The Epic of Gilgamesh is best known from its first-millennium rendition, the Standard Babylonian Version, a sequence of twelve tablets that detail the adventures of Gilgamesh, king of the Sumerian city of Uruk. The epic appears to have been composed in the early second millennium, however, and so the Old Babylonian (OB) period must be the focus of any exploration of its origins. Although we do not have access to the complete (or *a* complete) rendition of the OB epic, the existence of two tablets in particular confirm that a Gilgamesh Epic from this period existed on a smaller but no less impressive scale.[1] The six-column Pennsylvania Tablet ("Penn"), marked "Tablet II" of the series *šūtur eli šarrī*, "Surpassing above kings," covers the famed encounter between Gilgamesh, the aggressive king of Uruk, and Enkidu, his wild counterpart from the steppe. We then have the good fortune of having access to a copy of the third tablet in the same series, known as the Yale Tablet ("Yale"), which is also six columns long and shows evidence of having been produced by the same scribe.[2] In this tablet, which picks up where Penn leaves off, Gilgamesh persuades Enkidu to join him on an expedition to confront Huwawa, the fearsome guardian of the Cedar

---

[1] By the first millennium, reproduction of Gilgamesh seems to have settled into a more standardizing mode, with closer adherence to a fixed wording than is indicated for earlier copies. Even here, however, considerable variation is preserved in the available texts, and as much as twenty percent of the Standard Babylonian epic is still missing. As more tablets are discovered, the textual variability of the complete epic in its later form remains a constant consideration. For this issue and throughout our work, we benefit from the masterful and exhaustive publication of Andrew George, *The Babylonian Gilgamesh Epic: Introduction, Critical Edition and Cuneiform Texts* (Oxford: Oxford University Press, 2003). On "textual variants and recensional differences" in the Standard Babylonian epic, see pp. 419–431. George calls the term "epic" a "coinage of convenience" (p. 3), a coinage that we likewise retain.

[2] The Penn and Yale tablets were bought close to the same time from the same dealer. In his description of the two texts, George notes, "Very similar in clay, size and general appearance, they exhibit the same format of three columns on each side, the same orthographic conventions and, most importantly, they are inscribed in hands that are indistinguishable" (*Babylonian Gilgamesh Epic*, 159). Both tablets also have the unusual trait of clay lumps on the edges.

Forest. Given that Penn is marked Tablet II and that Yale concludes with the men just setting out for the forest, it is safe to say that this version of the epic would have covered at least four tablets, six columns apiece.

With good reason, Penn and Yale have generally been treated as deriving from the same authorial vision, notwithstanding the likelihood that these represent just one rendition of a text that could vary significantly in its reproduction.[3] In Penn, we are introduced to Gilgamesh, who is in the process of recounting two dreams that anticipate the arrival of Enkidu, his perfect match. In the second column of the tablet, the wild man Enkidu is ensconced with the harlot Shamkat, who informs him that he is like a god and should start behaving like one. She leads him to a shepherds' camp and introduces him to the trappings of civilization: clothing, bread, and beer. After this process of acculturation to life in human company, Enkidu heads to Uruk to confront the king, who, he has just learned, has been violating the brides of the city. The two engage in a ritualized wrestling match, which concludes with Enkidu's praise of Gilgamesh. In the next tablet, the two men form a partnership, apparently in the presence of the harlot.[4] Gilgamesh proposes an expedition to the Cedar Forest, and Enkidu, master of the steppe, promptly shoots down the idea. This exchange continues onto the reverse of Yale, until Enkidu finally concedes to serve as Gilgamesh's guide on the adventure. Gilgamesh then has them equip themselves with tools and weaponry before he sets out to persuade the citizenry and leadership of Uruk to endorse their plan. The tablets appear to fit neatly as two major components in an extended sequence. Penn closes with Enkidu's exaltation of Gilgamesh, whom he has just met, and although the first column of Yale is broken, it clearly opens with the two men in conversation, kissing and joining as partners. Penn exists to set up the relationship between

---

[3] George attributes original authorship of a coherent epic to the work of a poet who performed it without the involvement of scribes, so that even the earliest written text would have followed a long phase of oral transmission (*Babylonian Gilgamesh Epic*, 21). In spite of what he considers the probability of substantial change through repetition, George concludes that the OB material as a whole reflects the conception of a single creator. "Nevertheless, such is the beauty and power of the Old Babylonian fragments that one may be sure that the poem was originally the work of a single poetic genius, whether he sang it or wrote it" (p. 22).

[4] The first two columns of the Yale tablet are severely damaged, and this obscures the transition between the meeting of Gilgamesh and Enkidu in Penn and the direct concern with Huwawa in the rest of Yale. We will discuss this problem in detail in Chapter 5.

Gilgamesh and Enkidu that will be played out in the adventure they undertake together in Yale. The two tablets, as they stand, are inextricable from one another.

At the same time, the contents of Yale are rooted in a story that is known to stand on its own in other Gilgamesh material from the OB period. The tablet is preoccupied entirely with Gilgamesh's plan to confront Huwawa and to make a name for himself. It is safe to conjecture that this tablet would have been followed by an actual encounter with Huwawa, a notion encouraged by the fact that we have access to nine other OB tablets that cover the pair's journey to the forest and confrontation with the forest guardian. Even where these "Huwawa texts" reflect variant forms of the OB narrative, they likely match the broad outlines of Yale and what one would expect to follow Yale in the *šūtur eli šarrī* series.[5] The heroes' trek is punctuated by dreams that terrify Gilgamesh, while Enkidu offers comforting interpretations, yielding a prolonged, dramatic build-up to the actual confrontation. When they arrive, Huwawa is dispatched and trees are harvested.

The Huwawa story of Yale and the nine other OB texts is familiar as a separate Sumerian tale, found in two versions from the same period as the first Akkadian Gilgamesh. In spite of contrasts between the Sumerian and the Akkadian Huwawa tales, the areas of overlap demonstrate a direct relationship. Above all, the Sumerian versions show that the story of Gilgamesh and Enkidu's battle with Huwawa could—and did—stand alone.[6] The Akkadian Huwawa material therefore belongs to a tradition of telling this tale for its own sake, so that Penn somehow introduces the

---

[5] The specific evidence will be introduced in the next section. Potential parallel sections are only present in the much-copied Huwawa material. All of UM and the reverse of Schøyen-1 compare closely to parts of Yale, whereas the obverse of Schøyen-1 seems to be independent of Yale, and the dream content of Schøyen-3 appears to overlap with the fourth dream in the Nippur text without matching it closely.

[6] Although the Sumerian Huwawa adventure was generally treated as a distinct text and tale, the OB period copies do suggest some sense of their combination, whether or not by any association with the new Akkadian epic. The hymn that introduces Gilgamesh and Huwawa version B is found only in B:1–4, version A:130–135 and 164–171, and Gilgamesh and the Bull of Heaven 91–96 (unprovenanced text; cf. Me-Turan fragment D:39–41). It is very possible that all of these texts once existed in a form without this shared hymn to Gilgamesh, which is applied to different settings in each. With its current distribution, the hymn functions to join the two stories of the heroic victories of Gilgamesh and Enkidu over superhuman antagonists. Another indication that the Sumerian Gilgamesh stories of Old Babylonian scribal circles could be read in combination comes from the Hadad/Me-Turan source for Gilgamesh, Enkidu, and the Netherworld, which ends with a catch-line for Gilgamesh and Huwawa A, as the next in a sequence (see A. Cavigneaux

adventure in new terms. This origin of the Yale material in a separate
Huwawa story calls for explanation in relation to its combination with
Penn.

It is nothing new to conclude that the Huwawa episode in the OB
Gilgamesh Epic relies on a prior Sumerian tale.[7] The centrality of this fact,
however, was not evident without the texts gathered in Andrew George's
recent publications.[8] Ten out of the twelve attested OB Gilgamesh tablets
cover the Huwawa account. Moreover, because both the Huwawa and the
Bull of Heaven episodes of the Standard Babylonian epic have Sumerian
versions, it is not generally observed that only Huwawa receives full
narrative treatment in both the Sumerian and the known OB Akkadian
evidence.[9] Until now, all components of the OB Gilgamesh have seemed
equal, and without earlier Akkadian texts, there has been no basis to
disentangle further the relationship between the first epic and its sources.
With this project, armed with the litany of evidence now available, we aim
to take one major step in that direction.

---

and F.N.H. Al-Rawi, "La fin de Gilgameš, Enkidu, et les Enfers d'après les manuscrits d'Ur
et de Meturan," *Iraq* 62 [2000] 1–19). This evidence was brought to our attention by Paul
Delnero.

[7] In his examination of changes in the Gilgamesh Epic through time, especially the
contrast between OB evidence and the SBV, Jeffrey Tigay followed S.N. Kramer's ground-
breaking conclusion that the Akkadian epic was created under the influence of separate
Sumerian stories that had not yet been gathered into a single narrative; *The Evolution of
the Gilgamesh Epic* (Philadelphia: University of Pennsylvania Press, 1982); S.N. Kramer,
"The Epic of Gilgameš and its Sumerian Sources: A Study in Literary Evolution," *JAOS*
64 (1944) 7–23. For another early comparison of Sumerian and Akkadian material,
see Lubor Matouš, "Les rapports entre la version sumérienne et la version akkadienne
de l'épopée de Gilgameš," in Paul Garelli ed., *Gilgameš et sa légende* (CRRAI 7; Paris:
C. Klincksieck, 1960) 83–94. George emphasizes the diversity of texts and tales from
which the Old Babylonian Gilgamesh was drawn, including more than just the Sumerian
Gilgamesh stories of standard scribal training. Gilgamesh and Huwawa would have been
the best known of these (*Babylonian Gilgamesh Epic*, 18), but the Akkadian version
was composed without any attempt to translate the Sumerian, and it represents an
independent creative work. The variety and distinctness of OB Gilgamesh themes with
echoes in other Mesopotamian literature suggest to George the likelihood of an oral
component to the process of the epic's formation (pp. 20–22).

[8] Along with George's 2003 Gilgamesh edition, see his updates to the Schøyen texts
in *Babylonian Literary Texts in the Schøyen Collection* (Cornell University Studies in
Assyriology and Sumerology 10; Bethesda, MD: CDL, 2009), numbers 4–6, as Schøyen-1,
Schøyen-2, and Schøyen-3.

[9] For further discussion of the Bull of Heaven, see Chapter 3. It is still possible that this
tale was already incorporated into the Gilgamesh Epic in the OB period, but this cannot
be taken for granted. In the first millennium, the Sumerian tale of Gilgamesh, Enkidu,
and the Netherworld was translated into Akkadian and appended awkwardly to the end
of the epic as Tablet XII, a completely different phenomenon.

We propose that the Yale Tablet and the nine other Huwawa texts represent evidence of a once-independent tale that we call the "Akkadian Huwawa narrative." Rather than envision a primary creative act by a single epic poet, elaborated by countless imitators and copyists, we propose that there were at least two major acts of composition. The Gilgamesh Epic began above all with the Huwawa story, which we understand to have been known in Sumerian before any Akkadian rendition appeared. Between the Sumerian Huwawa story and the OB epic, there was an intermediate compositional stage in which the Sumerian tale alone was re-imagined in Akkadian. This tale can be shown to manifest a rather different perspective from both that of the Sumerian account and that of the epic writer. The primary goal of this book is to identify and interpret the Akkadian Huwawa narrative for the first time on its own terms. In the process, we aim to calculate the relationship of this first Akkadian Gilgamesh tale both to its new epic offspring and to its Sumerian predecessor.

I. *Early Second-Millennium Evidence for*
Gilgamesh in Akkadian and Sumerian

The number of known Old Babylonian Gilgamesh texts continues to increase, and the contents of future finds will provide the crucial test for this hypothesis.[10] We begin with what we have now, which includes three new tablets from the Schøyen collection. If we join George in attributing the cluster of Schøyen fragments listed as MS 3263 to a single tablet, there are now twelve OB texts.[11] As described already, by far the two largest blocks of writing survive in the six-column tablets of Penn and Yale, the first of which is nearly complete. Penn consists of 240 lines, while Yale would have had nearly 300. The labeling of Penn as "Tablet II" gives the impression of a standard division, though this could equally be the count of a single rendition.[12] Only two other texts display the same

---

[10] Iconography can offer further evidence for narratives known or implied. See the forthcoming doctoral dissertation on Huwawa by Sarah Graff (Institute of Fine Arts, New York University).

[11] George, *Babylonian Literary Texts*, 37, number 6.

[12] George remains agnostic on this question: the text of the Yale tablet shows considerable effort to reach a certain point in the narrative, evidently the heroes' point of departure, but we cannot assume that this goal follows a received pattern (*Babylonian Gilgamesh Epic*, 160).

format of multiple columns on front and back, neither of which preserves a colophon to indicate a series, though comparison with the two six-column texts could suggest such. Text UM, a fragment at the museum of the University of Pennsylvania, overlaps slightly with the contents of Yale.[13] The fourth multi-column text contrasts with Penn and Yale, having just two columns on each side, and a large top portion lost. This tablet, which we will identify by its apparent origin in Sippar, provides the only OB evidence for a Gilgamesh narrative that continues beyond the Huwawa account.[14] A Sippar location for this text would perhaps suit the unusual speaking role for Shamash, the patron deity of the city, though the sun god plays a part in defeating Huwawa, in any case.

Among the OB Gilgamesh texts so far discovered, the more common type has a single column on each side, with varying size and format. The Nippur text was found in House F, which contained the extensive literary remains of a scribal school, and the limited length of such tablets suggests no attempt to create a full series.[15] These appear instead to represent extracts from a longer text or tale, evidently as school exercises.[16] The longest of these extract tablets may have been those in the Schøyen collection. Schøyen-2 is completely preserved, with 84 lines, not quite filling the reverse side; and Schøyen-1 may have had room for up to 120

---

[13] This designation reflects George's "OB UM" (*Babylonian Gilgamesh Epic*, 216). With our focus on the Old Babylonian Gilgamesh, we omit the "OB" with names that otherwise follow those from George. There are both OB and MB texts from Nippur, but we will identify the OB text simply as "Nippur," with the later tablet not in view.

[14] The first publication of the probable "Sippar" tablet was by Bruno Meissner in 1902 (*Ein altbabylonisches Fragment des Gilgamos Epos. MVAG* 7/1), with a second piece published by A.R. Millard in 1964 ("Gilgamesh X: A New Fragment," *Iraq* 26, 99–105; with copy in *CT* 46 16). The tablets belong to collections in Berlin and London, but a direct join has been confirmed (George, *Babylonian Gilgamesh Epic*, 273–274). The original dealer stated that the tablet came from Sippar, which would fit the upstream orthography, but such a conclusion must remain tentative (p. 272). We nevertheless adopt the identification by tentative origin over the cumbersome identification by museum names as OB VA+BM, in part because we repeat the name so often in our exposition. The independent scribal tradition visible in the Sippar text, when compared to Penn and Yale, is reflected in different constructions for quoting direct speech; see Karl Hecker, *Untersuchungen zur akkadischen Epik* (Neukirchen-Vluyn: Neukirchener, 1974) 196.

[15] See Eleanor Robson, "The Tablet House: A Scribal School in Old Babylonian Nippur," *RA* 95 (2001) 39–66.

[16] We use the term "extract" to emphasize the continuity between these single-column texts and the Sumerian "Type III" texts of similar type, where both groups clearly represent only a fraction of a larger narrative. Our analysis thus parallels the framework adopted by Paul Delnero, "Sumerian Extract Tablets and Scribal Education" (under review by *JCS*, 2009/2010). We thank the author for sharing this manuscript with us.

lines.[17] Schøyen-3 is too broken for proper evaluation, though George considers it to have been a complement to Schøyen-2, so perhaps of similar scale.[18] Other examples were less ambitious. In descending order of probable size are Harmal-2, Ishchali, IM, Nippur, and Harmal-1, the last of which includes only 17 lines, all preserved.[19] This range of length compares generally with the Type III Sumerian extracts from literary texts used in scribal training.[20]

The most striking feature of the single-column extract tablets, taken together, is their content: all eight of them belong to the Huwawa narrative, with a remarkably generous spread. Schøyen-1 overlaps Yale and treats the period before Gilgamesh and Enkidu leave Uruk. Gilgamesh's dreams during the journey to the Cedar Forest were a popular subject, with four representatives: Schøyen-2 and -3, Nippur, and Harmal-1. Finally, Harmal-2, Ishchali, and IM address the sweep of events after they reach Huwawa, from first meeting through taking his life and selecting timber for a gift to Enlil. When scribes assigned themselves or their students the task of copying Gilgamesh in Akkadian, they chose the Huwawa narrative. Evidence for a larger OB epic comes only from the multi-column tablets. With the habit of writing segments from the Huwawa adventure, it is difficult to judge the nature of the narrative from which these were taken. Certainly we must beware of reconstructing an epic by numbered tablets from such material, and it is not immediately clear what kind of text provided the basis for such extracts.

Contemporary with the Old Babylonian Gilgamesh tablets are a multitude of Sumerian Gilgamesh texts, far more numerous than the Akkadian texts from the same period. These come from five stories, in which Enkidu plays a supporting role as faithful and capable servant of Uruk's king.[21] Although the theme of death, which already occupies the OB

---

[17] See the discussion of this tablet's length and contents in Chapter 5.

[18] George, *Babylonian Literary Texts*, 37.

[19] Stephanie Dalley tentatively identifies several fragments from early second-millennium Nineveh as belonging to Gilgamesh literature, if not part of any known text ("Old Babylonian Tablets from Nineveh, and Possible Pieces of Early Gilgamesh Epic," *Iraq* 63 [2001] 155–169). George finds no substantial connection, and we also decline to include them (*Babylonian Gilgamesh Epic*, 23).

[20] For the Decad of scribal training texts, the Type III tablets range from 13 to 73 lines in length (Delnero, "Sumerian Extract Tablets," Table 2). The unusual, even awkward, length of the Schøyen texts stands out.

[21] For Gilgamesh and the Bull of Heaven, see the edition by A. Cavigneaux and F.N.H. Al-Rawi, "Gilgameš et Taureau de Ciel (Šul.mè.kam). Textes de Tell Haddad IV," *RA* 87 (1993) 97–129. The first evidence for the Bull of Heaven episode in the Gilgamesh

epic, is central to two of these, The Death of Gilgamesh and Gilgamesh, Enkidu, and the Netherworld, one Sumerian story has particular importance for comparison with the earliest Akkadian Gilgamesh texts.[22] A freestanding account of Gilgamesh and Huwawa is known in two versions, typically designated A and B, with version A found in more copies than any other Gilgamesh narrative from the period.[23] When we consider the large proportion of OB Akkadian tablets devoted to the Huwawa narrative, including every extracted text, this phenomenon must be understood in light of the Sumerian evidence. At one level, the existence of both Sumerian and Akkadian Gilgamesh tales in the early second millennium must be considered part of a single intellectual world. Both sets

---

epic comes from the Hittite paraphrase of the 14th and 13th centuries, if we set aside the broken references to an ox and "its tail" in one of Dalley's Nineveh texts, without reference to any characters from the Gilgamesh tradition ("Old Babylonian Tablets from Nineveh," 162–163). George (*The Babylonian Gilgamesh Epic*, 23) observes that this episode "is not acknowledged by other Old Babylonian poems that cite Gilgameš's achievements, and occurs in art only from the Middle Assyrian period." He considers its original incorporation an open question. It is easy to envision the later addition of the Bull of Heaven story to the Gilgamesh Epic, based on familiarity with the Sumerian tale. The tale of Gilgamesh and Aga never found its way into the epic. See W.H.Ph. Römer, *Das sumerische Kurzepos 'Bilgameš und Akka'* (AOAT 209/I; Neukirchen-Vluyn: Neukirchener, 1980); Dina Katz, *Gilgamesh and Akka* (Groningen: Styx, 1993); Claus Wilcke, "'Gilgameš und Akka': Überlegungen zur Zeit von Entstehung und Niederschrift wie auch zum Text des Epos mit einem Exkurs zur Überlieferung von 'Šulgi A' und von 'Lugalbanda II'," in M. Dietrich and O. Loretz eds., *Dubsar anta-men. Studien zur Altorientalistik. Festschrift für W.H.Ph. Römer zur Vollendung seines 70. Lebensjahres* (AOAT 240; Neukirchener: Neukirchen-Vluyn, 1998) 457–485. There is disagreement over how to read the earlier Sumerian renditions of the name Gilgamesh, with some advocating the form "Bilgames" (see George, Chapter 2). Recently, Gonzalo Rubio has argued that the particular signs on which the /Bil-/ pronunciation is based are in fact to be rendered /Gil-/, and we therefore retain the same form for both Sumerian and Akkadian texts. See Rubio, "Excursus: The Reading of the Name of Gilgamesh," in *Sumerian Literary Texts from the Ur III Period* (Mesopotamian Civilizations; Winona Lake, IN: Eisenbrauns, forthcoming). We thank the author for pointing out his discussion and providing us advance copy of his manuscript.

[22] For "Gilgamesh, Enkidu, and the Netherworld," see the edition by Aaron Shaffer, "Sumerian Sources of Tablet XII of the Epic of Gilgameš" (University of Pennsylvania PhD, 1963); for "The Death of Gilgamesh," see Cavigneaux and Al-Rawi, *Gilgameš et la Mort. Textes de Tell Haddad VI* (Groningen: Styx, 2000); Niek Veldhuis, "The Solution of the Dream: A New Interpretation of Bilgames' Death," *JCS* 53 (2001) 133–148.

[23] Robson counted 92 exemplars of Gilgamesh and Huwawa A and 59 of Gilgamesh, Enkidu, and the Netherworld ("Tablet House," 54). Since that time, several joins have reduced the number of distinct copies, so that Delnero's score for Gilgamesh and Huwawa A now includes 85 total, mostly of the Type III extract category (*Variation in Sumerian Literary Compositions: A Case Study Based on the Decad*, University of Pennsylvania Ph.D., 2006).

of stories circulated at the same time, and apparently among the same scribal circles, as at Nippur, though they seem to have served different purposes. Based on the sheer numbers of copies, the Sumerian was rendered in writing far more often, evidently reflecting its widespread use in scribal training, where Akkadian literature appears to have played a smaller role than Sumerian. The contrasting perspectives of the Sumerian and Akkadian tales would have stood in tension or in conversation, with the Sumerian more oriented toward the attitudes of the Sumerian third dynasty of Ur, in the late third millennium. At another level, the Sumerian stories do appear to be older than the Akkadian, with actual roots in the Ur III period.[24] In the Huwawa story, this is manifest in the location of Huwawa's mountains in the east, to fit the political interests of the Ur kingdom, in contrast to the far western location in the OB Huwawa narrative. In spite of the contemporaneous copies, it is indeed likely that the Akkadian Gilgamesh tales were composed with awareness of existing stories in Sumerian.

The early second-millennium evidence for Gilgamesh shows considerable variation in both the Akkadian and the Sumerian texts. The Sumerian Huwawa version A has a much less common and apparently more archaic alternative in version B. Each of these maintains a generally consistent sequence in the plot and dialogue, yet with varied expression of repetition, shifts in wording, and occasional diversions.[25] There are far fewer copies of the Akkadian than of the Sumerian Huwawa version A, but the overlap of two fragments with Yale and the evident contrast between Nippur and Schøyen-3 suggest an at least equal diversity in the OB Huwawa material. There is still no sign that the basic elements of plot and sequence of dialogue were abandoned in any particular retelling. When we explore the role of new composition in the development of

---

[24] Gilgamesh and the Bull of Heaven is known from a brief Ur III fragment (see Cavigneaux and Al-Rawi, "Gilgameš et Taureau de Ciel," 101–103); and two otherwise unknown Gilgamesh fragments to be published in Rubio, *Sumerian Literary Texts*. None of these offers a direct textual continuity with the early second-millennium Sumerian stories.

[25] The degree and character of variation is particularly visible in version A, which is known from so many more copies. At line 148, with the account of taking Huwawa's terrors from him, the handling of the text varies considerably. On the one hand, the Isin text IsA condenses the account into a simple list of the terrors, in a single line, while on the other hand, two extract-length texts of unknown provenience (FLP 1053 and IM 11053) are entirely free accounts of this occasion, with no reference to the surrounding narrative. At the same time, this extensive freedom with the narrative is focused on a specific moment in the exposition and does not apply equally to every part of the text.

the Old Babylonian Gilgamesh Epic, we must keep in mind the reality
of variation in the reproduction of this literature. At the same time, the
concentration of Sumerian and Akkadian Huwawa texts allows us to see
what continuities of structure and perspective persisted in each narrative
tradition.

II. *The Case for an Independent Akkadian Huwawa Narrative*

A basic feature of the Old Babylonian evidence is diversity of origin and
variation of text, where overlap allows comparison. In light of the general
pattern, the continuity between Penn and Yale, as the longest available
texts, offers a unique opportunity to read an extended section of the
OB Gilgamesh Epic with certainty of a single hand and intent. Given
the single hand, we cannot help but expect continuity of voice, logic,
and perspective across the two texts, even as the scenes change and the
plot advances. We should find not only that Penn anticipates material
in Yale but also that Yale shows awareness of the events that took place
in Penn. At the outset, there is no reason to expect a disruption of this
continuity.

Our investigation of these sequential texts yielded unexpected results.
In the places where Yale appears to recall the events described in Penn,
we find that the details do not match. This is especially notable with
regard to the depictions in Penn and Yale of Enkidu's life in the steppe.
Whereas Penn has Enkidu roaming with the *nammaštûm*, for example,
Yale makes reference to Enkidu roaming about with the *būlum*. While the
former term may refer broadly to all animals and in its context denotes
wild animals, the latter term is used only for domesticated animals in the
early second millennium.[26] This subtle difference is tied to a whole host
of details that point toward a fundamental distinction in the authorial
visions of Penn and Yale. As we use the term, authorship is the composition of a new written work, with a profoundly new structure and point of
view, even if this work is developed from an existing composition.[27] By

---

[26] The distinct usages and contexts will be discussed in detail in Chapter 2.

[27] The OB Gilgamesh Epic appears to stand in literary relationship to the Akkadian
Huwawa narrative as its predecessor. While the Akkadian Huwawa narrative shows no
evidence of following either Sumerian Huwawa story directly, we consider it to represent
a conceptual recasting of the Sumerian as a known composition. Given the written
production of the Sumerian Huwawa texts, the setting for this recasting was evidently

authorial vision, we refer to the overarching structure and point of view that persist through every reproduction of a narrative.[28]

Because Penn and Yale were copied by the same scribe, it is significant and perhaps surprising that the two tablets preserve strong evidence for separate authorial visions. In Penn, Enkidu is depicted as a wild man who is removed from all human company, suckled by beasts. Yale, in contrast, envisions a different Enkidu, an Enkidu who is, in fact, a herdsman from the steppe. This Enkidu is known to have fought off a lion and young marauders in his efforts to protect his flocks. This Enkidu has expert knowledge from his life in the steppe, and for this reason, he is the best possible partner for Gilgamesh on his expedition. But this Enkidu was never a wild man separate from humans. This Enkidu, it seems, did not go through the transformation depicted in Penn. In sum, although Yale is part of the same series as Penn, it is not clear that the majority of its content assumes that of Penn or was constructed from the perspective that marks Penn.

We conclude that the contents of Yale are rooted in a once-separate story, the Akkadian Huwawa narrative. This separate Huwawa story had its own author, with an authorial vision distinct from that of the longer epic, though both would have been reproduced with the expected variability of form within these visions. After a transitional section that is damaged and difficult to assign securely, the Yale tablet settles into a consistent point of view that includes contrasts with Penn in both perspective and language. Enkidu is Gilgamesh's partner, not his passion. They are not godlike physical specimens but bold heroes with natural human limitations. Enkidu and Gilgamesh make equal contributions to the defeat of Huwawa, the one representing the capacities of the steppe and the other the ambition of the city.

From Yale alone, it appears that the Huwawa narrative was preserved with little adjustment. The epic author then took up this Huwawa tale and recast it according to a radical new vision, producing the change by adding material to the front and back of the received narrative. With the massive contribution represented in Penn alone, he re-imagined the partnership between Enkidu and Gilgamesh in passionate and heroic

---

among scribes, so that the new Akkadian Huwawa narrative is most easily understood to be a scribal creation, i.e. written. In spite of this preference, our basic ideas regarding the development of the Huwawa tale would also apply to oral composition.

[28] When we define the specific traits that distinguish the Akkadian Huwawa narrative in Chapter 3, these embody what we understand by authorial vision.

terms. Gilgamesh and Enkidu were recast as a fated match, both endowed like gods. To this end, Enkidu had to undergo a major transformation. Where he had been a hero among herdsmen, expert in the ways of the steppe, Enkidu was now recast as a wild man with tremendous strength, so that he could better serve as the king's perfect match. By creating and attaching an extensive new introduction to the front of his received story, the epic author managed to transform its reception without eliminating the distinct vision of the older tale. Certainly the Akkadian Huwawa narrative had to be adjusted at the beginning so that the new epic contribution would flow into it, and as it stands, the Yale Tablet cannot launch the beginning of a separate story. Yet it is not evident that the bulk of the narrative had to be altered in order to accommodate the new epic vision. The very contrasts between Penn and Yale, especially in their portrayal of Enkidu and his bond with Gilgamesh, suggest that much of the older Akkadian Huwawa narrative in the Yale text was simply retained and reinterpreted through the lens of the new material.

The discovery that Yale preserves a radically different authorial vision from that of Penn calls for the reevaluation of the rest of the OB Gilgamesh evidence in Akkadian. We find that of the ten other tablets, only Sippar seems to share the vision of the epic author. Gilgamesh's grief over Enkidu's death in Sippar suits the perspective of Penn, with its portrayal of the two as a perfect match. Further connections in language and motifs suggest that Sippar and Penn share a unified perspective, despite the fact that Sippar is not from the same series and seems to manifest its own set of local idiosyncrasies. Besides Sippar, we are left with a set of texts that cover only events related to the Huwawa adventure: the preparations, the nerve-wracking journey there, and the ensuing success. Close examination of these texts indicates that all of them share the distinct perspective of the Akkadian Huwawa narrative that is preserved in the Yale Tablet. Enkidu is repeatedly cast in terms similar to those of Yale: he is the one with knowledge of Huwawa and his domain; he is the one who advises Gilgamesh and reassures him when he falters. Though these texts demonstrate evidence of variation, their overall portrayal of Enkidu and Gilgamesh meshes with the picture presented in the Yale Tablet. We conclude that they, too, can be classified as relics of the "Akkadian Huwawa narrative," even if individual tablets were produced with awareness of the epic. This must remain an open question, to be addressed text by text, but all of them nevertheless preserve the contrasting perspective that marks the prior Akkadian narrative.

Whether or not the OB Huwawa material was produced with reference to or knowledge of a longer Gilgamesh Epic, the eight extract texts offer one concrete indication that the Akkadian Huwawa narrative was treated as a piece of literature distinct from the larger epic. These appear to reflect patterns of scribal education that are better established with the more numerous Sumerian literary texts. If the Akkadian Huwawa extracts indeed mirror the usage of Sumerian extracts, they show that this one Akkadian narrative was part of scribal curriculum across some portion of Babylonia, along with Sumerian literature. The larger Gilgamesh Epic does not appear to have been part of such training; at least, no evidence so far indicates it.

In his new study of Sumerian "extract tablets" as part of scribal training, Paul Delnero argues that single-column (Type III) extracts from the longer literary texts represent the first stage in mastery of this literature, before students would have to produce the full narratives as multi-column (Type I) tablets.[29] With the more frequently copied literature, it is possible to evaluate the relative proportions of single-column and multi-column tablets in the evidence as a whole, as well as the length and text selection in the extracts. The extracts are not selected according to popular episodes or meaningful units, and they are distributed evenly across each full narrative, so that all sections of the narratives are equally represented in extract evidence. On average, roughly four extract tablets would cover the contents of a full narrative, and among actual finds, there are roughly four times as many single-column as multi-column tablets. Thus, it appears that we have a random sampling of the remains from a practice whereby each scribe would have to produce one version of a literary work in extracted segments, and then copy the whole work on one multi-column tablet.

The OB Huwawa evidence offers an unexpectedly close approximation of this phenomenon, given the limited number of texts and their range of separate origins. As observed already, the Huwawa extracts are distributed across the whole narrative, with little overlap. Where two tablets come from the same find spot, like Harmal-1 and -2, and evidently Schøyen-2 and -3, they cover sequential and non-overlapping material. There are far too few texts to constitute a proper sample, but the initial impression fits the Sumerian pattern remarkably well. The extract

---

[29] "Sumerian Extract Tablets and Scribal Education," see above. The manuscript was provided to us by the author, in pre-published form.

format of itself is important and suggests that the OB Gilgamesh also con-
tributed to scribal training, though its use is much less widely attested
than the Sumerian literature. Only the Huwawa narrative, however, was
extracted, according to existing evidence, and only this Akkadian literary work can be considered part of such education. So far, there is no
sign that the larger epic was copied in this phase of scribal training,
because it is only known from two multi-column tablets, Penn and Sippar. The fact that only Huwawa material was extracted for this training
process appears to offer indirect evidence that the Akkadian Huwawa
narrative once held a place in the scribal repertoire as an independent
text.

III. *The Sumerian Pedigree of the Huwawa Tale*

The relationship between the Akkadian Huwawa narrative and the surrounding epic material is only one part of the equation. Once we manage
to isolate and characterize the distinct logic of the Akkadian Huwawa
narrative, it is equally necessary to determine the relationship between
this tale and its Sumerian predecessor. The Akkadian Huwawa narrative,
as represented in Yale and the other nine Huwawa texts, is not a direct
translation or even an approximation of the Sumerian Huwawa tale. Just
as the epic represents a radical repackaging of the old Akkadian Huwawa
tale, so too does the Akkadian Huwawa tale manifest a fundamentally
new perspective with respect to its Sumerian antecedent. As such, it displays, like the epic, the work of what we identify as an author, with a new
authorial vision that marks this creative composition. It should be noted,
however, that these two phases of authorship are marked by radically different processes. Where the epic author took up the old story and built
around it, the author of the Akkadian Huwawa narrative worked internally, thoroughly rewriting the older Sumerian piece more or less from
scratch.

Between versions A and B of the Sumerian tale, the latter is shorter and
probably preserves a more archaic form of the story, as stated above.[30]
The two versions diverge in a number of important ways, yet they have

---

[30] As with the OB Akkadian texts, actual copies of the two Sumerian versions of the
Huwawa story are contemporaneous, and judgment of version B as more archaic is based
on evaluation of content, partly with respect to the Akkadian Huwawa narrative. For full
discussion, see Chapter 4.

much more in common than either one has with the Akkadian Huwawa narrative. In both Sumerian versions, Gilgamesh, suddenly aware of his own mortality, informs his servant Enkidu that he wants to make the perilous trek to the highlands for felling cedar in order to bring back timber. Without much discussion, the two head to the forest and are struck by the tremendous force of Huwawa's auras. In both, the two manage to trick Huwawa into giving them his auras and to capture the forest guardian. Unfortunately, the end of version B is broken, and it is difficult to determine how the text would have concluded. At the end of version A, Enkidu lops off Huwawa's head, an act that angers Enlil but does not lead to the death of either Enkidu or Gilgamesh.

The Huwawa account from the OB evidence represents a drastically new rendition of the old Sumerian story, which survives most essentially in the simpler version B. On the one hand, the Akkadian loosely follows the plot of the Sumerian tale. Gilgamesh proposes his plan to Enkidu; the two make arrangements to head to the forest. Just as in the Sumerian story, Gilgamesh experiences fear along the way, this time depicted by a series of nightmares that Enkidu interprets favorably. The two confront Huwawa; in the Ishchali tablet, Gilgamesh lops off Huwawa's head as per Enkidu's advice. On the other hand, the Akkadian Huwawa narrative represents a changed and much more extensive version of the old Sumerian tale. In the Sumerian version B, the period before Gilgamesh and Enkidu set out covers 56 lines; in the Yale tablet, this is covered by six columns with almost 300 lines! In the Sumerian, Enkidu is Gilgamesh's trusty servant from Uruk, while according to the recollection in Yale IV 151–153, Enkidu was summoned from the steppe by Gilgamesh because of his great fame among herdsmen. As a free agent, Enkidu is free to reject Gilgamesh's idea, and he resists stubbornly before finally consenting to serve as Gilgamesh's guide. Where the appearance of Huwawa comes as a complete surprise in the Sumerian version B, the desire to battle Huwawa is central to Gilgamesh's plan from the very beginning. Strictly speaking, the Akkadian tale is more a "Huwawa narrative" than its Sumerian precursor.

The differences between version B and the OB Huwawa evidence are triggered by specific transformations in the logic from the Sumerian to the Akkadian, such as Enkidu's shift from servant at Uruk to partner from the steppe, and Huwawa's move from unexpected antagonist to Gilgamesh's anticipated target. In light of these straightforward changes, the relationship of version A to these tales becomes clear. Both D.O. Edzard and more recently Tzvi Abusch have proposed that version A may reflect awareness of the OB Gilgamesh Epic.[31] In other words, the relationship between the Sumerian and the Akkadian tales is two-way. While the Sumerian tale doubtless prompted the first rendition of the tale in Akkadian, the ensuing dialogue between Sumerian and Akkadian perspectives on Gilgamesh and Enkidu in the Old Babylonian period also had particular influence on the most popular Sumerian Gilgamesh story. We further propose that version A may reflect awareness of the Akkadian Huwawa narrative alone, without reference to the specific perspective of the OB epic. The divergences between versions A and B seem therefore to precede the composition of the epic, or at least its supplanting of the Akkadian Huwawa narrative.

In the end, our goal has been to find a way beyond the impasse in investigating the origins of the Gilgamesh Epic. Readers are faced with significant textual variability in both Akkadian and Sumerian Gilgamesh material, at the same time as the OB epic displays an enormous range of likely and potential sources. It has not been clear how to discern any specific process behind the creative act of epic composition. We conclude that beneath the surface of the OB Gilgamesh Epic, an earlier compositional phase can be discerned, still in Akkadian, and comprised only of the Huwawa adventure. This narrative, the unique perspective of which is still preserved in the Yale tablet and in the nine other Huwawa texts, has long been read and interpreted through the lens of the epic framework. It is our goal to unearth this old Akkadian Huwawa story and to reconstruct it to the best of our ability, with the intention of reading it on its own terms. As we reconstruct the relationship between the epic and the Huwawa narrative, with their particular linguistic and thematic contrasts, we envision a literary rather than an oral process of expansion. A written expansion better accounts for the incorporation of a long received narrative into a wholly new product without smoothing out the tensions created by the contrasts between old and new material. Our proposal is intended, however, to be adaptable to different notions of narrative transmission, including an early oral phase for the Akkadian in particular. Upon isolation of the Akkadian Huwawa story's logic from

---

[31] See Edzard, "Gilgameš und Huwawa": Zwei Versionen der sumerischen Zedernwalde-pisode nebst einer Edition von Version "B" (Munich: Bayerischen Akademie der Wissenschaften, 1993) 53–59; Abusch, "Hunting in the Epic of Gilgamesh: Speculations on the Education of a Prince," in M. Cogan and D. Kahn eds., Treasures on Camels' Humps: Historical and Literary Studies from the Ancient Near East Presented to Israel Eph'al (Jerusalem: Magnes, 2008) 17.

that of the epic, we are in a better position to understand the early evolution of the Huwawa episode from the Sumerian to the Akkadian. The distinction between the logic of the Akkadian Huwawa narrative and that of the epic also allows us to evaluate the contributions of the epic writer in a new light. By our estimation, this visionary was no less inventive than past assessments have allowed, but he did have at his disposal a lengthy work in Akkadian. By separating out the perspective of the old Huwawa narrative from that of the later epic, we can better assess and appreciate the ingenuity of the epic writer, the first creator of the OB Gilgamesh Epic.

CHAPTER TWO

ENKIDU'S FIRST STEPPE:
COMPETING PORTRAITS OF ENKIDU
IN YALE AND PENN

The starting point for our analysis is the character of Enkidu, which is presented in sharply different terms in the Penn and Yale tablets. Although the two texts were copied as part of one Gilgamesh series, they offer mutually exclusive accounts of Enkidu's origins and associations.[1] The contrasting renditions of Enkidu are generally treated as reflecting his development in the Penn text from a wild man to an *awīlum* ("gentle-man"). What has been overlooked, however, is that the Yale tablet's portrait of Enkidu's life in the steppe does not match the account of this life in Penn. At precisely those moments where Yale appears to recall the events described in Penn, the details do not match, and it becomes evident that Yale does not assume the contents of what precedes it in the sequence created by combination with Penn. Enkidu's supposed evolution in Penn is thus an inadequate explanation for the contrasting depictions of his experience in the steppe. Instead, we conclude that the two versions of Enkidu reflect the work of two different authors, one of whom recast an existing narrative. The tension between the Penn and Yale tablets has been obscured by the fact that these belong to one Gilgamesh series, the clearest indication of an OB epic.[2] It is thus appropriate to begin

---

[1] In terms of phrasing, only the recurrent discourse formulae show significant similarity, evidently demonstrating the same copyist's hand without further signs of deeper compositional unity. When Gilgamesh or Enkidu is about to speak, the Yale tablet frequently introduces the discourse by the phrase, "he opened (more literally, 'used, read-ied'?) his mouth" (*pīšu īpušamma*, II 83, 89; III 104, 117, 127; IV 138; VI 232), a formula that appears twice in the Penn tablet (III 94, the harlot to Enkidu; IV 147, the traveler to Enkidu). There are a variety of possible ways to introduce direct speech in Old Babylonian literary texts, as seen in Gilgamesh alone. This particular turn of phrase occurs commonly with speech by a single person, with many examples also found in the OB copies of Atrahasis (I 47, 85, 91, 105, 111, 118; etc.).

[2] In the following analysis, the contrasting logic of each text is significant for the very fact that the two tablets were certainly produced by the same scribe. Their characteristics do not therefore reflect variation from two scribal renditions of the same narrative, and they must derive instead from prior developments.

a reevaluation of the OB material with the two texts that long have been assumed to represent expressions of a single voice.

The competing portraits of Enkidu in Penn and Yale are most striking in references to his origin in the steppe. Penn excludes any human company from Enkidu's early life, while Yale assumes that he moved in the circles of herdsmen. In particular, the Yale text places Enkidu with *būlum*, livestock kept by human herders. Because the word *būlum* takes on a broader range of meaning in the first millennium, we devote a separate section to its usage in the OB period. In the Huwawa narrative as a whole, Enkidu represents the best of herdsmen, those who inhabit the dangerous back country far from city centers. In the epic, as reflected in Penn, the steppe that Enkidu inhabits is identified only with the wild and its beasts. This contrast between how Enkidu is portrayed in Penn and Yale lays the foundation for a sweeping reevaluation of all the OB Gilgamesh evidence.

I. *Enkidu in the Steppe*

The question of Enkidu's origins holds no interest in any of the five Sumerian Gilgamesh tales. There is never reason to doubt that he, like Gilgamesh, hails from Uruk. In contrast, the Penn and Yale tablets of the OB Gilgamesh present Enkidu as some polar opposite or complement to the city. Because both Penn and Yale set up these dual identities, based in city and steppe, it has been easy to miss the contrast between the two tablets. In fact, the two tablets offer deeply divergent pictures of Gilgamesh and Enkidu, both of which are rooted in the portrayal of Enkidu. The Penn tablet introduces Enkidu as one born in the wild, nursed by beasts, while Yale presents him as the progeny of herdsmen. Whereas the former is raised among animals and must be introduced to human company, the latter is familiar with the wild but needs no special acculturation in order to join society.

According to the Penn tablet, Enkidu "was born in the steppe (*ṣērum*), and the highlands (*šadûm*) raised him" (I 18–19). While making love with the harlot Shamkat, Enkidu forgets the land of his birth (II 47). Shamkat then tells Enkidu that he is "like a god" and challenges his way of life: "Why do you roam about the steppe (*ṣērum*) with the beasts (*nammaštûm*)?" (II 54–55). She leads him to a community of herdsmen, defined not by grazing lands but by the enclosures of their camps. In Penn's account, Shamkat's choice represents a first step toward a change

that is essential to meeting Gilgamesh at Uruk. At the camp, the inhabitants regard him as one removed from human society: "the milk of the
beasts (*nammaštûm*) he used to suck" (III 85–86).[3] He does not even
know that bread and beer constitute the standard fare of humans living
in communities. After Enkidu embraces these basics, along with oil for
the body, he arms himself and guards the shepherds from wolves and
lions (III 110–116). Enkidu's use of a weapon represents one more sign
of his acculturation to the ways of human communities. Upon his arrival
at Uruk, the city folk still identify him as one born in the mountains and
suckled by beasts (V 186–189), despite his recent transformation.[4]

At first glance, Yale seems to recall the same origins.[5] The Yale tablet
twice mentions Enkidu's back country beginnings, first, when Enkidu
tries to dissuade Gilgamesh from his quest, and second, when Gilgamesh
attempts to shame his companion into surrendering his fears. Enkidu
speaks of what he knows, referring to his time "in the highlands (*šadûm*),
when I used to roam with the herd (*būlum*)" (III 106–107). Later, Gilgamesh responds by reference to the same background: "You were born
and grew up in the steppe (*ṣērum*). A lion raided you, and you knew all,
young men robbed your …" (IV 151–153).

---

[3] The term *nammaštûm* may simply mean "animal," in a global sense, without any
modern sense of "wild" as opposed to domestic. The examples listed in *CAD* and *AHw*
do not list specific animals that must be "wild." The basis for distinction in the Penn tablet
comes not from the word itself but from the statement that the animals nursed him. Any
idea of Enkidu as the "noble savage" comes only from the full OB epic, without any basis
in the original placement of his origins in the steppe. For the Old Babylonian Enkidu,
assuming a unified portrait, see Aage Westenholz and Ulla Koch-Westenholz, "Enkidu—
The Noble Savage?" in A.R. George and I.L. Finkel eds., *Wisdom, Gods and Literature:
Studies in Assyriology in Honour of W.G. Lambert* (Winona Lake, IN: Eisenbrauns, 2000)
442–443. They attribute Enkidu's recommendation to kill Huwawa to his impetuous
ignorance of the laws governing proper behavior. No such connection is warranted in
the Huwawa narrative.

[4] Interpreters follow only this Penn version of Enkidu's origins when reading for an
OB epic. For example, Nathan Wasserman links the suckling of wild animals' milk to
Enkidu's ignorance of bread and beer, in portrayal of the man as wild ("Offspring of
Silence, Spawn of a Fish, Son of a Gazelle …: Enkidu's Different Origins in the Epic of
Gilgameš," in Yitschak Sefati et al. eds., *"An Experienced Scribe Who Neglects Nothing":
Ancient Near Eastern Studies in Honor of Jacob Klein* [Bethesda, MD: CDL Press, 2005]
597).

[5] The characterization of Enkidu in the Yale tablet is visible almost entirely through
columns III–VI, in part because the first two columns are badly damaged. At the same
time, columns I and II probably represent a transitional section of the text, where the
original introduction was adapted to fit the Penn narrative (see Chapter 5). In any case,
the material relevant to this discussion appears entirely in the last four columns.

The theme of birth in the back country is shared by both tablets, expressed by the words ṣērum and šadûm, "steppe" and "highlands." This feature would seem to offer the most direct occasion for mutual reference, and thus the contrasting treatments of the theme propel a reconsideration of the assumption that both texts reflect the same authorial vision. Of themselves, the terms ṣērum and šadûm do not require separation from human company. In Penn, this notion stems above all from the beasts (nammaštûm) that suckle Enkidu. Yale then introduces a new word for Enkidu's company: the "herds" (būlum). The primary meaning of būlum refers to domestic grazing animals: cattle, sheep or goats, and horses or donkeys. We are not aware of any OB reference to būlum that envisions wild beasts, though the word allows for this in the first millennium.[6] Without the prompting of Penn, it is most natural to understand Enkidu of Yale to belong to the herding communities of the back country.

The second reference to this theme in Yale reiterates the location in the steppe but adds another element. In the first reference, Enkidu identified his own background among the highland herds; this time, it is Gilgamesh who speaks of Enkidu's reputation, as rooted in his experience in the steppe. From Gilgamesh's view, Enkidu should not hesitate to join him in pursuit of Huwawa, when Enkidu was known for protecting flocks from both a lion and from young marauders. This diverges from what we have in Penn, where Enkidu only confronts lions after abandoning life in the wild and taking up residence at the shepherd's camp. Penn and Yale also lack a direct verbal connection in their treatments of this theme. "A lion raided you" offers no direct reference back to the plural lions and wolves of Penn, where Enkidu plays the active role. Although the wording is close enough to facilitate an easy transition from Penn to Yale, the lack of matching details indicates an underlying contrast in narrative perspectives. When Enkidu is said to have encountered a lion in Yale, this is part of a larger defense of herds against both animal and human predators that has no place in Penn's treatment of the theme. In Yale, the verbs "to raid" (šahāṭum) and "to rob" (habātum) form a parallel between lines 152 and 153, with the lion and the young men (eṭlūtum) representing the most dangerous antagonists. George translates line 153, "Grown men fled from your presence," evidently following the SB rendition of the hunter's response to seeing

---

[6] CAD s.v. būlu 2.

Enkidu.[7] It is only possible to read these lines as consistent with Penn by introducing an artificial division between the setting of line 151 and the rest, so that the steppe is restricted to Enkidu's early life, and the role of guardian follows his meeting with Shamkat and first movement toward Gilgamesh. Such produces an awkward and unnatural reading, the result of forcing content from Penn into the Yale text. Joined to the *būlum*, Enkidu's defense against marauders assumes the steppe to be a human home, and he thus is portrayed as the hero of herdsmen in his very origins.

II. *Herdsmen and Cities: The* būlum *as Domestic Livestock*

In the first millennium, the word *būlu* becomes a commonplace, with application both to domestic herds and wild animals.[8] In the Standard Babylonian Gilgamesh, *būlu* becomes a standard category for the wild population of the mountains and the steppe, even as the word keeps its old association with domestic livestock.[9] Given the explicit emphasis on Enkidu's wild condition when he is introduced in the Penn tablet, there has been no reason to question an interpretation of "wild animals" when the term appears in Yale.[10] In fact, however, the word *būlum* was used less widely in the early second millennium and with a decidedly narrower range.[11]

---

[7] George, *Babylonian Gilgamesh Epic*, 201. In all Babylonian dialects and through most Akkadian usage, the meaning "to flee" is an N form, while Yale IV 153 would have to be read as a G stem, which is only attested for Old Assyrian, as *ēbut-* (*CAD* s.v. *abātu* B).

[8] See *CAD* s.v. *būlu* 1 versus 2.

[9] See Tablet I 111 (with gazelles), 118, 127, 132 (as hunter's prey), 145 (estranged), 154, 159 (as hunter's prey), 163, 166 (estranged from Enkidu), 172, 176 (with gazelles), 187 (estranged), 196 (gazelles, estranged), 200; III 66; VIII 6 (with mother as gazelle, father as wild ass), 17 (mourned by them, listing bear, hyena, panther, etc.); X 260 (what Gilgamesh hunts, with similar list); XI 85 (loaded on the flood boat).

[10] This is displayed in the translation of *CAD* s.v. *būlu* 2a, "when I (Enkidu) used to roam the highlands with the wild animals" (Yale III 107). George renders the term nicely as "herd," which limits the meaning to grazing animals, without seeming to question the continuity with the Penn version (cf. R.J. Tournay and Aaron Shaffer, *L'épopée de Gilgamesh* [LAPO 15; Paris: Éditions du Cerf, 1998] 84, "je vagabondais avec la harde"). In general, translators may apply domestic language yet without observing any contradiction with the portrayal of Enkidu in Penn; see Stephanie Dalley, *Myths from Mesopotamia: Creation, the Flood, Gilgamesh, and Others* (Oxford: Oxford University Press, 1989) 143: "when I used to go with the cattle."

[11] The *CAD* entry concludes, "While *būlu* in mng. 1 clearly denotes a herd (of domesticated animals) rather than cattle as a collective designation, the usage in mng. 2 has to

Old Babylonian texts consistently apply the word *būlum* to herds of domesticated animals.[12] The greatest detail is provided by various letters found at Mari, where the royal archives preserve a remarkable range of correspondents and interests for the purposes of the king Zimri-Lim and his two predecessors. In these texts, *būlum* is a sweeping category that encompasses all the domestic herds and flocks affiliated with a given city-based administrative responsibility. Within the Mari kingdom, this could be one of the district centers, as in one case, for the most northern district of Qaṭṭunan.[13] One letter defines the *būlum* by the entire "land" (*mātum*) governed from the central cities of Karana and Andarig, two significant sites in the Sinjar region between the Tigris and the Habur Rivers.[14] The writer's real concern is that the herds of Mari's Zimri-Lim could join the others as prey to Išme-Dagan of Ekallatum, a perennial enemy from the east:

> No one has heard where his face is set—whether he set (his) face to plunder the *būlum* of the land of Karana, whether the *būlum* of the land of Andarig, or even the *būlum* of the steppe (*ṣērum*) of my lord—no one knows.[15]

For the Mari king, the writer specifies the steppe (*ṣērum*) as the particular domain of the *būlum*, which is linked to the state through livestock that falls under royal purview.[16]

---

be established by context whenever the word occurs alone (i.e., without the specification *ṣēri* or the apposition *nammassu*). Administrative texts use *būlu* rarely in OB (Sippar and Mari), but more often in NB."

[12] *CAD* s.v. *būlu* mentions both letters (1a) and extispicy texts (1b), including the *Šumma izbu* series. The *AHw* s.v. *būlu(m)* distinguishes 1) "Vieh der Herden," including OB texts, from 2) "Getier des Feldes," among which the only OB text cited is the reference from Yale.

[13] In ARM XXVII 112, the governor based at Qaṭṭunan writes to his lord expressing concern that the *būlum* will become a target for enemy attack. See lines 19–23; [19] *ù i-nu-ma bu-lu-um i-na Qa-aṭ-⟨tú⟩-na-an*^(ki) [20] *pa-ah-ru a-na na-ak-ri-im* [21] *ša i-še-em-mu-ú* [22] *um-ma-a-mi bu-lu-um i-na Qa-aṭ-ṭú-na-an*[^(k)]^i [23] *pa^l-hi-ir*, "And as soon as the *būlum* is gathered at Qaṭṭunan, the one who hears about it (will say) to the enemy: 'The *būlum* is gathered at Qaṭṭunan.'"

[14] During the early second millennium, the *mātum* was the basic unit of large-scale politics, most often defined in combination with rule by kings as "lands" but also representing a population distinct from its ruler. For extended discussion, see Daniel Fleming, *Democracy's Ancient Ancestors: Mari and Early Collective Governance* (Cambridge: Cambridge University Press, 2004) Chapter 3.

[15] ARM XXVI 430:31–35, [31] *ù a-šar pa-nu-šu ša-ak-nu ú-ul iš-še-me* [32] *lu-ú a-na bu-li-im ša ma-at Ka-ra-na*^(ki) [33] *lu-ú a-na bu-lim ša ma-at An-da-ri⟨-ig⟩*^(ki) [34] *ú-lu-ma a-na bu-lim ša ṣí-i-ir be-lí-ia* [35] *ša-ha-[ti-im pa-na-a]m ša-ki-in ú-ul i-de.*

[16] Other Mari references to the term *būlum* include ARM II 45:7′, 9′, 11′, the mass of grazing animals identified with a person of substance; ARM II 140:30, sheep owned by

In light of the body of early second-millennium evidence for the term, Enkidu's *būlum* must be domestic livestock. As made explicit in the report about Išme-Dagan, the standard location of the *būlum* is the "steppe." Both the Penn and the Yale tablets identify Enkidu with this back country, in tandem with the "highlands" (*šadûm*) in which he was roaming "with the herd" (Yale III 107). Because the Penn text transforms Enkidu into a creature of the wild, it avoids a term that specifies domestic herds and instead utilizes the more versatile *nammaštûm*. Yet by the time of the Standard Babylonian epic, when the application of the word *būlu* had broadened to include all animals, the term reenters the text. Based on the Mari evidence in particular, we must recognize in the *būlum* not only domestic livestock but also an affiliation with urban centers and the realms attached to them. When Enkidu is said to have roamed with the *būlum* in Yale, the implication is that he keeps company with human herdsmen, whose animals are associated with the cities and their dominions, even when grazing at great distances from them. Whether or not Enkidu's herds are meant to have ties to Uruk, they do not represent a world isolated from its people. Enkidu's defense against attacks by the lion and by young men then confirms what the word *būlum* alone suggests: he grew up not among wild animals but rather with herding communities that are most likely assumed to participate in the Uruk economy. This detail offers an explanation for how Gilgamesh would have heard about Enkidu in the freestanding Huwawa narrative. Especially if Enkidu and his fellow herdsmen are to be understood as associated with the Uruk economy, in the logic of the Yale storyline, it is simplest to imagine that the king would have heard about Enkidu's famous capacities through regular contact between city and steppe. With this knowledge, Gilgamesh would have summoned Enkidu to Uruk to accompany him on his expedition to the Cedar Forest.

Taken on their own, then, without assuming the backdrop of Penn, the Yale references never present Enkidu as living in the wild, raised by animals. Instead, the Yale text envisions only two stages in Enkidu's transition, with a single (and temporary) movement from steppe to city. In this schema, Enkidu is never isolated from human contact. As Gilgamesh is the hero of the city and the pinnacle of what it can produce,

---

a particular person; ARM V 81:19, sheep belonging to the king; VI 27:10, with reference to an enclosure for herds or flocks.

so Enkidu is the hero of the steppe, manifesting its greatest strengths.[17]
For an adventure in the highlands, Gilgamesh needs an expert, and
Enkidu is the perfect candidate. Gilgamesh and Enkidu thus embody the
cooperation of city and steppe, especially for what the representative of
the city hopes to accomplish in the steppe, far from the city's power.

In the Penn tablet, the epic author retains Enkidu's association with
shepherds but transforms its place in his representational scheme. Here
the steppe is defined not by livestock and herdsmen but rather by wild
inhabitants that have no human contact. Although Enkidu interacts with
shepherds, his identification with them is diluted, and the team of Gilgamesh and Enkidu no longer represents the collaboration between the
populations of the city and of the steppe. The shepherds only represent
outliers to civilization, and their camp is just a first step for Enkidu toward
the glories of Uruk.[18]

---

[17] The Yale tablet presents a positive view of the steppe that is somewhat unexpected.
Westenholz and Koch-Westenholz observe that "For the Babylonians, the wilderness
normally held only negative connotations. It was the uncultivated steppe, and nothing
but evil could come from there" ("Enkidu—The Noble Savage?" 443). This statement
is unnecessarily narrow and reflects only the most restrictive ideas of southeastern
Mesopotamia.

[18] There is a first reference to the shepherds at the end of Shamkat's invitation to
Enkidu, already anticipating the initial destination at their camps (II 64–65). These lines
are among the most tantalizing of the Penn tablet, with the signs almost entirely visible
but their sense far from obvious: *al-ka-ti-ma i-na qa-aq-qa-ri ma-a-AK re-i-im*, which
George renders, "You are familiar (enough) with the territory where the shepherd *dwells*."
For an overview of the interpretive and translation issues, see George's notes on lines 64–
65 (*Babylonian Gilgamesh Epic*, 184). The rendering, "You are familiar" is attractive for
al-ka-ti-ma, understood as a stative/predicative verb (2ms), if we can accept an alternate
form for **alkāta*. It does not make sense, however, to attach the sequential conjunction
-*ma* and then to follow with no further verb. The next line begins a new segment. We must
therefore still consider the reading of these signs uncertain. The "ground" is then clear,
and the question is how it relates to the herdsmen at the end of the line. In the Cuthaean
Naram-Sin legend as found at Hattuša, the *qaqqaru* is set against the "town" (*ālu*), as
what *CAD* translates insightfully as "open country" (KBo 19 98 col. B 6f, s.v. *qaqqaru* 6).
Benjamin Foster renders these lines without recognizing the social/geographical contrast:
"City, in the face of them, was no city, Ground, in the face of them, was no ground"
(*Before the Muses*, vol. I [Bethesda, MD: CDL, 1996] 261 b' 6'–7'). In the Penn tablet,
the open country is suggested by the herdsman at the end of the line. The second to last
word is clear but unknown. Neither Wolfram von Soden's derivation from *niākum* ("to
have intercourse"; see *AHw* s.v. *majjakum*) nor Dalley's translation from *mâku* ("absence,
lack"; see with this line, her *Myths from Mesopotamia*) provides a satisfactory relation to
the herdsman and his land.

Although a solution remains elusive, we wonder whether the noun may relate to a
category of personnel found in Mari letters, along with the verb from which it is derived,
both associated with roaming the steppe. In ARM XXVI 420:10–11, an emissary of
king Zimri-Lim reports that "Išme-Dagan has sent out scouts to scout out the steppe

Taken on its own, Penn never explains why Enkidu must undergo a transformation at the shepherds' settlement. He is already "like a god" (II 53), with the magnificence that will make him a match for Gilgamesh (cf. V 194), and for that bond, the experience with the shepherds is super-fluous. Read as the revision of a prior composition, however, the shep-herd scene in Penn displays its crucial purpose as the solution to a narra-tive obstacle created by the redefinition of Enkidu's origins. According to Yale, Enkidu served as the protector of herding communities and their animals, and this text displays no awareness of any previous life apart from all people. In the epic, the steppe becomes the setting for Enkidu's life among the wild beasts, and his entire identification with herdsmen is thereby lost. In order to maintain continuity with the received Huwawa narrative, Enkidu somehow must become the man he already is known to be. To this end, the author adds an intermediate stage to his basic move-ment from steppe to city.[19] In this light, the location of Enkidu's social-ization scene among the shepherds confirms that in the Huwawa narra-tive he was portrayed as a guardian of the flocks. After learning to eat, drink, and adorn himself properly for life among humans, Enkidu com-mences an unspecified period of service to the herdsmen. In doing so, Enkidu is prepared to be exactly the character attributed to him in Yale, but in the process, this character is no longer associated with his life in the steppe.

---

of Suhûm" ([lu.meš]*ma-ki-i a-na na-wi-im ša Su-hi-im ma-ki-im Iš-me-*[d]*Da-gan iṭ-ṭa-ra-ad*). The same scouts, with the same oblique case and long final vowel with the plural, appear in ARM XIV 84+:36, 39, 43, and in XXVI 30:12. It is not clear whether the root is third weak. With caution, we read the line in Penn as a bound form of the noun. The attraction of this root lies in its consistent connection with land away from settlements. In ARM XIV 84+, the scouts report on whether the population of the countryside has been gathered into fortified towns. In ARM XXVI 30, a high official tells the king that he has ordered scouts to accompany a group of Hana, the mobile herdsmen who fight on behalf of their kinsman who rules from Mari. Through all these examples, we have no basis for regarding the core action as "spying," as in "watching," as opposed to moving through open country, keeping away from settlements.

We know of no evidence for a cognate noun *$m\bar{a}kum$, which in this context would make best sense as the "wandering place" of shepherds. The last part of the line would then read, "... in the open country, the shepherd's range."

[19] The addition of Enkidu's intermediate stop with the shepherds is a fine example of what we envision as part of the epic author's work, in that it addresses the tension created by the redefinition of Enkidu's origins and character when he becomes a man of the wild. Such a change would not be the result of textual variability in regular transmission, but rather reflects a full-scale re-imagining of the basic narrative schema. The Penn tablet itself represents only one expression of a text that could vary in reproduction, yet we expect the authorial vision to survive in all copies.

III. *Enkidu and the Steppe after Ur III Sumer*

We do not propose that the Akkadian Huwawa narrative and the epic represent separate historical moments, with clearly distinguished social conditions and attitudes. Both Akkadian-language compositions would have been created in the first centuries after the fall of Ur III Sumer. There is no need to envision a special time when herding communities were more appreciated in the social circle of Babylonian scribes. More likely, the singular appearance of the sentiments underlying the Huwawa narrative reveal one current in early second-millennium society and thought that was generally present yet rarely visible in this scribal milieu. Even in the celebration of Enkidu as hero of the steppe, the Yale narrative assumes the importance of this domain and its herdsmen without explicitly stating it. Enkidu is not identified specifically as a shepherd, and moreover, shepherds are not given a direct role in the Huwawa tale. The displacement of Enkidu to the steppe from Uruk, where he is located in the Sumerian Gilgamesh tales, is what expresses the most powerful respect for those who move through the highland back country. When the author of the epic wished to reinterpret Enkidu's origin in the steppe as isolated from human company, it was not difficult to prompt a new interpretation of the description known from Yale in light of what now precedes it in Penn. This act was by all accounts successful, given that the contents of Yale continue to be read in light of Penn.

The relocation of Enkidu from Uruk to the steppe remains a striking and surprising choice in a literature about great Sumerian kings. Gilgamesh belongs to a tradition that glorified memorable rulers of Uruk from time gone by: Enmerkar, Lugalbanda, and Gilgamesh. Most of the Sumerian stories about these three kings probably first took form in the Ur III period, at the end of the third millennium, in service of a royal ideology at Ur that hearkened back to ancient Uruk for validation.[20] While the literary spokesmen for the Sumerian world under kings at Ur did not generally denigrate non-Sumerians as subhuman, the mountains could be regarded as the homeland of dangerous peoples who were ignorant of

---

[20] See Piotr Michalowski, "Épopées, hymnes et lettres," 251–252, in "Sumer," *Supplément au Dictionnaire de la Bible* XIII (Paris: Letouzey & Ané, 1999–2002). The ruling house at Ur, which had built a kingdom of considerable size that reached beyond the traditional region of Sumerian language use, in fact originated at Uruk. Shulgi, the second representative of this house, took up a notion initiated by his father of ancestry back to Gilgamesh. He cast himself as the issue of Lugalbanda and Ninsumuna, so that he was in effect a brother to Gilgamesh, sharing his divinity.

life's proper necessities. In the Curse of Agade, the Guti and the Martu (Amorites) are both defined as highland peoples, the Guti in animal-like terms and the Martu as "not knowing barley," a phrase reminiscent of Enkidu "not knowing" the custom of eating bread (Penn III 90–91).[21] One of the poems about Lugalbanda envisions that even in his time, Uruk needed ramparts to defend against the Martu, "who know no barley."[22]

Consistent with this trend, the Sumerian Gilgamesh tales do not associate the people of Uruk with pastoralism. Enkidu is from Uruk, like his master Gilgamesh, and is therefore separate from the herding country and its population. When the Huwawa narrative moves Enkidu to the steppe and identifies him with *būlum* livestock, it consciously embraces the possibility of relationship between Sumerian city and upland steppe. Somehow, the perspective that highlighted the cultural identity of a unified urban Sumer, an ideal of the Ur III regime, gave way to a view that now spotlighted collaboration with the high country beyond Sumer. At the same time as Enkidu is identified with the highlands, Huwawa's location is specified with familiar geography. The highland home of Huwawa in the Sumerian Gilgamesh tales is across seven ranges, with no named direction or point of reference (version A:60–63; B:59–61).[23] In the Akkadian Huwawa narrative, the Cedar Forest is securely attached

---

[21] The Curse of Agade, lines 46 (Amorites, mar-tu kur-ra lu$_2$ še nu-zu), 154–157 (Guti, "with human instincts, but canine intelligence, and monkeys' features ..."). These and similar texts are discussed in Jerrold S. Cooper, *The Curse of Agade* (Baltimore: The Johns Hopkins University Press, 1983) 30–33; the translation is his. The end of the Marriage of Martu includes a long and disparaging account of the Martu people as obnoxious to the gods, primitive highland-dwellers with tents, and having no civilized eating habits (lines 127–141). This speech, however, comes from a friend of Martu's would-be bride, who ignores the insult and declares that she will in fact marry the man. For the text, see Jacob Klein, "The God Martu in Sumerian Literature," in I.L. Finkel and Mark J. Geller eds., *The Sumerian Gods and Their Representations* (Groningen: Styx, 1997) 99–116. Michalowski (personal communication) will make the case in forthcoming work that even the Sumerian signs usually rendered mar-tu were read as Amurru(m).

[22] "The Return of Lugalbanda," lines 304 and 370; in Herman Vanstiphout, *Epics of Sumerian Kings* (WAW; Atlanta: Society of Biblical Literature, 2003) 153, 155.

[23] So far as a general location was in view, this is more likely in the Iranian highlands than to the west. A full argument for the eastern location is offered by Gerd Steiner, "Huwawa und sein 'Bergland' in der sumerischen Tradition," *ASJ* 18 (1996) 187–215. The sun god Utu is especially associated with sunrise in the east; the "seven mountains" to be crossed are typically placed in Aratta and Anshan, vaguely east of Mesopotamia; and the seven monsters "know the way to Aratta." Jacob Klein and Kathleen Abraham propose that in the Sumerian, the trees need not have been western "cedars" ("Problems of Geography in the Gilgameš Epics: The Journey to the 'Cedar Forest,'" in L. Milano et al. eds., *Landscapes: Territories, Frontiers and Horizons in the Ancient Near East* [CRRAI 44; Padua: Sargon srl, 2000] 65–66).

to western Syria. Ishchali places Huwawa in the vicinity of Sirion and Lebanon (rev. 31′), and Schøyen-2 offers a western definition in two stages. If George's new reading is correct, Huwawa's highland home is first associated with "the land of Ebla" (obv. 26) and then with the specific name of (H)amran, "where the Amorite lives" (rev. 55–56).[24] With this location for Huwawa, Enkidu's home in the steppe is also given a specific address. With Enkidu's removal from Uruk to the steppe, the region with these positive associations is now the Mesopotamian upstream, which reaches into Syria toward the Mediterranean.

The combination of Enkidu's origins in the steppe and the location of Huwawa in western Syria suggests a perspective that has shifted from that of the Ur III kingdom, which reached mainly from the Tigris toward the high country to the north and east.[25] The Akkadian Huwawa narrative appears to reflect the realignment of political power in the earliest second millennium, when lines of contact were open and acknowledged between old Sumer and regions further west than Ur's preoccupations. After the fall of Ur, leaders with West Semitic names are increasingly prominent throughout Mesopotamia, in what is commonly regarded as "Amorite" influence.[26] We see glimpses of the new alignments in Old Babylonian documentation from southeastern Mesopotamia, where certain rulers

---

[24] See George, *Babylonian Literary Texts*, text no. 5. The name Hamran is not otherwise known for second-millennium Syria and should be further west of Ebla, in the high mountains, which could suit the land of Amurrum, between the Orontes River and the Mediterranean Sea.

[25] For the expansion of the Ur kingdom under Shulgi, see Walther Sallaberger, "Ur III-Zeit," in Pascal Attinger and Markus Wäfler eds., *Mesopotamien: Akkade-Zeit und Ur III-Zeit* (OBO 160/3; Göttingen: Vandenhoeck und Ruprecht, 1999) 156–159.

[26] A basic discussion is provided by Dominique Charpin, "Histoire politique du Proche-Orient amorrite (2002–1595)," in Pascal Attinger, Walther Sallaberger, and Markus Wäfler eds., *Mesopotamien: Die altbabylonische Zeit* (OBO 160/4; Göttingen: Vandenhoeck und Ruprecht, 2004) 57–60. It is not clear where the Martu or Amurrû had their core territories, or even whether these terms were defined originally with geographical limits. The association with West Semitic language and the links between groups found in southeastern Mesopotamia (Sumer) and regions to the north and west indicate a strong connection with lands toward Syria. Anne Porter offers a completely new interpretation of the late third-millennium evidence, both archaeological and specifically textual, for the Amorites as an integral part of the Mesopotamian social landscape, urban and non-urban alike ("You Say Potato, I Say …: Typology, Chronology and the Origin of the Amorites," in C. Marro and C. Kuzucuoglu eds., *Sociétés humaines et changement climatique à la fin du Troisième Millénaire: une crise a-t-elle eu lieu en Haute-Mésopotamie?* [Varia Anatolica XVIII; Paris: De Boccard, 2007] 69–115). According to Porter, while eastern Mesopotamian leaders could define the Amorites as a foreign people, distinguishable as western nomads, the evidence indicates instead a period of settlement shifts in the context of overall social continuity. Amorites are mobile pastoralists, generally.

acknowledge affiliations with groups that link peoples up and down the river system. The most famous is Hammurabi of Babylon, who was affiliated with groups called the Amnanu, the Yahruru, and the Numha. The family of Kudur-mabuk at Larsa was linked to the Yamutbal, and that of Sin-kashid at Uruk was associated with the Amnanu.[27] All of these groups constitute major players in the politics of the middle Euphrates and Habur regions documented in the Mari archives for the same period as Hammurabi at Babylon, conventionally dated to the 18th century BCE. The Amnanu and the Yahruru belonged to the Binu Yamina coalition of peoples with ties to grazing lands in western Syria.[28] In the Hammurabi period, the Numha and the Yamutbal were identified with the kingdoms of Kurda and Andarig, just south of the Jebel Sinjar, north of Mari.[29] The palace archives from Mari are particularly attuned to the contribution of herdsmen to the society of the entire region, and its correspondence shows how much the integration of upstream and downstream Mesopotamia was dependent on the role of pastoralism in the larger economy.[30]

In the Akkadian Huwawa narrative, Enkidu hails from the steppe, a radical reorientation from the Sumerian setting. The new tale now brings Enkidu to Uruk because he knows Huwawa from the highlands where he roamed with the *būlum* (Yale III 106–107). This region is elsewhere identified with the mountains of western Syria. Gilgamesh and Enkidu collaborate in an undertaking with no interest in sheep and goats, or even the lions that may prey on them. Nevertheless, Enkidu can assist Gilgamesh because of the life he shares with herding peoples who move in lands far from Uruk and the cities of southeastern Mesopotamia. This social orientation contrasts both with the perspective of the Sumerian

---

[27] See Fleming, *Democracy's Ancient Ancestors*, 159–160.

[28] This is demonstrated above all by a text that defines the range of the Binu Yamina by three lands west of the Euphrates: Yamhad, Qaṭna, and Amurrum; see Fleming, *Democracy's Ancient Ancestors*, 29 and n. 7; "Mari and the Possibilities of Biblical Memory," *RA* 92 (1998): 61 and n. 91.

[29] For Kurda, see Bertrand Lafont, "L'admonestation des Anciens de Kurdâ à leur roi," *FM* II (1994): 209–220. Somewhat later, king Ammi-ṣaduqa of Babylon mentions the sons of the Numha, the Emutbal, and a people of the upper Habur drainage called Ida-Maraṣ (the edict of Ammi-ṣaduqa sects. 18'–19'). A text from Eshnunna, slightly earlier than the Mari archives, describes a treaty between "the Akkadians, the Yamutbal, the Numha, and Ida-Maraṣ" (TA 1930-T575:7–8, cited in Marten Stol, *Studies in Old Babylonian History* [Te Istanbul: Nederlands Historisch-Archaeologisch Instituut, 1976] 64).

[30] Fleming, *Democracy's Ancient Ancestors*, Chapter 2: "The Tribal World of Zimri-Lim."

tales and with the epic vision of Penn, in which Enkidu's original herding affiliations were set aside in favor of his representation as a man endowed with the powers of nature.[31]

IV. *From Servant to Sage to Savage: Enkidu as the One Who Knows*[32]

The evolution of Enkidu's character, and subsequently, his relationship to Gilgamesh, undergoes two major changes in the transmission of the tale. These may be characterized simply as shifts from "servant to sage" and from "sage to savage," with the essential middle step defined by Enkidu's knowledge. In the Akkadian Huwawa narrative, Enkidu knows Huwawa and his world, because he has lived in the highlands shared by the guardian of the Cedar Forest. This theme is particularly visible in the Yale tablet, with its long discussions before departure. In introducing the theme here, we focus primarily on the evidence of Yale, especially as it contrasts with the portrayal of Enkidu in Penn.

In the Sumerian tales of Gilgamesh and Huwawa, Enkidu is Gilgamesh's devoted servant from Uruk, free of all associations with the steppe, including prior knowledge of Huwawa. With the shift of Enkidu's origins to the steppe in the Akkadian Huwawa narrative, Enkidu is repeatedly characterized by Gilgamesh and the elders as one who "knows," by way of his experience in the realm of herdsmen. In this context, Enkidu's knowledge is crucial to his role as Gilgamesh's partner on the expedition. As reflected in Penn, the epic author in Penn then reinterprets Enkidu's back country origins as wild, recasting this past as a source of vitality and vigor as opposed to one of knowledge. Yet rather than remove the theme of knowledge entirely, the author displaces Enkidu's wisdom onto the three leading women in the epic: Gilgamesh's mother, Shamkat, and the tavern keeper.

---

[31] In the Penn tablet, the reading of Enkidu's character in relation to the back country is turned on its head, and his ignorance of bread is a social lack that must be remedied to allow contact with Uruk and its king. As such, the epic writer reverts to attitudes more like those of traditional Sumerian literature. Enkidu must be brought to the association with herdsmen that the Huwawa narrative already assumed, and the shepherd scene in Penn serves to give Enkidu a secondary connection with these people.

[32] So far as Enkidu's character may be discussed in light of the folk concept of the "noble savage," the theme is relevant only to the final OB portrayal, as seen in the Penn tablet. Enkidu is admired for his strength and takes offense at Gilgamesh's royal excesses. See Westenholz and Koch-Westenholz, "Enkidu—the Noble Savage?" 437–451.

The reorientation of Enkidu's origins in the Huwawa narrative prompts a transformation in his relationship to Gilgamesh. Enkidu's role as Gilgamesh's counselor, an element already present to some extent in the Sumerian tales, becomes crucial to the notion that the adventure requires a partnership.[33] Gilgamesh intends to make a name for himself by confronting Huwawa (Yale IV 148–150), and Enkidu knows Huwawa and his environs, through his experience among the herdsmen (III 106–107). Whereas Enkidu is solely a servant in the Sumerian texts, his new origins in Yale and the other Huwawa material render him Gilgamesh's comrade-in-arms (*ibrum*), his advisor (*mālikum*),[34] his dream interpreter,[35] and even his guide. Despite Enkidu's well-founded hesitations, Uruk's elders trust him to lead Gilgamesh on the journey, for "he has seen the path; he has traveled the road" (VI 252). Among these titles, the one that comes to characterize the relationship between the two heroes in Yale and the other Huwawa texts is *ibrī*, "my comrade." We have chosen this translation over the common rendering as "my friend" to emphasize the equality of status indicated by the word, rather than emotional content.[36] In fact, the standard reading "my friend" may represent another effect of the Penn tablet as introduction, casting every aspect of the relationship between Gilgamesh and Enkidu in terms of the passion and attraction felt by Gilgamesh in his dreams in Penn.

---

[33] The appearance of this counselor theme in both versions A and B indicates that it precedes all Akkadian renditions of the Huwawa story. Upon hearing of Gilgamesh's proposal to enter the highlands for felling cedar, Enkidu advises the king to consult the sun god Utu for assistance (A:8–12; B:22–28). After the two have captured Huwawa at the close of the tale, Enkidu then opposes his master's inclination toward pity. Gilgamesh suggests that they permit "the captive bird" to return untouched (A:161), but Enkidu doubts the wisdom of this choice, saying, "One who is tall, yet has no forethought, fate will consume" (A:170–171; cf. B:139a) According to version A, Enkidu takes matters into his own hands and lops off Huwawa's head (179); in B, it is unclear whether or not Huwawa dies.

[34] In Schøyen-1 obv. 2′, a fragment that appears to overlap with the material lost in the badly fragmented column I of Yale, the harlot refers to Enkidu as Gilgamesh's counselor (*mālikum*). It is significant that the elders, too, are referred to as Gilgamesh's *mālikū* (Yale V 201).

[35] See Schøyen-2, Nippur, and Harmal-1, with further discussion below.

[36] At the end of the entry in *CAD* s.v. *ibru*, the editor observes, "The word denotes an institutionalized relationship between free persons of the same status or profession which entailed acceptance of the same code of behavior and an obligation of mutual assistance. In Sum. the connotation 'comrade-in-arms' is well attested .... The term occurs after the OB period only in literary texts, mostly in the hendiadys *ibru u tappû*. The translation 'friend' should be used only for the latter, since *ibru* was originally devoid of emotional connotation."

The emphasis on Enkidu's knowledge is expressed especially in the recurring use of the verb *edûm*, "to know." This term occurs five times in the Yale tablet, almost always with respect to Enkidu. The first occurrence encapsulates both Enkidu's reluctance and his potential contribution due to his experience of Huwawa and the highlands. Enkidu tells Gilgamesh, "I knew (him), my comrade, in the highlands, when I used to roam with the herd ... Huwawa—his voice is the Deluge, his mouth is fire, his breath is death!" (III 106–107, 110–112). The word appears once more before Enkidu consents to go, in Gilgamesh's last effort at persuading him. Gilgamesh attempts to turn Enkidu's knowledge of Huwawa into an asset, as opposed to a reason to decline the adventure. He returns to the same theme of Enkidu's origins in the steppe, but instead of referring to his companion's knowledge of Huwawa, Gilgamesh recalls Enkidu's fame as a defender against all attacks. "A lion raided you, and you knew all, young men robbed your ..." (IV 152–153). These first occurrences of *edûm* occur in the two sections in Yale that permit the most direct comparison with Enkidu's characterization in Penn. In the Huwawa narrative, the theme of Enkidu's knowledge is essential to what distinguishes his birth and subsequent life in the steppe. When this story was elaborated into a longer epic, the link between Enkidu's knowledge and the steppe was discarded.

Not only do these discussions equate Enkidu's experience in the steppe with knowledge, but they also imply Gilgamesh's lack thereof. More direct declaration of this deficiency is asserted by the elders of Uruk, who do not hesitate to criticize Gilgamesh on just this point. Having gathered the people to announce his plan, Gilgamesh addresses them through the city elders (cf. IV 178–180, restored from 189–190). In response to Gilgamesh's confident boast that he can overcome Huwawa in the Cedar Forest (V 184), they open with a reference to Gilgamesh's ignorance: "You do not know (*lā tīde*) what you are doing" (192). Finally, after the elders have invoked both Enkidu's essential value as guide and the necessity of the gods' assistance, Enkidu offers himself as a balm against all fear. This time, his knowledge of Huwawa is positive, a reason for optimism: "I know (*īdeam*) his dwelling [in] the forest" (VI 275).[37]

---

[37] In lines 251–254, the elders ask Gilgamesh to accept Enkidu's help, letting Enkidu lead the way, because of his familiarity with the route. Line 253 is broken, but George tentatively restores [*i-d*]*e*? *ša* TIR *né-re-bé-tim*, "[He kno]ws(?) the entrances into the forest."

By the time of the heroes' departure, all of the key participants have reinforced the link between Enkidu's knowledge and his experience in the steppe.

Enkidu's role as the knowledgeable counselor reverberates throughout the rest of the Huwawa tale, and it becomes a reference point for distinguishing the voice of that story from that of the epic narrator. In the first section of the story, as represented in Yale, this role is defined by the verb *edûm*, "to know." Although this word may not occur elsewhere in the surviving evidence for the Huwawa narrative, Enkidu is consistently the one who advises and reassures Gilgamesh.[38] By its association with the particular theme of his origins in the steppe, Enkidu's "knowing" is central to the profound tension between the portrayals of Enkidu and Gilgamesh in Yale and in Penn.

In Penn, which represents the epic expansion, Enkidu's origins undergo a further shift, which by necessity impacts both his relationship to Gilgamesh and the expression of the knowledge motif. Now, Enkidu is utterly detached from all human company, a notion that appears to borrow from the tradition of Huwawa's origins, as found first of all in the Sumerian texts. Both Sumerian versions apply the motif of wild upbringing to Huwawa: "My mother who bore me was a hole in the highlands; my father who begat me was a hole in the hill-country" (B:152–153).[39] This creature is deprived even of the companionship of parents. Enkidu is described in similar terms in Penn, as one suckled by wild beasts (III 85–86). We see further evidence of this transference in Gilgamesh's second dream, with his description of the axe that symbolizes Enkidu: "its form was strange" (*šani būnūšu*, I 31). The elders of the Yale tablet describe Huwawa with exactly the same phrase: "We hear that Huwawa's face is strange" (*šanû būnūšu*, V 193). The familiar Huwawa imagery, with its overtones of both wildness and strength, serves the new objectives of the epic creation.

---

[38] In his first edition of Schøyen-2, George read the beginning of line 58, *i-[d]e-šu-[m]a*, "he knew him," which he has now revised. That interpretation envisioned Enkidu as subject and Huwawa as object, whereas George now considers Huwawa the subject of another verb (see translation note to lines 58–60). At this point, the reading of these lines remains in doubt.

[39] Compare version A: "Utu, I knew neither mother who bore me, nor father who raised me. I was born in the highlands, and you yourself raised me" (155–156). In this version, Huwawa addresses this statement to Utu right after his capture, before Gilgamesh pities him (159). In version B, the exchange occurs after Enkidu has advised Gilgamesh against letting him go (139–146).

According to the perspective of the epic author, Enkidu represents the physical power of untamed nature; this is what renders him the ultimate match for Gilgamesh. Here it is less important that Enkidu serve as a comrade or advisor than that he compare to Gilgamesh in physical glory: he is "a match to Gilgamesh in build" (V 183), with a smaller stature but bigger bones (184–185). Gilgamesh anticipates the arrival of a figure who is like him (I 17), one whom he loves "like a wife" (I 33). The close companionship between Gilgamesh and Enkidu in the Huwawa narrative is repackaged in Penn as equality of splendor, for only this equivalence can account for Gilgamesh's sorrow at Enkidu's death, the driving theme of the OB epic. Recurring vocabulary cements their likeness: Shamkat tells Enkidu he is "like a god" (II 53); she then leads him, "like a god" (II 74), to the shepherds' hut. In column V, the people declare that an equal has been provided for Gilgamesh, who is "like a god" (194–195). The concluding wrestling match only further confirms their equality, as Gilgamesh's apparent victory is understated, without explicit demonstration of physical superiority.[40]

The new notion of Enkidu as wild in Penn contributes to the likeness of Gilgamesh and Enkidu through divinity. Gilgamesh represents the city and its power, yet his mother is Ninsunna, "the wild cow of the fold" (VI 236–237). So far as divinity is linked to the force of undomesticated nature, Gilgamesh participates in this force, at the same time as Enkidu's godlike character is associated with his life in the steppe among the wild beasts, in the vision of the epic author found in Penn. It is significant, then, that neither Gilgamesh nor Enkidu is described explicitly as divine or godlike in the texts of the Huwawa narrative.[41]

---

[40] It is thus possible for Thorkild Jacobsen to conclude that when Gilgamesh kneels in VI 227, this is in recognition of Enkidu's victory ("The Gilgamesh Epic: Romantic and Tragic Vision," in Tzvi Abusch et al. eds, *Lingering Over Words: Studies in Ancient Near Eastern Literature in Honor of William L. Moran* [Atlanta: Scholars Press, 1990] 237). The manner of breaking off contact may also reflect the ritualized aspect of the bout, which occurs after Enkidu has been selected as the king's "equal" (V 195); see the discussion in George, *Babylonian Gilgamesh Epic*, 169–170.

[41] It appears that the scribal handling of the three main characters by the choice whether or not to mark their names orthographically with the divine determinative "dingir" operates at a level conceptually distinct from the direct description of the narrative. Although even Gilgamesh is not described as a god in the Huwawa material, his name is consistently marked with dingir wherever it appears (Penn, Yale, UM, Schøyen-2, Harmal-2, Ishchali, and Sippar). Enkidu's name is marked as divine in Penn, Yale, and the two Schøyen texts, but not in UM (I 4′), Ishchali (obv. 6′, 10′, 14′; rev. 23′, 39′, 40′), and Sippar (II 2′). Huwawa is only mentioned by name in four texts, two of which mark it with the dingir (Yale and Schøyen-2) and two of which do not (Harmal-2 and

The Penn tablet also contrasts with Yale in how it invokes political roles. In Yale, as throughout the Huwawa narrative, Gilgamesh is never called "king," even if he may be assumed to occupy such a role. Certainly the Sumerian tradition is based on the notion that Gilgamesh was one of the great kings of Uruk, and there is no indication that the Akkadian Huwawa narrative strips him of this position. He is outfitted lavishly by the craftsmen; he assembles together the people of the city and its elders, and it appears that he has arranged for Enkidu to join him on his expedition. At the same time, the lack of the royal title may reflect the relative insignificance of this role with regard to the plot in general. Gilgamesh hopes to make his name not as ruler of Uruk, a position that appears to offer no lasting tribute, but rather through what he accomplishes by individual daring, representing no one (IV 148–150). For Penn, the royal title expresses a power that is respected and perhaps feared. It is used in association with the abuses of Gilgamesh on the people of Uruk (IV 154, 156), yet Enkidu also praises Gilgamesh as one who must have received his kingship by Enlil's recognition (VI 238–240). In the epic, then, Gilgamesh's kingship is one expression of his uniqueness, born to Ninsunna "as one alone" (*kīma ištēnma*, 234–237).

With all the emphasis on Enkidu's likeness to Gilgamesh and on the pair's godlike character, the theme of Enkidu's knowledge is conspicuously absent from Penn. In contrast to Yale, the author of Penn only utilizes the verb *edûm* once in finite form, this time in negative terms, for what Enkidu does not yet know about normal social habits. "Enkidu did not know (*ul īde*) that bread was for eating; that beer was for drinking he had not been taught" (III 90–93). At this point in the narrative, Enkidu exists in a liminal state of not knowing; he has forgotten his birthplace (II 47) but has not yet acclimated to society. Whereas Yale touts Enkidu's familiarity with the steppe as an explicit advantage, Penn emphasizes the systematic eradication of Enkidu's former life: his diet of grass and milk is replaced with bread and beer; his hairy body is anointed and clothed; and his jaunts with the animals are supplanted by offensive attacks on predators. In essence, Enkidu's success depends upon the rejection—not the recollection—of his past, in that he now must identify with the city, abandoning his previous life in the steppe.[42]

Ishchali). We do not accept George's reading of Harmal-2 rev. 42 as repeating the epithet of Gilgamesh's mother, "the wild cow of the fold."

[42] As observed by Abusch, the Standard Babylonian version then transforms this departure from the steppe by having Enkidu attempt to return to the animals, who spurn

We recognize, then, a particular discontinuity between Penn and Yale in their perceptions of Enkidu's background. Whereas in the Yale text, Enkidu's experience equips him with crucial knowledge, rendering him essential as Gilgamesh's guide to the Cedar Forest, Penn associates Enkidu's life in the steppe with wild habits and sheer physical strength. This physical magnificence is the basis for an overwhelming emotional attachment that is described in sexual terms, when Gilgamesh caresses the axe in his dream and loves it like a wife (I 33–34). Such passionate love and the devastation at its loss provide the driving motivation for Gilgamesh in the latter part of the epic, after Enkidu has died. With Penn's eclipse of Enkidu's herding past and the recasting of his origins as feral, the source of Enkidu's knowledge is subsequently eliminated. Nonetheless, the theme of knowledge is not simply dropped. Rather, Enkidu's knowledge is displaced onto the central female figures in the epic, each of whom plays a pivotal role with regard to the pair's relationship and to the greater themes of mortality and loss, the primary contributions of the OB epic creator.

V. Enkidu's Heirs: The Knowledgeable
Women of the Gilgamesh Epic

It appears that the role of Gilgamesh's mother as her son's dream interpreter is an outgrowth of Enkidu's role in the Huwawa narrative.[43] Her recurring epithet, "knower of all" (*mudeat kalâma*),[44] resonates with Gilgamesh's declaration to Enkidu in Yale IV 152: "A lion raided you and you

---

him and force him to give up his life in nature ("The Courtesan, the Wild Man, and the Hunter: Studies in the Literary History of the Epic of Gilgamesh," in Sefati et al. eds., *"An Experienced Scribe Who Neglects Nothing": Ancient Near Eastern Studies in Honor of Jacob Klein* [Bethesda, MD: CDL, 2005] 422–424).

[43] For previous discussion of these characters, see Rivkah Harris, "Images of Women in the Gilgamesh Epic," in *Lingering over Words*, 219–230. Citing A. Leo Oppenheim (*The Interpretation of Dreams in the Ancient Near East, with a Translation of an Assyrian Dream-Book* [Philadelphia: American Philosophical Society, 1956] 221–222), Harris notes the frequent association of Mesopotamian women, human and divine, with dream interpretation (p. 221 and n. 12). Whereas Harris notes that the importance of women in the epic concerns their relationship with and assistance to Gilgamesh (p. 220), we focus on the role each of the three women plays with regard to the sweeping themes of the OB epic. Unlike Harris's synchronic analysis of women in the whole Gilgamesh Epic, especially as known in the SBV, our comments on the representation of women are confined to the OB epic.

[44] See Penn I 15, 37.

knew all (*kalâma tīde*)."[45] When Enkidu interprets Gilgamesh's dreams in the Huwawa narrative, the verb *edûm* is not applied, yet the mother's title in Penn indicates that this gift also belongs to the realm of knowledge. The interpretive skills of Gilgamesh's mother likewise serve as a tool for prediction, forecasting Enkidu's arrival and Gilgamesh's passion for him: "When you see him, you will rejoice ... You will embrace him, and you will lead him to me" (I 20–23). As the sole figure in Penn explicitly associated with knowledge, the mother's primary role is to anticipate the compatibility of Gilgamesh and Enkidu, the central focus of this tablet.

Although the term *edûm* is not used in connection with Shamkat, she too functions as a knowledgeable guide in the text, leading Enkidu to Gilgamesh and instructing him in the basic customs of human communities.[46] In II 56–74, "leading" verbs (*redûm, warûm*) are linked repeatedly to the harlot: twice, she proposes to lead Enkidu to Gilgamesh (II 56, 59); in a third instance, the narrator states, "Grasping his hand, she was leading him like a god" (II 73–74).[47] Furthermore, Shamkat is said to give Enkidu advice (*milkum*, II 67–68), an act that recalls the advisory role attributed to Enkidu and the elders in the Huwawa narrative.[48] The pair's interactions mainly consist of Shamkat's speech and instructions to the silent Enkidu. We are told in II 66 that "he heard her instruction, he agreed to her proposal."[49] In III 90–98, which begin with the negative use of *edûm* to describe what Enkidu does not know, Shamkat

---

[45] Compare the similar line in Schøyen-1 rev. 4'.

[46] Harris notes Shamkat's use of "proverbial language," which links her to both Gilgamesh's mother and the wise alewife ("Images of Women," 224). According to Harris, Shamkat's unexpected role is just one example of "status inversion" in the Gilgamesh epic (p. 223). Rather than present Shamkat as the lustful seductress, the author chooses to depict her as a maternal, wise woman (pp. 222–223). Harris's categories are stereotypes that need not apply to ancient Mesopotamia. If anything, Shamkat and the tavern keeper might be taken as proof that prostitution could be associated with wisdom.

[47] This element already appears in the Huwawa material; cf. Schøyen-1 obv. 4'–5': "Come, harlot, let me do something good for you, because you led me to the heart of Uruk-Thoroughfare-of-the-Land." We propose, however, that the harlot's original association with "leading" is then expanded in the epic, in which she facilitates Enkidu's acclimation to human society.

[48] See Schøyen-1 obv. 2' (Enkidu); Yale V 201; VI 248 (elders); cf. for Enkidu, IM obv. 19, as reconstructed by George (pp. 268–269): "the one born in the steppe was able to advise" (*waldam ṣērim mitlukam ile"i*). This designation is particularly instructive with regard to Enkidu's prior knowledge, as the author of IM explicitly ties Enkidu's origins in the steppe to his role as counselor.

[49] Compare Ishchali, in which Enkidu instructs Gilgamesh regarding Huwawa; Gilgamesh "heard what his comrade said" and behaves accordingly (rev. 19').

functions as the implicit counterpoint: *she* knows that bread and beer are for consumption and instructs her protégé accordingly. In sum, Shamkat's position as advisor is essential to Enkidu's transformation into Gilgamesh's equal.

Finally, it is worth mentioning the tavern keeper, who appears in the Sippar tablet, a text that we include with the Penn narrative as belonging to the larger OB epic.[50] Like Gilgamesh's mother and Shamkat, the tavern keeper represents yet another wise advisor tied to the central themes of the epic, namely, the heroes' partnership and Gilgamesh's confrontation of mortality. Once again, we witness a woman whose role is to instruct—in this case, advising Gilgamesh in the simple pleasures of mortal life: "Let your garment be clean, let your head be washed, bathe yourself with water. Bask in the little one who holds your hand, let a partner always take pleasure in your loins" (III 10–13). With Gilgamesh's reply, "With your heart, you have seen all …" (*amrātīma libbaki kal*[*a*] …, III 22), we recall both his mother's epithet (*mudeat kalâma*) and its possible origin in the Huwawa narrative with Enkidu (*kalâma tīde*).

We find then that elements of Enkidu's role as knowledgeable guide in the Huwawa narrative are transferred onto the three women of the OB epic. Gilgamesh's mother anticipates Enkidu's arrival through dreams; Shamkat properly prepares Enkidu to meet Gilgamesh; and finally, the tavern keeper consoles and instructs Gilgamesh after his partner's death.[51] In turn, these three women systematically advance the overarching themes of partnership and mortality, as they play key roles at each juncture of the pair's fateful relationship. The theme of knowledge, tied so explicitly to Enkidu's herding past in Yale, is detached from his character and linked instead to the themes of partnership and loss within the extended OB epic.

The core contribution of the epic author, namely, Gilgamesh's confrontation of mortality, thus provokes a series of changes in the narrative, most of which are tied directly to the characterization of Enkidu. For Gilgamesh to be adequately destroyed by Enkidu's death, Enkidu

---

[50] Note that the name Siduri does not occur in the OB text.

[51] These observations stand, however one understands the initial approach by Gilgamesh to the tavern keeper. Abusch proposes that the hero wants to bind himself to the divine tavern keeper and so escape death ("Gilgamesh's Request and Siduri's Denial, Part I," in Mark Cohen et al. eds., *The Tablet and the Scroll: Near Eastern Studies in Honor of William W. Hallo* [Bethesda, MD: CDL, 1993] 1–14). Though the name Siduri is not used of the OB character in Sippar, the interpretive issues remain the same.

must be recast as Gilgamesh's physical equal. Gilgamesh is the mightiest of men, and the only possible match for him must come from the wild, the domain of divine beings like Huwawa. In preparation for this partnership, Enkidu will leave behind the animal habits that accompany his existence outside human society. The new composition transfers onto Enkidu the traits that had been identified with Huwawa, who already combined divinely granted power with feral origins.[52] Once Enkidu is detached from human society, the original sense of collaboration between city and steppe is lost. In order to prepare Enkidu for his characterization as guardian of flocks, however, the author creates an intermediate stage of interaction with shepherds in which Enkidu becomes a "gentleman" (*awīlum*, Penn III 109) and protects the herdsmen from wolves and lions. Enkidu's knowledge, originally associated with his experience in the steppe, becomes extraneous with respect to the larger themes. In the new material, the role of advisor is picked up by female characters who guide Gilgamesh and Enkidu through crucial passages in their partnership and separation by death.

Despite the far-reaching impact of these changes, it is important to note that each one stems from elements original to the Akkadian Huwawa tradition: Enkidu's origins in the steppe, the motif of knowledge, and the partnership between Enkidu and Gilgamesh. With the elaboration of the Huwawa narrative into a longer epic, however, the relationship between Gilgamesh and Enkidu undergoes a major shift, a development that triggers both the reshuffling of these elements and the complete transformation of Enkidu's character and capabilities. It is nothing new to observe that in the OB epic, Enkidu's likeness to Gilgamesh is the basis for the grief that will drive Gilgamesh to seek a way to avoid death.[53] We submit, however, that as Gilgamesh's equal from the steppe, Enkidu has been recast from a previously unrecognized antecedent in the Akkadian version of the Huwawa tale. Enkidu's origins undergo a double shift: first

---

[52] It is interesting to observe that in the dream interpreted by Enkidu in the Nippur text, it is Huwawa with whom Gilgamesh grapples *ki-ma le-i-im* (obv. 5–6), the phrase that describes the wrestling scene between the heroes in Penn VI 218 and 224. Whether this phrase is translated "in order to prevail" or "like a bull" (see note to Penn VI 218), it could represent another expression of how the epic transfers traits from Huwawa to Enkidu. For translation as "prevail," see Esther J. Hamori, "A Note on *ki-ma* LI-*i-im* (Gilgamesh P 218, 224)," *JAOS* 127 (2007) 67–71.

[53] See for example, Jacobsen, "The Gilgamesh Epic," 245; Tigay, *Evolution of the Gilgamesh Epic*, 29.

from Uruk in the Sumerian to the steppe in the Akkadian Huwawa narrative, and then deeper into the wild in the Penn tablet and the OB epic as a whole. With the next sections, we set out to define the bounds of this intermediate literary stage and to explore its relation to the Sumerian tradition of Gilgamesh and Huwawa.

CHAPTER THREE

DEFINING THE BOUNDS OF THE
AKKADIAN HUWAWA NARRATIVE

Having observed contrasts in the characterization of Enkidu across the Penn and Yale tablets, the entire body of OB Gilgamesh material must be reevaluated to decide what originated with the prior narrative and what reflects the extended epic. Although the OB texts are commonly read together as components of the earliest Gilgamesh Epic, their narrative range is in fact quite limited. Ten of the twelve texts involve various stages of the Huwawa adventure. Only Penn and Sippar treat events outside the planning and execution of this campaign, the former leading up to Gilgamesh and Enkidu's first encounter, and the latter reflecting the aftermath of Enkidu's death. Because the Penn tablet displays a perspective and themes that do not fit the Huwawa narrative, particularly in its portrayal of Enkidu, we submit that this text marks an expansion from some shorter composition. Sippar treats events far removed from those in Penn, yet it shows substantial parallels with Penn in thought and language, parallels that contrast with the Huwawa narrative. When viewed alongside the ten OB Huwawa texts, Penn and Sippar together represent the coherent extension of a shorter Gilgamesh tale defined by that one adventure. Sumerian Gilgamesh texts from the same period include two versions of a freestanding Huwawa tale, and the earlier Akkadian narrative must be related to that Sumerian story.

The expanded narrative reflected by Penn and Sippar incorporates key plot developments that characterize the later Gilgamesh Epic, and it is therefore appropriate to identify both texts as reflecting the early reproduction of that first "epic," already created in the Old Babylonian period. In order to evaluate the relationship of these two texts to the epic as a whole, we must consult later evidence for the longer narrative. According to the Standard Babylonian Version (SBV) of the first millennium, the defeat of Huwawa is just one of two exploits, along with slaying the Bull of Heaven, that show what Gilgamesh and Enkidu can achieve as companions. This partnership is preceded by a long account of Enkidu's creation and his meeting with Gilgamesh, and the joint venture is brought to an end by the death of Enkidu. Gilgamesh then seeks some way to

escape mortality, a possibility that is put within reach by a visit to Uta-
napishti, the man who survived the great flood. Already in the 14th–13th
centuries, the Hittite paraphrase attests all of these major episodes in a
Gilgamesh Epic, and it is not difficult to conclude that Penn and Sippar
constitute earlier evidence for the epic composition.[1]

In this section of our study, we elaborate the main elements necessary
to define a freestanding Akkadian Huwawa narrative. To this end, we
begin by identifying features of the Sippar text that share the distinct
voice and perspective found in Penn. The ten Huwawa-related texts
then become the basis for reconstructing the outlines of an Akkadian
Huwawa account. Together, they appear to offer a surprisingly complete
sampling of the whole narrative, notwithstanding significant gaps and
some variations. It must be established that these share a coherent plot
and point of view that can be distinguished from the "epic" view in
Penn and Sippar. Together, these features are central to the authorial
vision of the independent Akkadian Huwawa narrative: Enkidu is the
expert guide, born in the steppe; Huwawa is the central objective, and
the cedar follows as a benefit of his defeat; and Gilgamesh undertakes the
whole adventure in order to win fame from valor, not title. As a coherent
perspective, such elements of the OB Huwawa tale can be recognized
by comparison with the Sumerian story of Gilgamesh and Huwawa. The
Sumerian most likely preceded the Akkadian, in that Enkidu's identity as
the servant of Gilgamesh already at Uruk is shared by the whole Sumerian
Gilgamesh repertoire. In the Akkadian narrative, Enkidu's origins are
moved to the steppe, a radical transformation with associations that
ripple through the Huwawa tale. In the following chapter, we evaluate
how the Akkadian Huwawa tale evolved from and interacted with its
Sumerian predecessor, which continued to be learned and copied even
after composition of the Akkadian epic.

---

[1] See George (*Babylonian Gilgamesh Epic*, 25) for the extent of the Middle Babylonian
epic. Fragments of what George gathers as MB Boǧ₁ may belong to a single large tablet
that he reconstructs as covering a narrative from the tyranny of Gilgamesh and creation
of Enkidu through the Huwawa and Bull of Heaven adventures to Enkidu's death and Gilgamesh's lament (p. 309). The materials all date from about 1400, and George concludes
that the scribe was following a version derived from the late OB and earliest MB periods.
For the definition of an extended OB epic, it is not necessary to imagine that every element of the later epic was already present, and even our distinction of Huwawa narrative
from OB epic simplifies a process that may have involved further variants and stages of
development.

I. *The Sippar Tablet: The Epic and the Death of Enkidu*

The Sippar tablet introduces new characters and themes not present in the other OB Akkadian texts. Shamash the sun god, who was only invoked at a distance in Yale, now has a speaking role, as does Utu in the Sumerian Huwawa tale. The tavern keeper and the boatman Sursunabu are uniquely connected to the moments when each must help Gilgamesh move to the next stage in his journey. Gilgamesh demands to be shown Uta-na'ishtim, a man who lives across the waters of death. With so many new characters and situations, Sippar offers a particular test of the continuity of language and ideas first visible in Penn, so far as these contrasted with those of Yale. Moreover, the distinct four-column format and probable production at Sippar, far from the likely origin of Penn and Yale downstream (see below), prepare us for a completely different scribal practice. Notwithstanding the fresh themes and situations, along with its point of origin, Sippar shows several concrete points of connection with the Penn text.

At the start of the preserved Sippar text, the steppe represents a world apart from human society, as in Penn, so that Gilgamesh inhabits the world that had belonged to Enkidu before he came to Uruk. The first four lines conclude a broken section that describes Gilgamesh's search for life. He has hunted wild animals, dressed in their hides and eaten their meat (I 1'–2').[2] He has dug water holes where there had been none, a reflection of life beyond even the outer range of human movement.[3] Gilgamesh is now a predator in the country Enkidu had shared peacefully with the animals. Later, he characterizes his whole existence as that of a "hunter" (*hābilum*, II 11'), the profession of the man who first brings Enkidu to the attention of Gilgamesh in the SBV.[4] The author views the steppe as a realm foreign to human occupation, as in Penn, although Gilgamesh can never belong to the steppe as did Enkidu.

---

[2] Line 1 mentions two animals, the wild bull (*rīmum*) and another grazing animal (*tišānu*); see the discussion in George, *Babylonian Gilgamesh Epic*, 280–281. Jean-Marie Durand, "'Hittite' *tišanuš* = mariote *tišânum*," *N.A.B.U.* 1988/15, pp. 10–11, identifies the animal as an "ovin," a kind of wild sheep.

[3] The text of Sippar I 3'–4' is badly damaged, but references to wells in line 3' and to water in line 4' suggest that the issue is what Gilgamesh drinks.

[4] The word *hābilu* is more often applied to the "criminal" or "wrongdoer," but the references to beasts and hides indicate that Gilgamesh has in fact been hunting (cf. *CAD* s.v. *hābilu* A s., which cites this text and translates, "I am roaming like an evildoer in the midst of the desert"). In Tablet I of the SBV, the hunter who first encounters Enkidu is

Gilgamesh's time in the back country identifies him with Enkidu, even though he cannot live there as Enkidu did, at one with the animal inhabitants. Although Enkidu has died, he remains vividly present in the Sippar narrative, and that presence is defined in terms already familiar from Penn. As opposed to the working partnership developed in the Huwawa narrative, the relationship between the two men in Penn and Sippar is marked by a passion rooted in their unique likeness. In the Penn text, Gilgamesh's feelings for Enkidu are anticipated through the figure of an axe that he "loves" like a wife (*arâmšuma kīma aššatim*, I 33). When we find Gilgamesh speaking with a female tavern keeper at the start of Sippar column II, his first preserved words lament the loss of Enkidu, whom he "loves" mightily (*ša arammušu danniš*, II 2'–3', repeating lines 0'–1').

The theme of likeness unfolds in Sippar with language already found in Penn, while the application is distinct in each case. When the tavern keeper responds to the hero's plea for help in crossing the sea, she begins, "There has not been, Gilgamesh, one like you (*ša kīma kâta*)" (III 26). Even as she sets aside the very identity of Enkidu, and along with it the overwhelming grief felt by Gilgamesh, her words recall Enkidu's likeness to Gilgamesh in his first dream in Penn. Gilgamesh's mother tells him that there will be one "like" him (*ša kīma kâti*, I 17). At the very sight of this man like himself, Gilgamesh will rejoice, embrace him, and bring him to his mother (I 20–23). Both Gilgamesh and Enkidu are godlike (II 53, 74; V 194). Now, the tavern keeper appears to return Gilgamesh to his previous condition, alone in his astonishing capacity. Further, by rendering the statement in the simple past (*ul ibši*), she proposes to him that even Enkidu was not truly his match. Gilgamesh will pursue his quest for immortality as a unique hero, the one man capable of making the voyage necessary to attain it.

Neither the theme of love nor that of likeness is represented in the Huwawa evidence that stands between Penn and Sippar in the OB Gilgamesh narrative. For the Huwawa campaign, Gilgamesh and Enkidu are companions, each addressing the other as "my comrade," and their bond is demonstrated by dangers shared, not described directly.[5] The

---

usually called a *ṣayyādu*, but at his first introduction, this is elaborated by the term *ḫābilu* (I 113), which may also be translated as "hunter, trapper" (see *CAD* s.v. *ḫābilu* B s.). The later use of this term in connection with an intruder into the steppe only confirms the epic's perception of this domain as wild; the term itself offers no link with Penn.

[5] The whole epic then treats this relationship as having been established with the Huwawa adventure, so that in the Sippar text, Gilgamesh still speaks of his departed partner as "my comrade" (II 7'; III 18).

Sippar text provides the earliest evidence for extending the tale beyond Huwuwa. This is accomplished above all through the death of Enkidu, so that Gilgamesh is isolated as a solitary seeker, driven by his reaction to the loss. In this reorientation of the Akkadian Gilgamesh, the death of Enkidu overshadows his life, and the intensification of the bond with Gilgamesh in Penn anticipates the lament recounted in Sippar.

The character of Gilgamesh alone is also consistent across Penn and Sippar, especially through his inclination to act in anger. Although the experience of Enkidu's loss is presented in Sippar as having driven Gilgamesh away from human company, leaving him in unspeakable distress, he remains headstrong and sure of himself. Gilgamesh refuses to heed the sun god's warning to give up his search for life, and he declines the tavern keeper's advice to return home. Then, when he goes to Sursunabu, Gilgamesh rashly destroys what turn out to have been the Stone Things that allow the boatman to cross the sea to Uta-na'ishtim. Gilgamesh smashes the stones "in rage" (*uzzu*), an action characteristic of his confident right not to be opposed. The same confidence marks his combat with Enkidu in Penn, after which the narrator states, "His rage (*uzzu*) calmed, he turned away" (VI 229–230). Throughout the evidence for the Huwawa narrative, Gilgamesh never acts in anger, even when he and Enkidu finally agree to kill the Cedar Forest guardian. In a scene preserved in the Ishchali text, Gilgamesh dispatches Huwawa without emotion (rev. 19'–22'). For detail, we are offered only the axe and sword with which the deed is done. As in Gilgamesh and Huwawa version A, Huwawa is killed with a blow to the neck, but the Akkadian text lacks the statement of emotion provided by the Sumerian, where Enkidu is the one who acts in rage (A:179). Throughout the Huwawa narrative, Gilgamesh remains determined to attain his goal, yet he wins the support of Enkidu and the townspeople by charisma and persuasion, and at every stage of the expedition, he faithfully follows Enkidu's counsel. For all he has suffered, the Gilgamesh of Sippar resembles most the character presented in Penn.

Along with these characteristics of Gilgamesh and his relationship to Enkidu, Penn and Sippar share a key structural feature of what comes to be the extended epic: blocks of seven days and nights that occur at decisive moments in development of the plot. William Moran considers that in the SBV, three such blocks indicate essential transitions in the development of Gilgamesh. The first two of these are already present in OB evidence, one in Penn and the other in Sippar. Enkidu has sex with the harlot for seven days and nights (Penn II 48), launching him toward

Uruk and its king. After Enkidu dies, Gilgamesh spends the same length of time refusing to accept his death: "I would not let him be buried, lest my comrade arise at my cry, for seven days and seven nights, until the worm fell from his nose" (Sippar II 6'–9').[6] A third interval occurs when Gilgamesh finally faces the possibility of winning immortality, if he can only stay awake for seven days in the company of Uta-napishti (SBV XI 209, 225–230).[7] The seven days and nights give a ritual aspect to these moments of transition, so that each becomes a rite of passage. Since these blocks of time remain major signposts for narrative structure in the later Gilgamesh Epic, it is significant that the OB evidence preserves two of them on either side of the Huwawa narrative with none inside it. The seven-day unit has no role in that tale, at any stage of its preservation.

The Sippar tablet also displays noticeable contrasts with Penn, and the points of contact are perhaps all the more striking in light of these divergences. Aside from the fact that the text deals with Gilgamesh after his loss of Enkidu, far removed from the episodes found in Penn, the tablets have different formats and probably were produced at considerable distance from each other. The six-column Penn and Yale tablets are thought to come from Larsa, far downstream from Sippar, which, if the true origin of that four-column tablet, would be the furthest inland find-spot for the OB Gilgamesh evidence.[8] The strong thematic and verbal links between Penn and Sippar coexist with a noticeable difference in style that may reflect the textual variability characteristic of this period. At least, we cannot assume that the Gilgamesh series represented by Penn and Yale would have included exactly this form of the narrative found in Sippar. The speaking role for the sun god Shamash has no counterpart in Penn, which lacks any active role for the gods. Ninsunna plays her advising role

---

[6] It is not clear at which point Enkidu dies in the OB Gilgamesh. In the SBV, he dies at Uruk, where the heroes remain after slaying the Bull of Heaven (Tablets VI–VIII), and Gilgamesh's first call to mourning begins with the elders and the people of Uruk (VIII 9–10).

[7] Moran, "The Epic of Gilgamesh: A Document of Ancient Humanism," in *The Most Magic Word* (Washington, DC: CBA, 2002) 13. He credits the first observation that there are three seven-day blocks to Hope Nash Wolff, "Gilgamesh, Enkidu, and the Heroic Life," *JAOS* 89 (1969) 392 n. 2. The third seven-day unit may have originated in the OB epic as well, so far as Sippar suggests that Gilgamesh is headed for a meeting with Uta-na'ishtim. George (*Babylonian Gilgamesh Epic*, 183) argues that we should read "seven days and seven nights" in all OB contexts, as opposed to "six days and seven nights" in the SBV. The contrast is clear through comparison of the OB Sippar tablet with the SBV Tablet XI.

[8] Regardless of the exact origin, the tablet definitely shows many features of upstream or "north Babylonian" orthography (George, *Babylonian Gilgamesh Epic*, 272 n. 133).

as Gilgamesh's human mother, resident with him in Uruk. Given the particular affiliation of Sippar with Shamash,[9] it is conceivable that this element of the Sippar narrative reflects and perhaps even confirms the text's origin in that city and would not have belonged to every rendition of the OB epic.[10]

Despite the significantly different concerns of Sippar when compared to Penn, the specific traits in common, especially the themes of the wild steppe and Gilgamesh's love, along with the seven days of mourning, indicate a substantial literary connection between the two texts. They pertain to the character of Gilgamesh, the definition of his relationship to Enkidu, and the nature of Enkidu's domain, the steppe. The links are manifest in specific language shared by Penn and Sippar, and they appear in every major section of the Sippar text. There are other instances of specific terminology and usage shared by the two texts that would confirm their connection.[11] We conclude that Sippar also reflects the

---

[9] The Shamash temple Ebabbar was long central to the town of Sippar; see Dominique Charpin and Martin Sauvage, "Sippar," in Francis Joannès ed., *Dictionnaire de la Civilisation Mésopotamienne* (Paris: Robert Laffont, 2001) 782–784.

[10] Penn and Sippar present a noticeable difference in style that may reflect the variability of different copies from the OB epic narrative. More than any other part of the OB Gilgamesh material, Penn incorporates the narration of unfolding action as if the reader were watching (see the note to Penn I 11). Penn also has a higher concentration of repetitive parallelism in its poetry than the other texts, as visible especially in the scene at the shepherds' camp (III 87–116), a section with minimal direct speech. The speaking role for Shamash stands out in Sippar as the only such direct divine speech in the OB Gilgamesh evidence (I 5'–8'). Both Penn and Yale identify the city of Gilgamesh as Uruk-Thoroughfare (*rebītum*, Penn I 28; II 57; IV 154, 156; V 177, 180; VI 214; Yale IV 174, 176, 179, 180; V 189; cf. Schøyen-1 obv. 5', 7'), whereas Gilgamesh tells Sursunabu that he is from Uruk-Eanna (Sippar IV 9), a variant that perhaps follows a different local copying tradition. Without further evidence, explanation of these contrasts must remain elusive. The important continuities between Penn and Sippar, including characterization of the relationship between the heroes and the seven-day structuring component, indicate that both texts evidently reflect the authorial vision of the epic. Nevertheless, the contrasting styles suggest voices from different individuals, perhaps reflecting the distance of Sippar from the sites of text production downstream. These two voices show the degree of variation that could develop with different renditions of the epic in separate settings.

[11] Shamash begins his intervention with Gilgamesh by saying, "Where are you wandering?" (*e-eš ta-da-al*, Sippar I 7'). In Penn, the harlot confronts the wedding traveler with the question, "Where are you rushing?" (*e-eš ta-hi-š[a-a]m*, IV 145). In both cases, an important verbal exchange is launched with the question "where?" which interrupts a man's travel. Each time the question begins with vocative address, "Young man!" (*eṭil*) or "Gilgamesh!" The interrogative adverb *êš* represents a rare form of *ayiš*, "whither?" ("to what place?"), attested only in the Penn and Sippar tablets of the OB Gilgamesh (see also Sippar III 1), and in one lexical list, according to both *CAD* (s.v. *ayiš*) and *AHw* (s.v. *êš*). In all three lines, it is spelled *e-eš*.

composition of an extended narrative that may be called the first Gilgamesh Epic. Because the Sippar text constitutes the only OB narrative
after the defeat of Huwawa, and it shares the voice and vision of Penn,
the remaining evidence under consideration for a prior Akkadian Gilgamesh tale is confined entirely to the Huwawa adventure.[12] However an
earlier narrative may have ended, there is no basis for defining it in terms
beyond the Huwawa expedition, and the existence of a Sumerian story
with just this definition suggests that the first Akkadian account shared
this framework.

As a whole, the Sippar tablet directly develops the implications of
Enkidu's death, which becomes the catalyst for every act that follows.
In Sippar, Enkidu's only function is to die and leave Gilgamesh bereft.
The Huwawa material makes much of the bond between Gilgamesh
and Enkidu, in whose companionship the combination of heroic ambi-
tion and wise caution brings unprecedented human achievement. No

---

Two other features in Sippar offer possible continuities with Penn, though without
the direct match of rare diction. In lines I 10′ and II 10′, the Sippar text marks the
connection of current thought to past events with the use of *ištu* as a conjunction, "after."
This narrative construction is absent from the extant Huwawa narrative evidence, and
its only other occurrence in the OB material is in Penn VI 231, with the transition from
the fight to Enkidu's spoken admiration for Gilgamesh: *ištu irassu inē'u* ("Once he had
turned away …"). In Sippar II 10′, the conjunction is redundant, with *warkīšu*, "after
him."

The rare word *marhītum* derives from the verb *rehûm*, which describes the sexual
act in terms of the man's emission. A lexical list equates it with a "wife" (*aššatu*), but
the legal status surely has nothing to do with the tavern keeper's advice to Gilgamesh.
It is noteworthy that in Penn the verb *rehûm* is applied to Enkidu's sex with Shamkat
(II 49) and to the right of the king with a bride (IV 159). Here in the Sippar text, the
focus is explicitly sexual, with the noun *sūnu* ("lap, crotch, genitals") also defined in
terms of the man's role: "Let the partner (*marhītum*) always take pleasure in your loins"
(III 13). George objects to Abusch's suggestion that the *marhītum* may be a prostitute (in
Abusch, "Gilgamesh's Request and Siduri's Denial, Part I," 8–9; with further discussion
of the text in Abusch, "Gilgamesh's Request and Siduri's Denial, Part II: An Analysis and
Interpretation of an Old Babylonian Fragment about Mourning and Celebration," *JANES*
22 [1993] 3–17). In our analysis, the purely sexual role explains the term's usage, rather
than social standing. This naturally comes to be associated with a wife, as in the lexical
text discussed by Anne Draffkorn Kilmer, "The First Tablet of *malku = šarru* together
with its Explicit Version," *JAOS* 83 (1963) 436.

[12] While Penn and Yale together display the capacity for texts from the same scribal
hand to preserve evidence of two different authorial visions, Penn and Sippar allow us
to consider how texts from different hands and distant settings can preserve evidence
of authorial continuity. However much this four-column epic series may reflect the
variability of reproduction in its own idiosyncratic circle, not only the broad themes but
also specific language and motifs still match details found in the version of the epic found
in the Penn Tablet.

narrative tension, however, accompanies its basic existence. Penn and Sippar display a radical change, whereby the very formation of this friendship and its dissolution offer a drama of their own.

With Enkidu's death at center in the newly extended composition, the emphasis shifts to Gilgamesh the individual. The tale is no longer focused on what the two can accomplish by their collaboration; rather, the epic is finally about Gilgamesh alone.[13] It explores how an individual must live, must accept the good in life and cannot escape the limits of mortality. The tavern keeper exhorts Gilgamesh to enjoy the physical essentials: food and drink, dance and fine clothes, the intimacy of a sexual partner and the hope embodied in a child. Now, the ultimate point of the bond with Enkidu is its loss and how that loss affects Gilgamesh's psyche. Here we see the force of the fact that Gilgamesh is the one who loves Enkidu, while we learn nothing of Enkidu's emotions. Enkidu may be the perfect match for Gilgamesh, but in the epic, it is only Gilgamesh's passion that matters. After the loss of his partner in adventure, Gilgamesh's psychological state is the focus.

II. *The Huwawa Narrative as Preserved in Ten Old Babylonian Texts*

Outside of Penn and Sippar, which belong to an "epic" composition, all the remaining Old Babylonian evidence treats the Huwawa episode. Together, the ten remaining OB Gilgamesh texts, including Yale, present a remarkably full view of a coherent Huwawa narrative, in spite of the fact that no two of them appear to have been copied for a single series. In addition, the individual texts and fragments are in varied states of preservation, and they reflect diverse geographical origins and scribal purposes. Out of this mix of evidence, we must evaluate the nature of the OB Huwawa tale that emerges. None of the ten texts displays the innovations and language that characterize Penn and Sippar. All of them can be read as belonging to a single narrative that continues intelligibly from the six-column Yale tablet.[14] An expedition to find and defeat Huwawa is planned and carried out, with success only following a long journey marked by frightful dreams. Throughout, Enkidu and Gilgamesh

---

[13] When Wolff observes that only Gilgamesh undergoes real change in the epic, not Enkidu, she reflects this creation ("Gilgamesh, Enkidu, and the Heroic Life," 392).
[14] Among the ten, Schøyen-1 and UM overlap directly with the content of Yale.

are characterized in terms consistent with Yale, in contrast to Penn and Sippar. Even the sheer number of Akkadian Huwawa narrative texts may attest not only to the popularity of the tale but also to its capacity to stand alone, like the Sumerian Gilgamesh and Huwawa. In this light, it is possible to argue that the OB epic itself was still very much built around a Huwawa narrative, playing out a fresh vision of its implications for the hero Gilgamesh.

A. *The Scope of the Huwawa Narrative*

All ten texts for the OB Huwawa narrative date to roughly the same period, during the first Babylonian dynasty, like the Penn and Sippar texts, so that all may well have been copied with awareness of an extended Gilgamesh Epic. None of them was copied outside of Babylonia, although they cover a range from Uruk or Larsa downstream (Yale) to Nerebtum upstream, in the region of Eshnunna (Ishchali).[15] Eight of the ten texts, all but Yale and the fragment UM, were copied as single-column extracts, suggesting that the Huwawa story belonged to scribal training in literature, the one Akkadian text that evidently joined the mass of Sumerian literature in this function. As of now, no extract from the larger OB epic has yet been discovered, so we must conclude tentatively that the epic did not share this educational role. If anything, the evidence suggests that it was reserved for a more advanced stage, to be copied only in multi-column tablets, like the tablets for whole literary works in Sumerian.

As preserved in the available material, the plot of the Huwawa narrative may be divided into the following parts, each represented by more than one text:

1. The introduction presents special problems, to be discussed in detail in Chapter 5. Yale picks up directly from Penn, as expected from the physical evidence for their copying as a series, and columns I and II of Yale must have contained material that bridged the epic expansion of Penn and the already extant Huwawa narrative. The text for the original Huwawa introduction appears to be lost

---

[15] George discusses the origins of each tablet with its edition. Nippur, Harmal-1 and -2 (Shaduppum), and Ishchali (Nerebtum) have known provenance, while Yale (with Penn) is reputed to have come from Larsa or Uruk/Warka. Schøyen-1 and -2, UM, and IM are of unknown origin, although Schøyen-2 and IM show a blend of language and writing traits from upstream and downstream (*Babylonian Gilgamesh Epic*, 224–225, 267).

permanently, though Schøyen-1 offers details independent from the Penn scenario, especially as related to the first encounter between Enkidu and Gilgamesh and the formation of their partnership.

2. Yale columns III–VI are set entirely at Uruk, as Gilgamesh persuades Enkidu to join him, and the elders offer their caution and advice before departure. The fragment UM, which belonged to another multi-column tablet, would have treated most of the same material. Its first legible lines overlap with the end of Yale column II, and the tablet must have opened with content somewhere in that column.[16]

3. Schøyen-2, Nippur, Harmal-1, and probably the reconstructed Schøyen-3, follow Gilgamesh and Enkidu on their journey toward Huwawa, a journey that is defined entirely by Gilgamesh's terrifying dreams and Enkidu's reassuring interpretations. The dreams are presented as a series in two of the texts, none of which overlaps with another: the first and second in Schøyen-2, with the introduction of a third; a fourth in Nippur, with reference back to a preceding one; and an unnumbered dream in Harmal-1, which George therefore takes as the first in a distinct version of the narrative. Schøyen-3 includes one reference to Enkidu interpreting a dream and two lines with something "favorable," and though the traces suggest overlap with the fourth dream in Nippur, the line-by-line content appears to be entirely distinct from anything in the other three journey texts.

4. The confrontation with Huwawa is confined to Harmal-2 and Ishchali, both of which are severely damaged. As in the Sumerian tradition, Huwawa seems to be captured alive, so that he has opportunity to plead for his life (Harmal-2). Gilgamesh and Enkidu kill Huwawa nonetheless and dispatch his auras afterward, so that they are free to harvest the valuable trees of his domain (Ishchali, and perhaps the start of IM). Finally, they make plans to build Enlil a temple-door as a gift (IM). Much is lost from all three of these tablets, so definitive statements are difficult. Nevertheless, the legible contents caution us not to assume the events preserved in the later Gilgamesh Epic. There is no hint of divine disapproval, though the gift indicates a desire to placate Enlil in case he is annoyed, as he is elsewhere in

---

[16] The obverse of UM comes from the left margin of the tablet, so its first columns, and neither the upper nor the lower edge is preserved (see George, *Babylonian Gilgamesh Epic*, 216–217).

early second-millennium literature.[17] Although Enlil must be kept happy, there is no sign that any reprisal looms, and there is no reason to expect Enkidu's death.[18] In the Sumerian version A, Enlil is angered by the slaughter of Huwawa, yet he takes Huwawa's powers and distributes them according to his preference, keeping some for himself. Neither hero's life is threatened.[19]

As a collection, the ten texts cover the full range of the episode known to the later epic, from the formation of a partnership between Gilgamesh and Enkidu at Uruk, to preparation and journey, to confrontation with Huwawa and victory. In this Akkadian narrative, the dramatic tension occurs not in the conflict with Huwawa but in the anticipation. Should they even set out from Uruk? Huwawa is fearsome in Gilgamesh's dreams; dare they continue? Seven of the ten texts treat the period before they meet Huwawa, a pattern that underscores the attraction of the anticipation more than the conflict itself. Once the two arrive, we hear only of their success, and the one question is whether Huwawa must die. Although the ending is preserved in broken segments, it nevertheless appears optimistic, even celebratory. Against all fears, Gilgamesh has survived, and he makes his name not by dying in battle with Huwawa but by overcoming him. By the end of the Akkadian Huwawa narrative,

---

[17] Enlil's unreasonable annoyance dominates the Akkadian flood text, Atrahasis, and his irritation is blamed for the destruction of Sumer and Ur in the lamentation literature.

[18] The OB evidence also offers no explanation for how or why Enkidu dies in the first epic, as attested in Sippar. Two possibilities suggest themselves. If the Bull of Heaven story was not added to the epic until somewhat later, the slaying of Huwawa alone could have provoked Enlil to reprisal. In the Sumerian version A, Enlil is angry, though no punishment is evident. Alternatively, if the Bull of Heaven episode was incorporated into the extended epic during the OB period, it could have brought with it the cause of divine displeasure that survives in later versions. With only two OB texts outside the Huwawa material, however, it is impossible to gauge the possible role of the Bull of Heaven tale in the OB epic with any confidence. Our approach allows for the possibility of variant renditions of the OB epic, with and without inclusion of the Bull account, because this need not change the characterizations and plot development that result from the basic expansion beyond the Huwawa expedition. The hymn that begins the Sumerian Gilgamesh and Huwawa B offers some evidence that the two adventures were already associated in some terms in Sumerian literature in the early second millennium. In slightly varying forms, this praise to Gilgamesh occurs in all Sumerian literature only in the two Huwawa versions (A:130–134, 164–169; B:1–4) and in the Bull of Heaven tale (unprovenanced 91–96; Me-Turan Fragment D 39–41). The hymn appears to have been composed to expand a text that already existed, and wherever it appeared first, it finally displays a sense that these form a set, as George proposes for MB Boǧ₂ as an actual copy of the two episodes in Akkadian (*Babylonian Gilgamesh Epic*, 317–319).

[19] See lines 185–202; the end of version B is lost.

Gilgamesh is famous for an achievement that has nothing to do with his rule of Uruk. He has earned his name indeed, by the single act of defeating Huwawa.

B. *Huwawa as the Defining Center*

We define the Akkadian story that preceded creation of the Gilgamesh Epic as the "Huwawa narrative" because more than any other feature, Huwawa binds all the elements together as a unit.[20] Although the Sumerian counterpart has conventionally been called "Gilgamesh and Huwawa," it is only in the Akkadian rendition that Huwawa truly takes center stage, from beginning to end. Especially in the Sumerian version B, which shows less affinity with the Akkadian than version A and most likely preserves an earlier form of the narrative, Huwawa appears as a complete surprise, only present after Gilgamesh and Enkidu have cut down trees and piled them for transport. In contrast, Huwawa is the great obstacle and alluring challenge from the start of the Akkadian tale, and the valuable timber is only an outcome for victory.[21] His terror is already famous among the people of Uruk. The Yale tablet provides the first discussion of the expedition, with long debate over its feasibility, and the argument revolves entirely around the danger represented by Huwawa. When Gilgamesh has dreams along the way, as portrayed in Schøyen-2, Schøyen-3, Nippur, and Harmal-1, each one presents a vision of Huwawa.[22] Neither the debate nor the dreams is found in the Sumerian, so that all the major contributions to the story pertain to the feared guardian. More than the Sumerian story that preceded it, the first Akkadian Gilgamesh was indeed a Huwawa narrative.

---

[20] We understand the Akkadian Huwawa narrative to have been received by the epic author as a written work, who likewise created a written composition. The Akkadian tale recasts the main characters and their motives from a Sumerian story that we know circulated in writing, even though the new composition did not incorporate any part of the Sumerian as received text. This process thus contrasts with what occurred with the first Gilgamesh Epic, which was created by the massive expansion of a received text, the Akkadian Huwawa narrative.

[21] See already Abusch, "Hunting in the Epic of Gilgamesh: Speculations on the Education of a Prince," in M. Cogan and D. Kahn eds., *Treasures on Camels' Humps: Historical and Literary Studies from the Ancient Near East Presented to Israel Ephʿal* (Jerusalem: Magnes, 2008) 16–17.

[22] In Schøyen-3, Fragment 2:4′ introduces Enkidu's dream interpretation by "the seven auras," which pertain directly to Huwawa (cf. Yale IV 137).

Naturally, the characterization of Huwawa in the OB Gilgamesh material cannot be compared directly with Penn and Sippar, where he does not appear. It is nevertheless important to consider how the ten texts of the Akkadian Huwawa narrative are bound by a set of key features, several of which clash with the perspective of the epic. Together, these ten texts indicate that the Akkadian Huwawa narrative represents a massive transformation of the Sumerian story. In the Akkadian tale, Huwawa's characterization constitutes a major innovation that is central to redefining the relationship between Gilgamesh and Enkidu. Huwawa is prominent in every phase of the unfolding plot, and his presence provides an essential unifying feature through the different phases of the campaign against him.[23] Together, these texts offer a consistent portrait of Huwawa, while they suggest some variation in the vocabulary associated with individual renditions of the story, perhaps also reflecting the different geographical origins of the tablets.

The following traits are attributed to Huwawa throughout the set, with at least four texts attesting each one. All of the traits are present together in Yale, by far the longest text, as well as in Schøyen-2, which provides the second longest sequence of preserved material. First of all, Huwawa is guardian of the Cedar Forest. This job description contrasts immediately with the Sumerian tale, where Huwawa simply inhabits the wilderness that contains the desirable trees. In the Akkadian narrative, in which Enkidu already knows of this guardian role, Huwawa must be taken into account in advance. Enkidu explains at length how the Cedar Forest is guarded (*naṣārum*) by "Wer," who is somehow identified with Huwawa under the power of Adad (Yale III 129–135).[24] After the second dream in Schøyen-2, Gilgamesh and Enkidu continue on their way until they can hear Huwawa's constant roar (rev. 57). At this point, he is recognized as "the guardian of the cedar" (*maṣṣār erēnim*, rev. 58, 60). When slain, Huwawa is called "the guardian of the forest" (*maṣṣāru qištim*, Ishchali rev. 30′) or simply "the guardian" (*maṣṣārum*, Ishchali rev. 26′; IM obv. 20).

Huwawa is not portrayed as larger than a normal human, but he bears overwhelming power in two forms, one visual and one aural. The visual

---

[23] Of the ten texts, only Schøyen-1 and UM, the two small fragments that overlap directly with content from Yale, fail to mention Huwawa, at least by description.

[24] Gilgamesh's second dream repeatedly identifies the terrifying fire and darkness with Adad's thunder (Schøyen-2 obv. 34, 38, 45). Huwawa is not named, but all this represents the coming conflict with him.

power is shared with the Sumerian story, as the possession of "seven terrors" (*pulhiātum*, Yale IV 137), which are often described as having a luminous brilliance that cannot be borne. Enkidu expresses these as "seven auras" in Schøyen-3 (*melemmū*, Fragment 2:4′). In the Sumerian tale, these "terrors" (ni$_2$, or ni$_2$-te) make Huwawa invulnerable. There is no question of heroic courage or capacity. As long as he has these powers, which may be described as radiant "auras" (me-lam$_2$, like the Akkadian *melemmū*), he cannot be overcome, and this is why Enkidu proposes to trick him into giving them up voluntarily.[25] The Akkadian narrative borrows the idea of Huwawa's terrors from the Sumerian, without attributing to them the Sumerian tale's notion of unassailable power. References to Huwawa's particular powers are found both before the partners meet him and during the confrontation itself. In Gilgamesh's first dream, he also experiences these in the form of "terror" (*puluhtum*, Schøyen-2 obv. 20). Interpreting another dream in the Nippur text, Enkidu promises Gilgamesh deliverance, though he naturally fears (verb *palāhum*) Huwawa's "awesome radiance" (*šalummatum*, rev. 4′). In two texts for the encounter itself, the terrors are called "auras" (*melemmū*, in Ishchali obv. 12′–13′; Harmal-2 rev. 37); also as a set of seven in Ishchali rev. 35′; alternatively, they are called "dazzling beams" (*namrirū*, Ishchali obv. 13′; also Nippur obv. 3).[26]

The Akkadian texts then introduce a second dimension of Huwawa's power that expands the depiction in the Sumerian. Huwawa's roar (*rigmu*) has mythic power. In Yale, the power of Huwawa's raised voice is cast in dragon-like terms: "his voice is the Deluge, his mouth is fire, his breath is death" (III 110–112; V 197–198). The second two statements occur in Nippur with the same phrasing (obv. 14; rev. 3′). Gilgamesh's second dream in Schøyen-2 is filled with fire and thunder, "Adad's roar" (*rigim Adad*, obv. 38); after that dream, we are told that the two heroes "kept hearing Huwawa's roar" (*rigim Huwawa*, rev. 57). Ishchali adds to Huwawa's guardianship the legend that the massifs of Sirion and Lebanon were cloven into two by his roar (rev. 31′). Yet for all that sound seems to amplify Huwawa's power, it is accompanied by a new vulnerability

---

[25] In version B, this is what is meant by Gilgamesh's statement after he awakes from Huwawa's unexpected attack: "Against the warrior, there is no strength" (B:89, ur-sag-e usu nu-mu-e-da-gal$_2$). It is not a question of whether Gilgamesh admits his own inadequacy or points out that of Enkidu.

[26] The translation of these three terms is somewhat arbitrary, attempting to capture in each case the association with light, joined to their overwhelming power.

that contrasts with the simple potency of his seven terrors. According to Enkidu, Gilgamesh can overcome Huwawa with the help of superior divine force, in the form of Shamash and Lugalbanda (Schøyen-2 obv. 21; Nippur rev. 6′; Harmal-1 rev. 12–16). The Sumerian scheme envisions no such special intervention. Utu does provide seven companions to lead Gilgamesh through the mountains, but they do not join in combat with Huwawa.[27] Huwawa's vulnerability in the Akkadian narrative, in spite of his power, accompanies a crucial change from the Sumerian conception. In the Sumerian, the auras serve as Huwawa's personal protection, as long as he retains them. With Huwawa now the forest guardian, the Akkadian composition shifts the primary purpose of the auras, so that they now protect the forest itself rather than Huwawa (see Chapter 4).[28] When Enkidu first glimpses their destination, he says, "I beheld the cedar, its auras covering the peaks" (Schøyen-2 rev. 69–70). Here, the auras directly emanate from the trees.

The Akkadian material adds one more major change to Huwawa's character. The Sumerian tale renders Huwawa a mysterious mountain man, born and raised in the wild, with no known parents (A:155–156; B:152–154). He is difficult to distinguish from the wild Enkidu of Penn, except that Huwawa is endowed with seven terrors that render him indomitable.[29] Version A has Gilgamesh awake from the stroke of Huwawa's terrors and declare, "until I have found out whether that man is human or divine, the foot that I have set toward the highlands I shall not set back toward the city" (A:93–94). Huwawa is so fearsome that Enkidu is ready to head back to Uruk immediately. Still, there is nothing intrinsically inhuman about Huwawa, beyond his terrifying powers. When stripped of these, he is subdued by an unarmed blow. In the Akkadian, however, Huwawa is put in contrast to other people,

---

[27] This is especially evident in the description of version B, where the sun god bestows stars on Gilgamesh to show him the way (B:45–50). It is not clear that version B ever calls these "warriors" as in version A (line 36), where they still serve as mountain guides (A:45).

[28] The damaged text of Yale IV 136–137 appears to state this directly, and the notion is confirmed by the fact that Huwawa can be captured without the auras (Ishchali obv. 12′–13′).

[29] In the preserved text of version B, Huwawa's name is never marked with the divine determinative (see lines 129, 155), yet certain copies of version A add the determinative to both Enkidu and Huwawa (Enkidu, KiA 106, 160, 176; UnB 176; Huwawa, UnD 148f; IsA 152; KiC 152; UnB 152, 185, 201; SiB 201; both Enkidu and Huwawa, KiA 175; UnB 175).

his appearance somehow "altered" from what is normally human. Uruk's elders recall that "his face is strange (*šanû būnūšu*)" (Yale V 193), a notion echoed in Gilgamesh's fourth dream of an Anzu-bird (*šunnû pānūša*, Nippur obv. 13). When Enkidu interprets Gilgamesh's first dream in Schøyen-2, he repeats a similar idea in mysterious terms: "Now, Huwawa, the one to whom we journey, is he not the mountain? Everything is altered (*nukkur mimma*)" (obv. 14–16). The exact phrase is repeated when Enkidu interprets the bull dream of Harmal-1 (rev. 11).

C. *Enkidu and Gilgamesh in Pursuit of Huwawa*

Although Huwawa appears only in the Gilgamesh material devoted to the campaign against him, his portrayal is intertwined with that of Enkidu in a way that allows for comparison with Penn and Sippar. Enkidu comes to Gilgamesh as one famed for his prowess in the steppe; based on this prowess, he will serve as a reliable guide for the ruler of Uruk. In every case, Enkidu's expertise is tied specifically to Huwawa. In the discussions in the Yale tablet, Enkidu describes Huwawa's deadly nature and elaborates upon his role as guardian of the Cedar Forest. Later, Enkidu confidently interprets Gilgamesh's dreams, and although promises of success replace warnings of disaster, Enkidu's knowledge still has Huwawa as its principal object.

Throughout the Akkadian Huwawa narrative texts, the relationship between the two companions is characterized by Gilgamesh's dependence on Enkidu for crucial insight on what to think and how to act, especially with respect to Huwawa. Before departure, the elders perceive Enkidu as essential to Gilgamesh's success. When they offer advice, before invoking the gods' protection, they insist that Enkidu go in front, as one who knows the road and Huwawa's tricks (Yale VI 251–254). This perspective continues beyond the Yale tablet. After the two set out, Enkidu is always there to reassure Gilgamesh through optimistic interpretation of his nightmares. When they finally reach the Cedar Forest, Enkidu is repeatedly the one to propose the right course of action. This trend is epitomized in IM, when Enkidu prompts Gilgamesh to choose a tree for a gift to Enlil, an elaborate temple door. The narrator states, "The one born in the steppe was able to advise (*waldam ṣērim mitlukam ile"i*)" (obv. 19; also cf. Harmal-2 rev. 47). This function as advisor (*mālikum*) is attributed to Enkidu by the harlot at their first meeting (Schøyen-1 obv. 2'). Enkidu tells Gilgamesh not to trust Huwawa's offer of service (Harmal-2 rev. 47–48); he suggests that they kill Huwawa first and pursue his auras later (Ishchali obv. 14'–15', edge 16'–18'); and he gives particular counsel regarding how to approach the rich harvest of cedar (Ishchali rev. 40'–43').

In the Yale text, Gilgamesh must convince Enkidu that an expedition to the Cedar Forest is even feasible, with Huwawa as its guardian. Gilgamesh resists Enkidu's advice only when it would discourage him from the whole enterprise. The relationship itself is defined only by the category of comradeship and is reciprocal, with each calling the other "my comrade" (*ibrī*).[30] For the OB material, actual contact between Gilgamesh and Enkidu is contained almost entirely in the Huwawa account, so it is difficult to compare how this contact is handled in Penn and Sippar. The one direct exchange between them centers on the wrestling match at the end of Penn, through which neither combatant says a word. Enkidu breaks this silence only after Gilgamesh turns away as victor, and his praise ends the tablet: "As one alone, your mother bore you; the wild cow of the fold, Ninsunna. Your head is raised above men, the kingship of the people Enlil designated for you" (VI 234–240). Although Enkidu is a physical match for Gilgamesh, he bows entirely to Gilgamesh's superiority as king in a way that recalls the opening line of the epic, as quoted in the colophon: "Surpassing above kings."

Such flattery is not typical of Enkidu's relationship with Gilgamesh in the Huwawa narrative, where Enkidu offers confident advice with frank awareness of his companion's weakness. Before agreeing to join Gilgamesh, Enkidu only observes obstacles, based on Huwawa's fearsome nature (Yale III–IV 106–116; 129–137). When the two are on the verge of departure, Enkidu reassures Gilgamesh, telling him that he need not fear, because Enkidu knows his forest home (VI 273–276). Enkidu interprets Gilgamesh's dreams in full acknowledgement of the terror they inspire, each time with a reminder that a god will sustain Gilgamesh.[31] The conversation that accompanies Huwawa's slaughter is businesslike, without praise for Gilgamesh (Ishchali). Only when Enkidu suggests building a door for Enlil does he compliment his companion, based on action alone,

---

[30] For example, Yale II [79] (Gilgamesh), 85 (Enkidu), III 106 (Enkidu), 119 (Gilgamesh), etc.; Ishchali obv. 11' (Gilgamesh), 15' (Enkidu). This term occurs in every Huwawa narrative text: UM I 6'(?); Schøyen-1 obv. 6'; Schøyen-2 obv. 4, 14, 33, rev. 66, 69, 75, 84; Nippur obv. 1, 9; Harmal-1 obv. 3, rev. 10; Harmal-2 obv. 4, 14, rev. 48; Ishchali obv. 11', 15', rev. 23'; IM obv. 19.

[31] See Schøyen-2 obv. 14–22, obv. 45—rev. 53; Nippur obv. 1–8, rev. 1'–6'; and Harmal-1 rev. 10–17. The same pattern is suggested in Schøyen-3 Fragment 2:3'.

without epithet: "By your own strength you slew the guardian. What can put you to shame?" (IM obv. 20–21). Gilgamesh's achievement in the Cedar Forest is exactly what he desired in order to gain lasting fame, as opposed to any name that is defined by his role as king of Uruk. In this respect, Enkidu's praise in Penn is exactly what Gilgamesh does not seek, when he strikes out on the expedition to defeat Huwawa.

D. *Huwawa, Enkidu, and Their Back-Country Origins*

Another dimension of Huwawa's character permits comparison with the extended epic, in spite of his absence from Penn and Sippar: both Huwawa and Enkidu hail from the back country. The Sumerian tale places Huwawa in the highlands (kur), which for the purposes of Gilgamesh's journey are called "the highlands for felling cedar" (kur ^{giš}eren-ku$_5$).[32] The Akkadian Huwawa narrative preserves this highland association as the general setting for the entire expedition. According to the elders, Enkidu will prepare the highlands (*ša-di-a*) for his companion's foot (Yale VI 261), though they are directed ultimately toward "the river of Huwawa (*na-ri ša* ^{d}*Hu-wa-wa*)" (VI 266).[33] In Gilgamesh's first dream, Huwawa himself is a "mountain" (*šadûm*/kur, Schøyen-2 obv. 5–6, 15–16), and the scene of his defeat is linked to mountains.[34] Consistently, however, Huwawa's home is described as a "forest," and his guardian role is defined in relation to that forest, which represents the riches of this distant terrain.[35] When captured, Huwawa offers to serve as Gilgamesh's personal forester, in contrast to the Sumerian version B, where Gilgamesh envisions a guide.[36] This identification with the forest is absent from the Sumerian and forms part of the new characterization of Huwawa for the Akkadian writer.

In the Akkadian Huwawa texts, the particular category of the "steppe" (*ṣērum*) appears only in connection with Enkidu, as the place of his birth.[37] Further detail is provided only in Yale, where we learn that

---

[32] A:12, 18; B:25, 28, 33, 59.

[33] See also Schøyen-2 obv. 27–28, where Gilgamesh has his second dream on top of a mountain (kur), still somewhere along the route toward Huwawa; and Harmal-1 obv. 1, where another dream is associated with a "mountain cliff" (*sú-ri-im ša* kur).

[34] References to kur/*šadûm* occur in damaged contexts in Harmal-2 rev. 43 and Ishchali rev. 32′.

[35] See Yale III 108–109, 130; V 184, 195; VI 253; Nippur obv. 1; Ishchali obv. 12′; edge 17′; rev. 29′, 37′; IM obv. 17, 21.

[36] Harmal-2 rev. 46–47; cf. Gilgamesh and Huwawa B:138.

[37] Yale IV 151 (edin); Harmal-2 rev. 47 (edin); IM obv. 19 (*ṣe-ri-im*).

Enkidu was known for driving off marauders in the form of a lion and young men (IV 151-153). Together with the fact that Enkidu used to roam with the domestic herds (III 107), this portrays a man who lives in contact with other people. As seen in Penn and Sippar, the extended OB epic takes over the terminology of the "steppe" and transforms it into a place marked by its lack of human inhabitants, except for the hunters that pursue their prey there. Consistent with the epic's received material, Penn observes that Enkidu was born in the steppe (I 18, II 47), a domain that is paired with "the highlands" (*šadûm*, I 18). This combination allows the writer to rework another part of Enkidu's origins from the Huwawa narrative. Enkidu knows Huwawa from the time of his "roaming with the herd (*būlum*)" in the highlands (Yale III 107), and in Penn, the harlot asks him why he "roams the steppe with the animals" (II 54-55). The same verb and stem are used.[38] The Penn author reinterprets the *būlum* as wild animals, however, and must replace the term with the more versatile *nammaštû*, "beasts" that now are said to nurse Enkidu (V 188-189). For the epic, Enkidu's steppe was removed from human society. After Enkidu's death, Gilgamesh returns to his companion's world, refusing to accept his role at Uruk. When Gilgamesh answers Shamash in the Sippar text, he evokes the same action: "After roaming, wandering the steppe, there will be plenty of rest in the world below!" (I 10′-11′).[39] Likewise, he explains to the tavern keeper that he has been roving the steppe like a hunter (II 11′).

For the author of the Akkadian Huwawa narrative, the highland back country is what links Enkidu with Huwawa. Enkidu's collaborative relationship with Gilgamesh depends on his knowledge of Huwawa and his domain. For Enkidu's birth and life at the fringes of human society, this back country is called the "steppe" (*ṣērum*), a term reserved for these particular associations. In the epic, this application is set aside in order to oppose the social constraints of the city to the wild back country. Enkidu derives his superhuman strength from this identification with the animals in a realm without human contact, and perhaps only in this setting is an escape from mortality possible.

---

[38] This is the Gtn of *alākum*, "to go."
[39] Once again, the first verb is a Gtn form of *alākum*.

E. The Possibility of Epic Influence in Huwawa Narrative Texts

As a whole, it appears that the epic builds an extended story around the core Huwawa narrative without major adjustment to the received material. By its evident expansion from a received narrative, which seems to be left relatively intact, the epic appears to have been composed in writing, from the Huwawa narrative as a written source. It is difficult to be certain about the degree of epic influence on our extant Huwawa texts, though we must acknowledge that the new composition, whether at its first creation or in reproduction, could have left its mark within the body of the older narrative as well. While the ten Huwawa narrative texts generally do not exhibit the characteristics of the two epic texts, it is likely that all of them were copied after composition of the whole Gilgamesh Epic. The argument for the prior creation of an Akkadian Huwawa narrative proceeds from contemporaneous evidence: the concentration of Huwawa texts, especially in the eight extracts, and the contrasting perspective of Penn and Sippar. With all OB Gilgamesh tablets copied in roughly the same period, we cannot exclude the possibility that bits of epic language or perspective could have intruded into the Huwawa narrative, perhaps to varying degrees with different reproductions of the material.[40] While Yale was definitely produced for a complete epic series,

---

[40] Direct verbal connections between the Huwawa narrative texts and Penn are rare. The most striking instance occurs as a response to Enkidu's dream interpretation in Schøyen-2. After Enkidu has finished an optimistic rendition, Gilgamesh rejoices: "his heart exulted and his face shone" (*īliṣ libbašuma pānūšu ittamrū*, obv. 24), the exact response of Enkidu after drinking seven jugs of beer in the Penn tablet (III 104–105). It is hard to tell which text depends on which, although a direct allusion is likely, with such a close verbal match. In the Schøyen-2 text, the line belongs to a framing response, rather than to the dream or its interpretation, and it may reflect casting as part of an epic version that included the section known from Penn. A second example would be equally specific and direct if George's reading is correct. When Huwawa begs for his life in Harmal-2, George has him say to Gilgamesh, "The cow of the cattle-pen, Ninsumuna, bore you (*ūlidka littum ša supūri Ninsumūna*)" (rev. 42). After their fight at the end of the Penn tablet, Enkidu praises Gilgamesh in similar terms, by reference to his divine mother: "As one alone, your mother bore you, the wild cow of the fold, Ninsunna" (*kīma ištēnma ummaka ūlidka rīmtum ša supūri Ninsunna*, VI 234–237). The reading in Harmal-2, however, envisions significantly different orthography and requires substantial reconstruction. It is difficult to be sure that the reading itself is not influenced by the epic text attested in Penn. Finally, a third example may only reflect common idiom and a shared theme. The dream accounts in two extract tablets include the same formula for repetition as that found in Penn, when Gilgamesh announces, "Mother, I saw a second one (*ummi ātamar šanītam*)" (I 26; see also Schøyen-2 obv. 33, rev. 84; Nippur obv. 9). None of these similarities touches the core features that we identify as separating the Huwawa

the intrusion of epic features in the Huwawa extracts need not reflect copying from the epic, though such features may well reflect awareness of the separate epic.

The one block that offers the strongest possibility of this process is found on the reverse of Schøyen-2, after the second dream. A third dream is introduced, without copying the content, following a long conversation between Gilgamesh and Enkidu that reverses the attitudes exhibited in the first two sequences of dream and interpretation. Whereas Enkidu had been providing Gilgamesh with hearty reassurance, now he reverts to the fear that had made his face pale upon first hearing about the Huwawa enterprise (rev. 61–81; cf. Yale II 71–88).[41] The specific response of the face turning pale recalls Enkidu's reaction to the wedding traveler's account of Gilgamesh as king in Penn (IV 165–166). In Schøyen-2, the section is highly repetitive, without introducing new ideas.[42] At the end of this section, the third dream is introduced in terms completely different from those of the first two. This time, there is no occasion for sleeping; they simply lie down (rev. 82; versus obv. 27–30). Both of the first two dream sequences begin, "In the middle watch, his sleep startled him" (obv. 2, 31), with no reference to the night, as found in rev. 82–83. This third dream is introduced by the notion that Gilgamesh himself "loosens" (i.e., "relates") what he saw (rev. 83), using the same application of the verb *pašārum* as found in his dreams in Penn (I 1; II 44). With the first two Schøyen-2 dreams, Enkidu is the one who "loosens" (i.e., "interprets") the vision (obv. 13, 44).

One further indication that this section may reflect epic influence may be the speech formula in rev. 68 and 77: "Enkidu/Gilgamesh opened his

---

narrative from the rest of the OB epic in the Penn and Sippar tablets. These core features belong to what we consider the authorial vision of the Akkadian Huwawa narrative.

[41] In Schøyen-2, we are told three times that Enkidu's face turned pale (*īriqū pānū*, rev. 63, 66, 75), and fear (*adirtum*) has entered his heart (rev. 64, 67, 76). In Yale II 71–88, completely different language is used: Enkidu's eyes fill with tears, his heart is sick, and he is wearied; his neck is knotted, his arms are limp, and he has lost his strength. The very contrast of language leaves the Yale text entirely distinct from the section of Schøyen-2 that we examine here, and if both reflect epic influence, then this is accomplished without attempt to link the two episodes.

[42] Enkidu's fear is repeated three times, as in the previous note. He explains himself in lines 69–70 in terms that introduce the section in lines 61–62, where he first sees the cedar and its auras. Lines 71–74 involve a full repetition in A:B:: A':B' format, a compositional element that is common enough, but which adds little content here. Only in lines 78–81, when Gilgamesh finally offers Enkidu a substantial answer to his fears, do we encounter fresh ideas that pick up on elements from before their departure, as found in the Yale Tablet.

mouth (*pâšu īpušamma*) and spoke to Gilgamesh/Enkidu." While variants of discourse introductions are ubiquitous to OB Akkadian narrative, the particular idiom with the verb *epēšum* ("to do, make") is distinct. In the OB Gilgamesh material, it marks the particular scribe responsible for copying Penn and Yale as part of an epic series. In terms of diction, the repetition of this idiom is one of the only marks of compositional continuity between the two tablets. Outside of Penn and Yale, through the ten remaining tablets, only these two lines in Schøyen-2 employ this version of the speech formula.[43] When viewed together with the features just discussed, the use of *pâšu īpušamma* adds to the impression that the scribe who produced Schøyen-2 elaborated on a sequence of dreams and interpretation with material inspired by the epic and its contrasting perspective.

The narrative structure of Schøyen-2 could also suit the notion that lines 61–81 reflect the hand of this particular copyist, or at least that of whoever first produced this specific extract. Schøyen-2 is built around the recounting by Gilgamesh and the interpretation by Enkidu of two dreams on the way to confront Huwawa. The final line introduces a third dream without attempting to explore its content, only to remind the reader that the extract belongs to a longer dream sequence. In effect, then, lines 61–81 represent the last section of the tablet as such, an elaboration that wanders from the consistent structure of report, interpretation, and travel that frames the first 60 lines. All the repetition of Enkidu's fear leads to an exhortation by Gilgamesh that plays on ideas from early in the Huwawa narrative, prior to their departure.[44]

If these lines in Schøyen-2 were added to the received Huwawa narrative, the purpose may have been to enhance Gilgamesh's heroic character, which could be seen to suffer somewhat from all his fear in dreaming. With Enkidu the fearful one, he can share Gilgamesh's disability, so that Gilgamesh may take his turn at offering reassurance, returning to the confidence that had marked his mentality while still in Uruk. At the

[43] Elsewhere in Schøyen-2, the dream accounts are introduced, "He arose (and) addressed his comrade: 'My comrade, I saw a dream'" (obv. 3–4, cf. 32–33). Each time, "Enkidu interpreted the dream, he spoke to Gilgamesh" (obv. 13, 44).

[44] If George's new reading is correct, Gilgamesh begins with an acknowledgement of the heedless confidence for which the elders once chided him: "Did not my heart carry me …?" (rev. 78; cf. Yale V 191). He then seems to recall a promise of divine sustenance, the preoccupation of the last two columns of Yale, before instructing Enkidu not to fear and to guard Gilgamesh, as the elders had told the hero to guard himself (rev. 80; cf. Yale VI 250). Gilgamesh then promises unprecedented battle as if that in itself was a comfort, with an attitude familiar to his confidence before their journey.

end of this exchange, Enkidu is to find comfort in a thing that he did *not* know, combat that Gilgamesh will initiate (rev. 81), reversing the theme of Enkidu's knowledge that dominates the Huwawa tale as a whole. Such an addition may have restored the power balance we see at the close of the Penn tablet, when Enkidu praises Gilgamesh's capabilities.

Beyond Schøyen-2 rev. 61–81, we do not propose any intrusions into the Huwawa narrative from a scribe familiar with the extended epic, though we do not exclude the possibility. Yale columns I and II represent a special case, where the introduction to the Huwawa composition had to be bridged into a comprehensible connection with the long new sections represented by Penn and the tablet that preceded it. This particular issue will be addressed more fully in Chapter 5.

In sum, the ten texts that treat the adventure to the Cedar Forest reflect the existence of a freestanding Akkadian Huwawa narrative that became the foundation for the composition of the longer Gilgamesh Epic. At the center of this composition stood Huwawa himself, with Enkidu as guide and counselor to Gilgamesh based on his firsthand knowledge of Huwawa's domain. Before their departure, the elders of Uruk speak to Gilgamesh and Enkidu, but only Gilgamesh, Enkidu, and Huwawa play any significant role in the story.[45] The epic adds at least four important individual players, visible in Penn and Sippar alone: Gilgamesh's mother, the lady tavern keeper, Sursunabu the boatman, and Uta-na'ishtim. With such a range of new characters, the epic greatly expands the narrower drama of the prior Huwawa story.

The Huwawa narrative finds its drama in a long delay to the projected goal. First, Gilgamesh wants to enlist a guide who turns out to know the antagonist all too well and is not eager to join the expedition. Then, he encounters for himself the terror of their target in a series of dreams along the way. The two appear to enjoy straightforward success upon arrival, though they are forced to decide Huwawa's fate, as in the Sumerian tradition. Although the Akkadian Huwawa narrative adds new themes and a long plot development to the early phases of the story, it keeps the bounds of the Sumerian tale, which is constructed entirely around the expedition to obtain cedar in the distant highlands.

---

[45] Given her appearance in both Schøyen-1 and column I of the Yale tablet, we conclude that the harlot was originally present in the Akkadian Huwawa narrative, though her role may have been limited. Her role then underwent a major shift with the creation of the OB epic. For further elaboration, see Chapter 5.

In defining the character of an Akkadian Huwawa narrative, we have focused on the OB material itself. In light of the proposition that Penn and Sippar represent a new view of Enkidu and Gilgamesh, separate from what we find in the remaining OB evidence, we are left with a prior narrative centered on an expedition to overcome Huwawa. This conclusion leaves us face to face with a Sumerian narrative known from texts copied in the same period and clearly defined by the same adventure. In order to define properly the Akkadian Huwawa narrative, and to understand its logic and character, we therefore must consider more precisely how the Akkadian composition relates to and evolved from the Sumerian tale of Gilgamesh and Huwawa.

CHAPTER FOUR

FROM SUMERIAN TO AKKADIAN:
MAJOR INNOVATIONS IN THE AKKADIAN
HUWAWA TALE

Having concluded that the Yale tablet and nine other OB texts point to the existence of a once-independent Akkadian Huwawa narrative, the Sumerian evidence becomes even more crucial for reconstructing the Akkadian Huwawa tale that preceded the OB epic. The initial Akkadian composition began as a variant of one Sumerian story, that of Gilgamesh and Huwawa. As such, the relationship of the Akkadian Huwawa narrative to the Sumerian Gilgamesh and Huwawa defines the first major step in creation of what eventually became the Gilgamesh Epic. It is thus necessary to consider both the continuities between them and the principal changes undertaken in composing the Akkadian tale.

Among the independent Sumerian texts about Gilgamesh, the tale of Huwawa was perhaps the most widely copied. The longer version A formed part of what Steve Tinney calls a "Decad" of standard Sumerian compositions associated with scribal education in early second-millennium Babylonia.[1] In a study of specific tablet finds in the most productive school site for the period, Eleanor Robson counts ninety-two tablets or fragments that include Gilgamesh and Huwawa A for all of Babylonia at this time, seventy-two of which come from the city of Nippur, and twenty-one of which were found in the building under

---

[1] Tinney, "On the Curricular Setting of Sumerian Literature," *Iraq* 61 (1999) 159–172. Three primary groups of standard texts are the Tetrad, the Decad, and the Fourteen, in his terminology. Tinney defines the Decad by the ten texts that appear at the beginning of curricular catalogues, especially one from Nippur. Also, several copies of multiple literary texts follow the order of the Decad (pp. 159, 168–170). In a recent article, Paul Delnero challenges the identification of the key catalogue texts as curricular lists and presents evidence that they are in fact tablet inventories, like other texts of similar type, with uncertain relationship to training students ("Sumerian Literary Catalogues and the Scribal Curriculum," *ZA*, forthcoming in 2010). The appearance of Gilgamesh and Huwawa A in such scribal circles, then, may well reflect the educational process, but more simply, it displays a general interest in the text among scribes at the attested centers.

study.[2] In contrast, just one Akkadian fragment of Gilgamesh (OB Nippur) was found in this house, which yielded a thousand or more reconstructed literary and scholarly tablets. In written terms, the Sumerian version A was the Huwawa story best known to most scribes of the Old Babylonian period in southeastern Mesopotamia. The Akkadian Huwawa tale was probably recounted in some of the same circles, yet its rendition in writing was a relative rarity. The eight OB extract tablets suggest that it could be included in student training, though somehow less universally than the Sumerian version A. Version B of Gilgamesh and Huwawa was also much rarer than the Sumerian version A, with only five tablets included in the edition by D.O. Edzard.[3]

In this chapter, we begin by examining the major changes made in creating an Akkadian Huwawa narrative from the Sumerian Huwawa tale. Comparison of the Sumerian versions A and B suggests that B preserves an older, simpler rendition of that composition, one that shows no awareness of the contents of the Akkadian story. We therefore work first of all from version B, with focus on the specific features that reflect these changes. Because version A displays many more continuities with the Akkadian Huwawa narrative, we then undertake a fresh comparison in order to evaluate the possible influence of the Akkadian on this contemporary Sumerian rendition. In the process, we return to some of the same features that define the Akkadian Huwawa narrative against version B, with this new objective in view.

I. The Priority of the Version B Narrative

Although there are significant differences between the A and B versions of the Sumerian story, the two have much more in common with each other than with the Akkadian evidence as a whole. Version B is shorter

---

[2] Robson, "The Tablet House: A Scribal School in Old Babylonian Nippur," *RA* 95 (2001) 39–66. We leave this count for its proportions and its reference to House F as primary location. In his more recent compilation of all copies for the Sumerian Decad, Paul Delnero condenses these numbers based on several joins and a careful check of all evidence (*Variation in Sumerian Literary Compositions: A Case Study Based on the Decad*, University of Pennsylvania Ph.D., 2006). There are 85 representatives of Gilgamesh and Huwawa A, with 59 from Nippur; 4 from Isin; 3 from Kish; 4 from Sippar; 1 from Susa; 8 from Ur; and 6 without known provenience.

[3] Edzard, "*Gilgameš und Huwawa*", 14–15. Three of these five (texts A, B, and C) come from Nippur, a fourth from Uruk (W), and the last is of unknown provenance (MM).

and simpler, with all of its primary elements included in version A. After a four-line hymn to Gilgamesh that does not appear to have been composed for this setting, the B text opens with Gilgamesh struck by the inevitability of death after seeing a floating corpse.[4] Faced with such a fate, the king of Uruk longs to accomplish something memorable and resolves to bring back timber from the fearsome highlands for felling cedar. At his servant Enkidu's suggestion, Gilgamesh approaches the sun god Utu for help, and Utu provides him with seven celestial guides. Gilgamesh is then joined on the road by young men from the city, and after crossing seven mountain ranges, he finds and chops down the cedar of his choice. In version B, Huwawa only attacks them after they have taken the wood, and his presence comes as a complete surprise. The text gives no hint that Gilgamesh knew about this specific danger in the highlands. Huwawa's terrifying brilliance brings a deep sleep, from which Enkidu awakes first and must rouse his master. Gilgamesh responds to the assault with despair: nothing can overcome Huwawa's powers. The unavoidable obstacle of these powers leads Enkidu to propose a different strategy: they must trick Huwawa into handing them over freely. They accomplish this and render Huwawa helpless, forced to beg for his life. Enkidu advises Gilgamesh against granting freedom, but Huwawa's fate is left unresolved, with just a few lines lost at the end

---

[4] In version A, Huwawa speaks the first three lines to Gilgamesh when they meet properly (A:130–132), and the full four lines also launch Enkidu's attempt to persuade Gilgamesh to kill Huwawa (A:164–167), before he criticizes his master in line 170: "Supple with oil, lasting offshoot, native son, splendor of the gods, stout ox, in fighting stance, young lord Gilgamesh, exalted in Uruk." In the Sumerian Gilgamesh and the Bull of Heaven, Enkidu makes the same speech as he seizes the bull's tail so that Gilgamesh can kill it (91–94). The hymn includes two more lines: "your mother knew just how to form a child; the wet nurse knew just how to feed a child on her lap" (95–96; Gilgamesh and Huwawa A:133–134, 168–169). These were not included at the start of version B. It is not clear whether either of the version A settings or the use in the Bull of Heaven story provides an original literary context for the words. The moment of Gilgamesh's waking after Huwawa's assault may offer the best narrative association, although even this may be secondary. Gilgamesh anoints himself with oil and then stands like an ox (A:86–87). The anointing is the basis for our translation of the opening as "supple with oil" (see note to A:130–134). Because the hymn is cast in general terms, however, this scene may be inspired by the well-known exaltation of Gilgamesh. It is possible that the opening hymn of the OB Akkadian epic, as preserved in the SBV I 29–30, could refer to motifs that derive from the Sumerian Gilgamesh hymn, especially the hero as formidable bull and as native to Uruk: *šūtur eli šarrī šanu'udu bēl gatti qardu lillid Uruk rīmu muttakpu*, "Surpassing above kings, praiseworthy, a perfect specimen, heroic offspring of Uruk, charging wild bull." At least, the texts share key elements of stock praise for the ancient king.

of the narrative. Version A follows the main lines of the plot in B, with several differences in perspective and a generally expanded text. In this version, Enkidu kills Huwawa, and they bring both Huwawa's head and auras to Enlil, who is not happy with the deed, yet imposes no punishment.

The contrasts between the Akkadian Huwawa account and the basic Sumerian tradition far outnumber the continuities, though it is worth noting the plot elements that the two do share. In both, Gilgamesh proposes that he and Enkidu undertake a long journey to a destination identified with highlands and precious trees, where the fearsome Huwawa dwells. In order to bring back timber, the pair must overcome Huwawa. As in the Sumerian narrative, Gilgamesh's proposal in the Akkadian account is tied in part to his sense of mortality. Huwawa produces petrifying fear, and the whole adventure is life-threatening, heroic, and ultimately successful. In both the Sumerian and the Akkadian accounts, Enkidu advises the king against his own final plans for Huwawa. Moreover, in the Sumerian version B, Enkidu both advises Gilgamesh to seek help from Utu and proposes the scheme for tricking Huwawa out of his auras. The seeds for Enkidu's role as Gilgamesh's advisor, the cornerstone of the Akkadian Huwawa narrative, are thus already planted in the Sumerian story.

Such parallels indicate that the Akkadian Huwawa account must be related to the two Sumerian versions of Gilgamesh and Huwawa. The precise relationship among the three distinct narratives, however, is less clear. Edzard concludes that the standard A version is later than B and was developed from it. Further, he proposes that version A may have been influenced by the contemporaneous Akkadian epic, an idea that we will address further in this chapter.[5] The two Sumerian texts show that a Huwawa story existed in a form that could stand alone, without reference to outside events. Our hypothesis of a freestanding Akkadian Huwawa narrative is supported by the existence of the Sumerian versions, and this Sumerian tradition must provide the backdrop to the retelling of the story in Akkadian. Before turning to the complex literary relationship between the Akkadian Huwawa story and the two Sumerian versions,

---

[5] Edzard, "*Gilgameš und Huwawa*", 53–59. The possibility that version A has been influenced by the Akkadian OB epic is only mentioned in passing at the very end of his discussion, without elaboration. See also Abusch, "Hunting in the Epic of Gilgamesh," 17.

we shall first examine how the Akkadian Huwawa story re-imagines the narrative in the Sumerian version B that surely predates it. In general, all of our references either to the "earlier" Sumerian story or to the Sumerian story on its own pertain to version B, even though much of version A follows B.[6]

We acknowledge here that we are constrained by the available written evidence and can only draw rough conclusions about the logical relationships between contrasting stories. In fact, the reproduction of literature in this period could allow for considerable creativity and combination.[7] The most striking aspect of the evidence is the dominance of Sumerian literature over Akkadian in the sheer number of copies found in scribal centers of early second-millennium Babylonia. For all the attention attracted by the first Gilgamesh Epic, its twelve known texts are far outnumbered by contemporary tablets and fragments that include the Sumerian Gilgamesh stories. Why is this? At the least, it seems that the Akkadian Gilgamesh may not have been copied as part of standard scribal training in the way that characterizes much Sumerian literature. Along with other newly minted Akkadian composition, Gilgamesh must have been important to OB scribes, but its role with respect to the scribal craft remains mysterious. The eight extract tablets indicate at least occasional use of the Huwawa narrative, though these numbers fall far short of Sumerian finds. At least at Nippur, where the largest numbers of Sumerian literary texts have been found, the Akkadian Gilgamesh played a relatively minor role. In spite of these contrasting functions, the Sumerian and Akkadian Gilgamesh stories, and the Huwawa tales in particular, must have been known by many of the same scribes, so that the reproduction of each would have occurred with knowledge of the others.

---

[6] The set of Sumerian tales of Gilgamesh are attributed generally to the Ur III period, even though the attested renditions themselves date to the eighteenth century (by the common middle chronology). Three Sumerian fragments, however, including one from Gilgamesh and the Bull of Heaven, do belong to the Ur III period; for discussion, see George, *Babylonian Gilgamesh Epic*, 7–8. The set of tales consistently portrays Gilgamesh as king and Enkidu as his servant at Uruk, a relationship that is changed dramatically in the Akkadian with the transfer of Enkidu to the steppe. It may be that the forms of the Ur III versions of the Sumerian Gilgamesh stories were considerably different from their early second-millennium expressions, which in themselves were fairly fluid.

[7] See, for example, Tinney, "On the Curricular Setting of Sumerian Literature," 159–172.

II. *Enkidu's Relocation to the Steppe: The Domino Effect*

One of the most significant changes introduced by the Akkadian author was the relocation of Enkidu from Uruk to the steppe. Although the transformation removed Enkidu from the glories of Uruk and service as the king's right-hand man, it finally placed Gilgamesh and Enkidu on more equal footing. Now Enkidu's participation could not be taken for granted, and he became a free partner in the adventure. Such a change in Enkidu's status both necessitated certain additions and opened up opportunities for expanding and revising original components of the Sumerian story. Together, these innovations expand considerably the period prior to contact with Huwawa, so that the bulk of the Akkadian narrative is focused on the anticipation of the encounter rather than on the encounter itself. Each of these changes warrants further discussion.

A. *The New Need to Persuade Enkidu*

The opening section of the Sumerian version B offers a sense of how quickly the adventure could be launched, when the story was told before evident influence from the Akkadian tradition. Enkidu's participation in the expedition is automatic, and he only recommends that Gilgamesh first consult Utu for support. The exchanges cover approximately fifty lines, and by line 57 Gilgamesh has already left for the forest. In the Akkadian, however, with Enkidu's participation no longer a given, this part undergoes a massive expansion. Enkidu's experience in the steppe prompts him to reject the proposal outright: "Why do you want to do this? The abode of Huwawa is a battle not to be faced" (Yale III 113–116). In turn, Gilgamesh must persuade Enkidu to accompany him, in spite of the expert herdsman's better judgment. To this end, Gilgamesh employs a variety of tactics—he expounds upon the certainty of death (IV 138–143); he claims that Enkidu is afraid and offers to walk in front of him (144–147, 156–157); he cites his own desire for everlasting fame (148–149; 160); and he recalls Enkidu's skill in fighting off attackers (151–153). By line 163, Gilgamesh and Enkidu finally head off to the forge for their axes, but they do not leave the city until after the conclusion of the Yale tablet.

The expansion of Gilgamesh's proposal to Enkidu also may reflect the development of a different political perspective in the Akkadian version. In the Sumerian, Gilgamesh accepts Enkidu's counsel, but the relationship is still defined in terms of king and servant. The Akkadian presents a more nuanced picture, in which Enkidu chooses of his own accord to participate in Gilgamesh's adventure. The fact that Enkidu now must be lured out of the steppe by the harlot suggests that the herdsman is an autonomous individual, not someone whom Gilgamesh can simply summon to serve via royal messenger. Given that this is part of the lost introduction to the Akkadian Huwawa narrative, this particular addition will be addressed in Chapter 5. It appears that the harlot's role was invented by the initial Akkadian Gilgamesh writer to facilitate this need to bring Enkidu to Uruk. In accordance with this portrait, the Akkadian author introduces into the plot the elders, who protest Gilgamesh's plan in terms that echo Enkidu's objections. When they chide Gilgamesh, "You do not know what you are doing" (*mimma ša tēteneppušu lā tīde*, V 192), their words play subtly on Gilgamesh's earlier existentialist statement to Enkidu: "Everything [humanity] does is wind" (*mimma ša īteneppušu šārumma*, IV 143). The elders then advise that Enkidu walk in front of Gilgamesh, for only he is familiar with the many "plots of Huwawa" (VI 254). In his efforts to convince both Enkidu and the elders that his plan is viable, Gilgamesh takes for granted a style of leadership in cooperation with a collective body. Such a political perspective may complement Enkidu's independence and value, as reflected in his identification with the *būlum* and indirectly with herding peoples.

This view of kingship at Uruk need not have a direct relationship to the representation of herding communities, as displayed in the figure of Enkidu. Both features coexist in a narrative that places the heroism and ambition of Gilgamesh in a framework of essential support. Ultimately, the view of kingship in the Akkadian Huwawa narrative is less critical than the extreme view offered in the full epic. The king in the earlier narrative accepts help and succeeds in his quest, while the epic's monarch infringes on the gods' domain and is finally confronted with mortality and failure.

B. *Establishing a Name*

Although consciousness of mortality is still part of the Akkadian story, the reason for the king's expedition is set in rather different terms. In the Sumerian version B, Gilgamesh laments the end of life and in turn proposes an adventure. Though several lines are missing at this juncture, there is no reason to assume that another motive underlies his proposal. Gilgamesh sets out not to battle Huwawa but instead to enter the highlands for felling cedar. The whole adventure is defined by the desire to obtain precious timber, with no mention of Huwawa until after the men have met this goal (line 67). In the Akkadian rendition, however, Huwawa becomes the central focus, and the purpose for Gilgamesh's adventure is given an entirely new spin. In this version, Gilgamesh's main desire is to make a name for himself. Mortality is put in the context of fame, and fame comes only from confronting such a fearsome being, as Gilgamesh tells Enkidu: "If I should fall, my name will stand. (People will say,) 'Gilgamesh joined battle with martial Huwawa'" (Yale IV 148–150). The cedar is only mentioned secondarily (line 159). With the bulk of the elders' and Enkidu's responses centered on Huwawa, the entire focus of the expedition is set in terms of the king's proposed confrontation with the forest guardian.[8]

This shift of attention to Huwawa, which is inextricable from Gilgamesh's desire for eternal renown, may be linked indirectly to Enkidu's new status as a herdsman of repute. As in the Sumerian tale, Gilgamesh is the driving force behind the expedition to defeat Huwawa, and his goals are the particular interest of the narrative. Nevertheless, Gilgamesh treats Enkidu as already having a measure of what the Uruk ruler wants. Gilgamesh's reference to the single lion that attacked Enkidu suggests familiarity with a particular legend that established Enkidu's fame as a formidable hero of the shepherds' realm. Enkidu's name traveled all the way to Gilgamesh in Uruk, so that he was handpicked for this adventure because of his unparalleled skill. Just as Enkidu earned a name for himself by fighting attackers in the steppe, Gilgamesh seeks fame that is based on feats of valor, not on his status as king of a great city. Even Huwawa's name is known to all because of his incredible power and the danger of facing him in the steppe, and Gilgamesh must likewise achieve renown outside the city and its support. Given that Gilgamesh desires a name from great deeds, not from his position at Uruk, it is fitting that the Huwawa narrative does not once refer to him as king (šarrum/lugal), one of his titles in the Sumerian story.[9] Kingship alone gains Gilgamesh nothing in his quest for a lasting name.

---

[8] This shift is reflected in Schøyen-2 obv. 1–22, in which Gilgamesh dreams of a mountain that buckles and hems him in. Unlike the Sumerian, in which Gilgamesh proposes to go to the highlands (kur = mountain), in the Akkadian the mountain itself symbolizes Huwawa, so that his defeat is identified as the main objective of the expedition. While in line 15 the Akkadian term for mountain is written syllabically as ša-du-um, line 16 uses the logogram kur, a direct match to the Sumerian word.

[9] In Huwawa B, after the opening hymn, Gilgamesh is "lord (en) of Kulaba" as he

In the Sumerian story, Enkidu is a servant whose very role casts him as an aide to his master's ambitions. Now that Enkidu has the separate status of a companion in the Akkadian narrative, his own past becomes significant. He is known for his courage in combat with dangerous characters of the back country. Huwawa represents the ultimate antagonist for one who stakes his name on such exploits, and according to this vision, the author recasts the adventure in terms of challenging the forest guardian, as opposed to acquiring cedar. This theme of confronting mortality by establishing a lasting name is then picked up and expanded by the OB epic narrator.

C. The Dream Sequence

The combination of Huwawa's centrality to the expedition and Enkidu's status as one who "knows" Huwawa fueled the development of a sequence of anticipatory dreams in the Akkadian story.[10] In the Sumerian tale, the first contact with Huwawa is through his sleep-inducing auras. After this encounter, Gilgamesh wakes and is overwhelmed by the recollection of his first glimpse of Huwawa (B:84–89). Enkidu then provides Gilgamesh with the verbal ammunition that will persuade Huwawa to surrender the seven auras. As represented in Schøyen-2, Schøyen-3, Nippur, and Harmal-1, the Akkadian story then picks up on this basic sequence with noticeable expansion and revision. By introducing a set of Huwawa-based dreams, the Akkadian writer again emphasizes the confrontation with Huwawa as the main focus of the undertaking. Here Gilgamesh's fear of Huwawa stems not from an actual encounter with the guardian, but rather from his contact with Huwawa in nocturnal visions. Enkidu's

---

entreats the sun god (31) and "king" (lugal) at the moment of departure (57). He is "young lord (en)" when Enkidu tries to rouse him (75). Huwawa version A only uses the title lugal with reference to Enkidu's deference to Gilgamesh as his master, always with the pronouns "my" or "his" (9, 96, 97, 103). Although the Sumerian lugal comes to be identified with Akkadian *šarrum* as the predominant title for rulers of hierarchical polities, Sumerian applies other titles to this position, especially en ("lord"). The contrast we describe does not depend on the specific title lugal.

[10] We know Gilgamesh sees a series of four dreams, for in the Nippur text he states, "My comrade, I have seen a fourth. It was beyond my three dreams" (obv. 9–10). Harmal-1 includes an additional dream, yet because it is not identified as a "fifth," it is difficult to say whether or not we can read it in sequence with the others. Alternatively, this may reflect the possibility (or likelihood) of narrative variants. Likewise, Schøyen-3 appears to elaborate the same scheme of dreams en route, without a textual match to any of the other dream texts. We must not assume a particular series of four.

knowledge of Huwawa then renders him a talented dream interpreter: he decodes the symbols of Gilgamesh's dreams and forecasts certain success. The dream sequence has the dual effect of expanding Enkidu's role as advisor and emphasizing the sheer terror of Huwawa, so that success in battle against him is rendered an incredible feat, one worthy of everlasting fame.

Each of these narrative innovations, no matter how far-reaching, develops some element of the Sumerian version B, which evidently preceded the Akkadian Huwawa narrative. Enkidu's contribution as advisor and dream interpreter derives from his role in the Sumerian, in which his service to the king takes the particular form of providing potent counsel. Though he does not protest the king's plan, he consistently offers guidance and reassurance. He instructs Gilgamesh to seek Utu's support, and after Gilgamesh's first frightening contact with Huwawa, he proposes the key scheme for defeating Huwawa. When Gilgamesh takes pity on Huwawa, wishing to set him free, Enkidu again serves as the wise one, telling Gilgamesh bluntly that even a tall man can lack forethought (B:139a).[11] Although the conclusion of version B is missing, we know that the same exchange in version A leads to the death of Huwawa, brought about by Enkidu himself.[12] Such a scene is echoed in Ishchali, in which Enkidu dissuades Gilgamesh from chasing Huwawa's auras, urging him instead to smite the guardian a second time (edge 18′). Thus, even though the relocation of Enkidu to the steppe permitted a promotion to true partnership with Gilgamesh, instead of servant status, his function as knowledgeable guide in the Akkadian is rooted in the Sumerian character.

Gilgamesh's series of monologues, in which he attempts to convince both Enkidu and the elders of his plan, is also grounded in details already present in the Sumerian. Version B opens with a speech detailing the inescapable end of life in terms that are echoed in Gilgamesh's persuasive

---

[11] This line can be restored based on A:170–171, "One who is tall, yet has no forethought, fate will consume, and he will know nothing of his fate."

[12] See Edzard, however, who argues that Gilgamesh may have permitted Huwawa to live in version B, whereas in version A, Enkidu slays Huwawa (*"Gilgameš und Huwawa"*, 11 and 53–59). His argument is based on the observation that the damaged conclusion of version B preserves a dialogue between Huwawa and Gilgamesh that does not appear in version A (B:151–156). According to Abusch, version A then reflects the same tradition as the Akkadian epic: both make the defeat of Huwawa the central objective of the mission ("Hunting in the Epic of Gilgamesh," 16–17).

speech to Enkidu in column IV of the Yale tablet. The change in Gilgamesh's motive for the expedition then represents a logical extension from the original circumstances. In the Sumerian version B, the inevitability of death prompts Gilgamesh to propose a journey to the highlands to fetch cedar. In the Akkadian narrative, the notion that Gilgamesh now aims to battle Huwawa in order to make a name for himself naturally follows from his confrontation with mortality. This way, Gilgamesh will make a name for himself whether or not he dies on the mission. Mortality is still a part of the Akkadian Huwawa story, but only insofar as it propels Gilgamesh's desire for fame. It is not until the OB epic that Gilgamesh's direct confrontation with mortality is restored as the driving theme of the narrative.

III. *Details Lost with Rendition in Akkadian*

The Akkadian rendition of the earlier Sumerian text did more than develop new themes. Two components of the Sumerian Huwawa story disappear almost entirely with adaptation into Akkadian: the exchange over Huwawa's auras and Utu's provision of seven celestial guides to aid Gilgamesh on his adventure. The elimination of these two features is associated with a series of other changes that reflect the larger shift in narrative perspective. With regard to the auras, although we have only broken accounts of the dialogue with Huwawa in Harmal-2 and Ishchali, it is clear that the heroes do not take the auras prior to capturing Huwawa, and they evidently had no need to do so. On the contrary, the auras immediately scuttle away when Huwawa is captured, no longer essential to his power. In the Sumerian version B, Gilgamesh apparently tricks Huwawa into giving up his seven auras in exchange for footwear, an exchange that undergoes considerable expansion in version A. Whereas Huwawa is stripped of power in the Sumerian account after surrendering his auras, the auras themselves lose power in the Akkadian after Huwawa is captured. In Ishchali, Enkidu eases Gilgamesh's concern for the escaping auras by telling him, "My comrade, catch a bird, and where will its chicks go? Let us find the auras afterward, (which are) like chicks running around in the thicket" (obv./edge 15′–17′). Eventually the two do slay the auras, but only after killing the forest guardian.

Such divergent strategies for defeating Huwawa point to two rather different perceptions of Huwawa and his powers. In the Sumerian, the seven auras serve to protect Huwawa. Once Gilgamesh gains possession of the auras, it is easy to strike and capture the one who had held them. In the Akkadian, however, Huwawa can be seized and killed without this first step. Here slaying the auras is a prerequisite not for killing Huwawa but instead for felling cedar, which the pair do immediately after demolishing the auras (Ishchali rev. 35'–39'). The link between these actions demonstrates that in the Akkadian narrative, the auras do not protect Huwawa but instead serve as his means of guarding the forest.[13] This contrast is reflected in the different portraits of Huwawa in the two accounts. In the Sumerian version B, Huwawa is described repeatedly as a "warrior" who dwells in the highlands, with no sense that he is the highlands' guardian.[14] The lack of the divine determinative before his name indicates that he is not considered a god in this text.[15] Moreover, the highlands are given no precise location in the Sumerian, a vagueness that suits Huwawa's lack of a specific role.[16] Only in the Akkadian is Huwawa described as a guardian, one divinely appointed to protect the forest with his "seven terrors" (Yale IV 137).[17] With the assignment of Huwawa to this particular task, the forest also takes on specific points of reference to western locations: the land of Ebla (Schøyen-2 obv. 26), (H)amran and the land of the Amorites (rev. 55–56), and the ranges of Sirion and Lebanon (Ishchali rev. 31').

---

[13] This association with the forest itself seems to be reflected in Enkidu's reaction to the cedar and its auras in the meditation on his fear in Schøyen-2 (rev. 61–62, 69–70).

[14] For Huwawa as "warrior" (ur-saĝ), see lines 85, 89, 95, 105, 127, 137. This characterization is largely abandoned in version A, where it survives only in the account of Huwawa's overwhelming power (A:99 = B:85).

[15] In version B, Huwawa's name is not written with the divine determinative (lines 129, 155). Some copies of version A do use the dingir for deity, though there is no consistent trend (see Chapter 3 for further discussion).

[16] The "road to Aratta" in B:47 does not describe the particular route of Gilgamesh and Enkidu, but rather applies to the range of knowledge provided by Utu's seven heavenly guides: "These (beings) shine in the sky, they know the route on earth. In the sky they shine …, they give light, on earth, [they know] the road to Aratta, they know the trails like merchants, they know the mountain niches like (carrier-)pigeons" (B:45–50). Based on these lines, one cannot locate "the highlands for cutting cedar" or Huwawa in or near Aratta. The phrase only displays an eastward orientation for this literature.

[17] For Huwawa as "guardian" (maṣṣārum) see Ishchali rev. 26', 30', 34'; IM obv. 20. The guardian's relationship to deity is uncertain, with significant textual ambiguities. The reading of dingir as ilam in Yale V 182 is unnecessary and unlikely (see translation and notes). In Nippur obv. 3–4, Huwawa is grammatically parallel to the auras themselves (namrirū), not to "the god," and it is not clear whether it is the auras themselves that are considered divine. Finally, while the word [i-l]um must be restored to Harmal-1 rev. 10, the parallel with Schøyen-2 obv. 14 has inanna in the same position. The most certain indication of Huwawa's own divinity may be the consistent use of the divine determinative in the Yale tablet, which also marks Gilgamesh and Enkidu this way.

The Sumerian scene in which Gilgamesh tricks Huwawa into giving up his seven auras was thus dropped because it no longer fit the Akkadian narrative framework. Gilgamesh goes to the Cedar Forest specifically to fight Huwawa and thereby gain everlasting fame. As noted above, Huwawa himself becomes the focus of the expedition, rather than the pursuit of cedar, and the connection between the old objective and the new is made by giving Huwawa the explicit role of forest guardian. In the process, the auras come to serve this guardian role as well, so that they protect the forest rather than Huwawa personally, and thus it is unnecessary to procure them before his defeat. With Huwawa's defeat the new focus of the mission, his characterization undergoes a major shift, so that he is elevated in status from ferocious mountain dweller to the divinely endowed guardian of the forest. Certainly the defeat of such a figure will enable Gilgamesh to earn a name for himself.

For all that the Akkadian expands the period before confrontation of Huwawa, it is curious that this version omits the detail of the sun god contributing seven guides to the preparations. Both the Sumerian and the Akkadian Huwawa stories give special prominence to the sun god as the hero's helper, but in entirely different ways. In both Sumerian versions, Enkidu insists that any journey to the highlands for felling cedar must involve Utu, and thus Gilgamesh addresses the god as follows: "I want to enter the highlands. May you be my ally!" (A:17–18; B:32–33). This request is made directly in the presence of Utu, who has appeared in concrete form.[18] Utu then provides seven guides to lead them along the way, not to protect them at their destination or to ensure victory in a showdown with Huwawa. When the duo decides to face Huwawa, neither Gilgamesh nor Enkidu opts to enlist divine help; rather, they set out to trick Huwawa by their own cleverness.[19] Utu only reappears at the end when the captured Huwawa approaches him with the reminder that Utu himself was responsible for raising him in the wild highlands (A:154–156; B:152–154).

The Akkadian tale preserves a particular relationship between Gilgamesh and the sun god Shamash, though the god's purpose is also changed in order to suit the transformed nature of the expedition. After

[18] In B:29–30, the narrator states: "Utu-of-the-Sky donned his lapis diadem and came with head held high." In version A, Utu is not said to "come," but he speaks "from the sky" and enters into direct conversation with Gilgamesh (A:19–20 ff.).

[19] The repeated oath by the life of Ninsun and Lugalbanda introduces a new thought or action and has nothing to do with special help for this challenge (see A:89, 92, 137, 141; B:81, 93, 103).

Enkidu is finally persuaded to join Gilgamesh, and the elders have expressed their hesitation, we find Gilgamesh praying to Shamash, possibly at Enkidu's advice.[20] Shamash neither speaks nor makes an appearance, and the prayer is cast in more remote or transcendent terms. Later, the elders finally accept Gilgamesh's plan and offer him a blessing, predicated on Enkidu's essential experience (Yale VI 247–256). They ask both Shamash and Lugalbanda to help Gilgamesh achieve his goal, and they expect Gilgamesh to pray to these deities nightly (257–271). Once the journey begins, these gods appear only in dreams, as the powers by which Gilgamesh is rescued from the terrifying presence of Huwawa. The first moment of Huwawa's capture is missing from the obverse of Harmal-2, and the sun god is next mentioned only by Huwawa in his plea for mercy, as in the Sumerian.[21] Again, the god is more removed from the exchange in the Akkadian text, without the direct speech found in the Sumerian.

The net effect of the sun god's transformed role is mixed. In the Akkadian narrative, the gods are less available for personal contact with humans than in the Sumerian, where Utu converses directly with Gilgamesh.[22] They are only reached through prayer and dreams. Equally, however, the gods' role in the Akkadian story is new, to suit Huwawa's centrality. Gilgamesh's initial goal in the Sumerian version B is to reach the "highlands for felling cedar" and bring back timber. He invokes the help of the sun god Utu, who provides what he needs in the form of seven celestial guides. Huwawa's opposition is not anticipated, and the heroes handle him without recourse to the gods. The Akkadian Huwawa narrative makes defeat of this superhuman figure Gilgamesh's primary goal. While the Sumerian tale's Huwawa cannot be defeated as long as he possesses his auras, his attack does not kill Gilgamesh and Enkidu—it only

---

[20] There is a break of six to eight lines, before which Gilgamesh is speaking to his "comrade" (V 203–204) and at the end of which someone is saying, "May your god ..." do something, presumably to enable Gilgamesh to return safely "to the port of Uruk" (213–215). The speaker naturally would be Enkidu, who likewise sends his companion to the sun god in the Sumerian story.

[21] See Harmal-2 rev. 44, "By the mouth of the warrior Shamash ..."

[22] This pattern applies specifically to the change in the Huwawa narrative and does not represent a universal change of perspective in the Akkadian Gilgamesh tradition. In the Sippar text for the extended epic, Shamash enters into conversation with Gilgamesh with the immanence familiar to the Sumerian Huwawa story. As discussed earlier, this prominence makes particular sense at Sippar, if the tablet does indeed come from that site.

anesthetizes them. In the Akkadian narrative, Huwawa's attack will kill an unprepared assailant, and Gilgamesh approaches Shamash and Lugalbanda for divine power to overcome this deadly opponent. With the primary goal of the expedition transformed, and the role of the gods along with it, the celestial guides are no longer necessary. Enkidu takes over their function, except that he leads Gilgamesh to Huwawa himself rather than just to the highlands for timber.

IV. *The Influence of the Akkadian Huwawa Narrative on the Sumerian Tradition*

In order to determine the relationship between the first Akkadian tale and the two Sumerian variants, it is first helpful to identify the key traits that distinguish version A from version B of the Sumerian Huwawa narrative. We must keep in mind that the copies of version B as a whole are no older than those for version A, so that their relationship must be evaluated based on comparison of content alone. Moreover, the longer and more widely circulated version A does not represent a direct revision of the shorter version B. Both versions follow the same essential sequence, and large sections of them do correspond substantially, yet each one includes significant differences of narrative order and detail. Version B offers a simpler development of the plot, with a more direct logical progression than version A. We understand therefore that version B preserves a more archaic form of the narrative, one that survived in parallel with what became the standard form.[23]

In general, Gilgamesh and Huwawa A represents a much longer narrative than B. It shares the same essential structure, yet it is not an expansion of the shorter version. The survival of version B, if only in limited circles, suggests that some scribes may have viewed it as a distinct story, rather than simply a variant of the same one. The longer version A includes a number of distinctive new elements that share perspective or details with the Akkadian story. In version B, Gilgamesh simply delivers a speech to Enkidu regarding his desire to enter the highlands; in version A, Gilgamesh presents two variations of the speech to both Enkidu and

---

[23] The definition of two distinct "versions" of Gilgamesh and Huwawa does not mean that each of these was itself completely fixed. Both versions have variant forms, visible especially with the numerous copies found for version A. For details, see Edzard, *"Gilgameš und Huwawa."*

Utu, the second of which is cast in persuasive tones. As in the Akkadian, Gilgamesh's main objective in version A is to make a name for himself by entering the "highlands of the living one" (A:1–2).[24] Fittingly, then, Huwawa's presence looms larger in version A than in version B: a description of him now precedes his entrance, and the author extends considerably the scene in which Huwawa surrenders his auras to Gilgamesh. Finally, when Huwawa's auras knock out Gilgamesh and Enkidu, *Enkidu* is the one who describes Huwawa to Gilgamesh, where in version B, Gilgamesh delivered the exact same description. The presence of these elements only in the Akkadian and in version A indicates one of two possibilities: either version A has influenced the Akkadian, or the Akkadian has prompted such changes in version A. Because the variants in version A can be explained repeatedly by the shift in Enkidu's origins to the steppe that marks the Akkadian narrative, we conclude that the popular Sumerian version was influenced by familiarity with the new non-Sumerian rendition.

A. *Launching the Expedition*

After the four-line hymn to Gilgamesh, version B opens with the hero's announcement that he plans to enter the highlands for felling cedar, for no man can escape death. As his loyal servant, Enkidu does not protest but only advises him to consult Utu before proceeding. Although the text is missing several lines at this point, it is clear that the exchange with Utu is brief: the king requests help from the sun god, who in turn furnishes him with seven celestial guides. In version A, this sequence is lengthened and altered. The first set of exchanges is similar: Gilgamesh proposes his plan to Enkidu, who suggests that he contact Utu. Gilgamesh then asks for help from Utu, in terms identical to version B. In this rendition, however, Utu responds unfavorably, reminding Gilgamesh that his status as a "native son" in Uruk carries no weight in the wild (A:20). Gilgamesh next launches a plea to Utu, stating as he did to Enkidu, "Since no man can elude life's end, I shall enter the highlands, I shall set up my name" (A:30–31). The petition is successful, and Utu in turn furnishes him with the same seven guides introduced in version B.

---

[24] Abusch argues that both the Akkadian Gilgamesh Epic and the Sumerian Version A "center upon the image of Gilgamesh as a hunter who seeks out and defeats a powerful enemy ..." ("Hunting in the Epic of Gilgamesh," 6).

The Akkadian Huwawa story offers a possible explanation for such a change. In the Yale tablet, Gilgamesh also delivers two parallel speeches to two parties, Enkidu and the elders. With Enkidu's firsthand knowledge of the steppe and the elders' general experience, both parties protest Gilgamesh's plan outright and tell him, "The abode of Huwawa is a battle not to be faced" (III 115–116; V 200). In the Akkadian narrative, the protests are rooted both in the shift of Enkidu's origins, so that he has firsthand knowledge of the steppe, and in the new political picture, in which the collective elders play an assertive role. In version A on its own terms, however, there is no analogous explanation as to why Gilgamesh must now persuade Utu for support. Rather, it appears that the Sumerian reflects the influence of the Akkadian, in which Gilgamesh pleads his case extensively before departing for the forest. Yet with Enkidu still Gilgamesh's servant, and no role for the elders, Utu becomes the character who warns Gilgamesh of the journey's danger. Such is a logical choice in the Sumerian, for the sun god already occupies a prominent position in the exposition of the story.[25]

The dual emphasis on Huwawa and fame as the expedition's objectives at the start of version A may also reflect the impact of the Akkadian tale. In version B, Gilgamesh merely wishes to enter the highlands, "because no young man can elude life's end" (line 14), with no indication that such an adventure involves either Huwawa or the acquisition of fame. In version A, however, as in the Akkadian, the problem of mortality is linked to the establishment of one's name as the logical solution. The importance of fame as the rationale for the expedition in the Akkadian Huwawa narrative can be seen in the dialogue between Gilgamesh and Enkidu before their departure. When Gilgamesh launches his final, successful, effort to persuade Enkidu that the expedition is worthwhile, he builds the argument around the value of an enduring name. Gilgamesh begins by comparing human mortality to the gods' life in the heavens. With death inescapable, a name is all that lasts: "If I should fall, my name will stand ..." (Yale IV 148). Then, he closes with return to the same theme, after which he leads Enkidu to the forge to begin preparations: "Let me

---

[25] The sun god is part of the Akkadian story as well, though here he is merely the recipient of Gilgamesh's pleas. With tears trickling down his cheeks, Gilgamesh promises to make Shamash "a shrine of luxuries" if he survives the journey (Yale VI 234). Likewise, in version A, Gilgamesh's promise to "set up the names of the gods" (line 7) is accompanied by tears, indicating that Utu's new role in version A combines elements of Enkidu, the elders, and Shamash, as they appear in the Akkadian version.

begin work and cut down the cedar, let me establish everlasting [fame]!"
(158–160). The Sumerian version A introduces the specific theme of the
"name" at the very beginning of the narrative. In contrast to version B,
the text opens with a reference to Huwawa, "The lord indeed set his
mind toward the highlands of the living one" (A:1), so that the idea of
a guardian is present from the start. Gilgamesh's first words to Enkidu
voice his ambition to set up a visible monument to his name in the distant
highlands (A:4–7). In version A, Gilgamesh then heads to the forge to
acquire weapons for battle, an event that does not occur in version B
but is detailed fully in the Akkadian.[26] Moreover, although the conflict
with Huwawa is already part of the older Sumerian story, only version
A includes the narrator's description of Huwawa, in which we learn that
no man ventures closer to Huwawa than "sixty rods," and that his gaze
is "the eye of death" (lines 120 and 122). These lines recall the identical
statements by Enkidu and the elders in the Yale tablet: "For sixty 'miles'
the forest is deserted. Who can penetrate to its heart?" (III 108–109;
V 195–196).[27]

B. *Enkidu's Knowledge of Huwawa*

Although Enkidu remains Gilgamesh's servant in the Sumerian tale,
he does undergo significant changes in version A. Most noteworthy
is his role in the scene after he and Gilgamesh are knocked out by
Huwawa's auras. In both texts, Enkidu is the first to arise from the
assault.[28] In version B, Gilgamesh is the one to see Huwawa first, and

---

[26] See Yale IV 163–171, according to which they cast axes and swords, evidently both
for cutting wood and for battle with Huwawa.

[27] It is difficult to evaluate the relationship between these two units of sixty that are
associated with Huwawa's fearsome nature. The Sumerian nindan is smaller, defined
more in terms of agricultural plots, while the Akkadian *bēru(m)* has to do with time and
distance for extended travel. In connection with Huwawa, the two terms produce quite
different impressions. So far as the distance has to do with Huwawa's circle of activity,
the larger measure makes more sense in both contexts. The Sumerian version A warns,
"When anyone comes as close as sixty rods, Huwawa has already reached his house in
the cedars" (lines 120–121), a degree of anticipation that works best at greater distance.
Nevertheless, the term nindan is consistent in the Sumerian copies.

[28] This is clear in version A, but it is uncertain in version B whether or not Enkidu
also was put to sleep by Huwawa's auras. It is evident, however, that Enkidu is awake
while Gilgamesh is sleeping, and he appears to rouse him (73–77). It must be noted that
the actual B text of version B (the only text for this section) has "Enkidu" in place of
Gilgamesh, where context demands the correction. First, Enkidu is clearly the speaker
in line 75, in which he states, "young lord Gilgamesh, how long will you sleep?" Second,

he describes him to Enkidu: "I my[self laid eyes on him(?)], so I am [dist]ressed. A warrior—his eye is a lion's glare, his chest is a raging flood. None can approach his head, which consumes the canebrake" (B:84–87, cf. A:98–102). Such a vision produces fear in Gilgamesh, and he questions his ability to challenge Huwawa. In version A, however, the same description of Huwawa is delivered not by Gilgamesh but rather by Enkidu, with Enkidu the one who hesitates. This time, the description is introduced with emphasis on the isolated aspect of Enkidu's experience: "My king, you yourself have not seen that man, so you are not distressed. I am the one who laid eyes on that man, so I am distressed" (A:97–98).

Although Enkidu's statement is not cast in terms of knowledge, his vision of Huwawa is cast as a solitary experience, and from this vantage, he seeks to abandon the mission. Gilgamesh then persuades him to stay by appealing to the force of their partnership: "You help me, so I shall help you. What then can anyone do against us?" (A:110). Such a deliberate change in the Sumerian requires some sort of motive, and once again, the logic of the Akkadian offers an adequate explanation. With Enkidu's origins now located in the steppe, he possesses special knowledge of Huwawa, knowledge that Gilgamesh does not have. He thus protests the proposal based on personal experience. Enkidu's knowledge in the Akkadian narrative appears to have influenced the Sumerian story, prompting a shift in the one who sees Huwawa first. Yet because the Sumerian tale retains Enkidu's position as a servant from Uruk, his vision of Huwawa can no longer be rooted in prior experience; rather, it must occur after he and Gilgamesh have commenced their journey together.

V. The Nature of the Akkadian Tale at the Time of Its Influence

Thus far we have argued that a significant portion of the distinctions between versions A and B can be explained by recourse to the Akkadian tale. The precise nature of the Akkadian tale at the time of its influence,

---

once the person in question arises and rubs his eyes, he begins, "By the life of my mother Ninsun, of my father, the pure Lugalbanda," (81) a remark that unequivocally points to Gilgamesh as the speaker (see Edzard, "Gilgameš und Huwawa", 25; and George, The Epic of Gilgamesh [London: Penguin, 1999] 164).

however, remains in question. Most of the Akkadian features shared by
the Sumerian version A derive from the Huwawa story directly, as should
not be surprising. Because the epic was built outward from the Akkadian
Huwawa narrative without major change to the received material itself,
any influence on the Sumerian from this block naturally displays no
specific themes of the extended epic.

As with our comparison in Chapter 2 between Penn and Yale from
the OB Akkadian Gilgamesh material, it is illuminating to compare the
Sumerian version A with material from the Akkadian epic where they
treat the same theme. This is possible with the interest in mothers that
appears in both Penn and the Sumerian version A, much more than in
either the Akkadian Huwawa narrative or the Sumerian version B. In the
Penn tablet, Gilgamesh's mother is one of the epic's wise women, the one
who can interpret her son's two dreams of Enkidu. It is likely that her
role in Yale column II, which is almost entirely lost, reflects that same
epic voice (see Chapter 5). The Sumerian story offers no speaking role
for any character from Uruk besides Gilgamesh and Enkidu, and version
B expresses no particular interest in mothers. Gilgamesh swears by his
mother and father (B:15, and *passim*), and Huwawa complains of his lack
of proper parents (B:152–153).

Version A, in contrast, makes mothers the principal victims, if their
sons fail to return from adventure. Where version B has Gilgamesh
muster men who have no wives and children (B:53–56), in the corresponding lines, version A defines such household commitments especially by a man's mother (A:50–53). Then, when Enkidu announces his
decision to go home without Gilgamesh, he concludes with concern for
the king's own mother: "I will tell your mother you are alive, so she will
laugh. But afterward, when I tell her you are dead, she will surely shed
tears for you" (A:104–105).[29] Through all this, we see nothing of the most
striking feature of Gilgamesh's mother in Penn, as the wise woman, "the
one who knows all," who can interpret her son's dreams. In the Akkadian epic, this characterization places her among the three wise women
who play key roles as knowledgeable guides, taking over Enkidu's position in the received Huwawa narrative. Although we cannot know for

---

[29] When Gilgamesh recites the same speech about Huwawa's fearsome power in
version B (B:85–88; cf. A:99–102), he moves straight to a simple statement that their
mission is impossible (B:89), so that the comment about Gilgamesh's mother in A is
undoubtedly found only in that version.

certain which Akkadian narrative colored the Sumerian version A, it would be surprising to add new attention to mothers and ignore the most important aspect of Gilgamesh's mother in the epic. It seems more likely, therefore, that version A shows awareness of the Akkadian Huwawa narrative alone.[30]

The conclusion that Akkadian influence on the Sumerian version A preceded creation of the OB epic would also be supported by the fact that the most characteristic epic elements are lacking from the Sumerian more generally. The portrait of Gilgamesh as an aggressive tyrant, for example, does not resonate with his depiction in either Sumerian story, in which he summons only unencumbered men to join him and allows those with wives, children or mothers to remain behind. The notion that Enkidu is Gilgamesh's fated, godlike match also has no place in the Sumerian tradition, in which the two are nothing more than master and right-hand man. Likewise, the issue of Enkidu's death, which stands at the center of the epic, is not anticipated at all in version A, even when Enkidu angers Enlil by chopping off Huwawa's head.

It appears, then, that the Sumerian Gilgamesh and Huwawa A developed its long form in dialogue with an Akkadian Huwawa narrative that was known in the same scribal circles. One of the most intriguing features of early second-millennium scribal education, so far as it has been reconstructed, is that in settings where Sumerian literature was standard, as in the "tablet house" (House F) at Nippur, Akkadian literature did not play a comparable role. Only the solitary "Nippur" text, selected from the hero's dreams about Huwawa, came from this building and represents the Akkadian Gilgamesh material for this body of writing. In the scribal curriculum as known from Nippur, the Sumerian version A held a central place next to an Akkadian tradition of Huwawa that was known but not copied in the same way by students. Possibly, the independent Akkadian Huwawa narrative continued to exist as a complement to this Sumerian tale. When the Sumerian Gilgamesh stories lost their special place in scribal practice, evidently by the end of the OB period, it may

---

[30] One feature of Gilgamesh and Huwawa A that could reflect the epic's treatment of Gilgamesh's mother could be the hymn to the hero that was placed also at the start of version B and that appears in the Sumerian Bull of Heaven tale (see "The Priority of the B Narrative" in Chapter 4). There, in parallel lines, the mother and the wet nurse "knew" how to form and raise this remarkable child. As lines that forge a link between the Huwawa and the Bull of Heaven stories, these may represent part of the latest shaping of the Sumerian stories in OB scribal circles.

be that the Akkadian Huwawa narrative also ceased to be attractive for copying as a separate text.[31] At some unknown point, in unknown circles, the Gilgamesh Epic became the one viable form of this venerable narrative tradition.

---

[31] On the reproduction of Gilgamesh as part of scribal education with Sumerian literary texts, see George, *Babylonian Gilgamesh Epic*, 8, 17. George remarks, "By the late Old Babylonian period court literature in Sumerian had dwindled almost to nothing" (17).

CHAPTER FIVE

BEHIND PENN:
OLD BABYLONIAN INTRODUCTIONS TO THE
HUWAWA NARRATIVE AND TO THE EPIC

Most likely, the original introduction to the Akkadian Huwawa narrative offered a simpler sequence leading up to the meeting of Enkidu and Gilgamesh than that detailed in the epic, as represented in part by the Penn tablet. In this earlier story, the harlot's role would have been simply to lure Enkidu from the steppe and bring him to Uruk, so that he could assist Gilgamesh on his campaign to confront Huwawa. Remnants of this role are preserved in Schøyen-1, in which Enkidu thanks the harlot for leading him to Uruk, and in Penn II 56–60, in which the harlot invites Enkidu to the Uruk temple. With the epic's introduction of new themes, however, certain elements of the earlier exposition became insufficient to set up the relationship between the two men. To this end, the harlot's role in bringing Enkidu to Gilgamesh was taken up by that of the wedding traveler, who now incited Enkidu to go to Uruk and confront the king in anger. As "Shamkat," the harlot was furnished with a completely new function in the epic, namely, to transform Enkidu from a wild man into a "gentleman" (*awīlum*) prior to his encounter with Gilgamesh.[1] The anticipatory dreams of Penn then introduced Enkidu not as Gilgamesh's guide, but rather as his destined match.

Because Penn and Yale were copied by a single scribe as part of the OB epic, the sequence should display how the start of the Huwawa

---

[1] It is possible that the harlot was anonymous in the original Huwawa narrative. She is called only "the harlot" in both Yale and Schøyen-1, as opposed to the Penn tablet, which utilizes both her title and her name interchangeably. In particular, if the harlot were named in the Huwawa narrative, one would expect the author to utilize it in the parallel line of Schøyen-1 obv. 3. Here Enkidu "speaks to her, to the harlot" (*ana šâšim issaqqaram ana harimtim*), yet the author uses the dative pronoun rather than the prostitute's name. In contrast, we see the interchangeable use of "harlot" and "Shamkat" in Penn (II 45–51; IV 135–143). It is especially worth noting Enkidu's address to "Shamkat," as opposed to the generic harlot, in IV 140. Notwithstanding the fact that the contexts for references to the harlot in Yale and Schøyen-1 are somewhat broken, it is possible to conjecture that along with the development of the harlot's role in the larger epic, she was endowed with a name.

narrative was adapted to fit the new material and purposes of the extended tale, except that Yale columns I and II are severely damaged. Even
in this condition, it is clear that column I of Yale cannot begin a new
narrative. Gilgamesh and Enkidu are already conversing in the opening
lines, and later in the column, the harlot is mentioned (I 43), though her
role must precede the Yale text. In sequence with Penn, Yale columns I–
II must address the period immediately after the fight between Enkidu
and Gilgamesh. However the Akkadian Huwawa narrative introduced
Enkidu and brought him to Gilgamesh, this has been subsumed in or
replaced by the epic introduction represented by Penn and is now largely
lost.

I. *Remnants of the Introduction to*
the Akkadian Huwawa Narrative

Although Gilgamesh and Enkidu have already met before the Yale tablet
begins, the exchanges between these two, perhaps along with the harlot and Gilgamesh's mother, could offer hints regarding the contents of
the original introduction to the Akkadian Huwawa narrative. Unfortunately, most of the first two columns are missing and tell us little. For
this opening stage of the Huwawa narrative plot, Schøyen-1 provides a
glimpse of several lines, which we cannot assume to match what would
have occurred in Yale, and these lines do include hints of an older introduction. In addition, it appears that the epic picked up a segment of the
prior Huwawa tale's introduction and incorporated it into the scene with
the harlot that is found in Penn. Such changes to the introduction are not
surprising, given the nature of narrative revision. As the logic of a story
is recast, and new material is placed in front of existing narrative in order
to lead the reader to respond differently, some substitution is necessary
so as to avoid contradiction.[2]

A. *Schøyen-1*

In the first legible line of Schøyen-1, a character refers to "Enkidu, the
advisor whom I observed ..." (obv. 2′), an assertion that is followed by
Enkidu's address to the harlot: " 'Come, harlot, let me do something good

---

[2] For thorough discussion of this phenomenon of "revision through introduction,"
see Sara J. Milstein, "Expanding Ancient Narratives: Revision through Introduction in
Biblical and Mesopotamian Texts" (New York University Ph.D., projected 2010).

for you, because you led me to the heart of Uruk-Thoroughfare-of-the-Land, because you showed me a good partner, (because you showed) me a comrade" (obv. 4′–6′). George renders line 2′, "Enkidu, the counsellor that I kept seeing [in dreams!]," which he fronts with a completely reconstructed line: "'[I] *have acquired a friend, the counsellor [that I kept] seeing [in dreams]*."[3] If Gilgamesh is the speaker of these first visible lines, such "seeing" only could have occurred in dreams, presumably the dreams of the Penn tablet. As evidence for his reconstruction of line 2′, George cites Yale I 24–25, two lines that themselves are quite broken. Though the term for dreams (*šu-na-tim*) is mostly visible in line 25, it is not at all certain that the line corresponds to Schøyen-1 obv. 2′.[4] For one, the two fail to share a single overlapping sign. Second, the reverse of Schøyen-1, though broken, indicates that the text is not identical to the corresponding section of the Yale tablet. Although lines 3′–5′ of the reverse overlap with Yale IV 151–153, lines 1′–2′ demonstrate considerable variation from the preceding lines in Yale column IV.[5] There is no reason to assume, therefore, that line 2′ of the obverse has any direct parallel in the Yale tablet.[6]

---

[3] Not one sign is read as certain, and only the lower half of several signs are visible at all (obv. 1′). Based on George's copy, the signs for the first half of line 1′ do not appear to parallel those of line 2′, so that his proposed repetition is doubtful.

[4] No part of the Schøyen-1 obverse aligns with preserved lines from Yale.

[5] Schøyen-1 rev. 1′ is almost entirely broken, though it begins with *lu-*, "Let me … (?)." The start of the next line is clearer, and has nothing in common with what should represent a parallel text in Yale: *at-ta nu-hi-dam ia-x-*[…] *x x a-na* […] *x x*, "you, alert me, … to …." The lines in Yale that correspond to Schøyen-1 rev. 1′–2′ offer nothing close to these signs or sentiments: "If I fall, my name will stand. (People will say,) 'Gilgamesh joined battle with martial Huwawa'." The three lines begin, [148] *šum-ma* … [149] ᵈGIŠ-*mi* … [150] *ta-qum-tam* … The only preceding line that begins with *at-ta* in Gilgamesh's statement to Enkidu reads, *at-ta an-na-nu-um-ma ta-dar mu-tam*, "Here, even you fear death" (144).

[6] A further important factor is the size of Schøyen-1. We find that the gap between the obverse and the reverse appears to cover considerably more of the Yale text than supposed by George (*Babylonian Gilgamesh Epic*, 219–221), so that the obverse of Schøyen-1 has no viable match with any nearby material from Yale. It is therefore likely that Schøyen-1 preserves a text that diverges significantly from that of Yale, in spite of the brief alignment of two lines from its reverse. George estimates from the curvature of what survives that "about five-sixths of the tablet are missing, perhaps more" (p. 219). This leads to an estimate of roughly sixty lines on each side, with a few missing at the beginning of the obverse and the end of the reverse. According to George, Schøyen-1 obv. 1′–2′ align with Yale I 24–25, and Schøyen-1 rev. 3′–4′ definitely match Yale IV 151–152. That leaves 125 lines between the two texts, but as George observes, at least 17 lines of poetry in the Yale section are divided across two lines, where Schøyen-1 consistently offers longer lines without such division. George concludes that the roughly 108 lines, or slightly fewer, that

Further, the notion that Gilgamesh would speak of an "advisor" whom he saw in dreams does not fit the pattern for visions elsewhere in the OB material. Before he meets Enkidu, Gilgamesh dreams of inanimate objects that represent him, an axe and a stone from the sky. On the way to Huwawa, Gilgamesh sees concrete images that are later identified with Huwawa, Shamash, and Lugalbanda. The descriptive title, "advisor," has no counterpart in either the dreams or their interpretations, as it has neither the visual specificity of the one nor the named referent of the other.[7]

would then define the gap between obverse and reverse on Schøyen-1 are just the right number to match the known quantity of text in Yale. Our analysis, based on George's description of the evidence without collation of the tablet, suggests that considerations of size add to the difficulty of aligning the obverse of Schøyen-1 with Yale column I. First, the reverse of Yale also tends to avoid splitting poetic lines, like Schøyen-1, so that the factor of adjusted line counts from divided lines applies only to Yale's obverse, which ends at line 135. Then, a more precise estimate of poetic line count for the Yale obverse must be proportional, defined by the poetic lines that can be defined for surviving text. That is, the split lines counted by George reflect only a fraction of the obverse text, and the overall number of split lines should be estimated by extrapolating the whole from the preserved part. This procedure produces the following results. Only 59 lines from Yale 1–135 can be evaluated, and out of these, 40 poetic lines are represented: 10–15 as 3, 16, 17, 18–19 as 1 (total 6 for 10); [20–71 impossible to assess]; 72–73 as 1, 74, 75–76 as 1, 77, 78, 79–82 as 2, 83, 84, 85–88 as 2, 89, 90; [91–97 uncertain or broken]; 98–103 as 3, 104, 105, 106, 107, 108, 109, 110, 111–116 as 3, 117, 118; [119–126 too broken to assess]; 127, 128, 129–132 as 2, 133, 134–135 as 1. This proportion may be applied in either direction. If we begin with Yale, we may conclude that if the proportion was consistent throughout, the 135 lines of the obverse would equal roughly 92 poetic lines. If we begin with Schøyen-1, and we follow George's estimate that five-sixths of the tablet survives, then the visible text of the obverse and reverse falls within lines * 1–10 and * 110–120, with approximately 100 lines to fill. The 13 lines of Yale IV 136–148 would match Schøyen-1 without splitting poetic lines, so that 87 lines in Schøyen-1 would remain to count according to the proportion from the Yale obverse. These 87 lines would match 129 from Yale, so that if we count backwards from Yale III 135, the last visible line from the obverse of Schøyen-1 should align approximately with Yale I 7, which is entirely lost. Nevertheless, this analysis leaves us with a highly problematic alignment between the two texts. The opening lines of Yale must provide a direct transition from Enkidu's praise of Gilgamesh in Penn VI 234–240. Presumably, Gilgamesh speaks next, perhaps already mentioning his dangerous plan, because Yale I 10–15 indicate Enkidu's discomfort in terms that he repeats in III 113–114. It is difficult to envision any place for the harlot, or any exchange between the harlot and Enkidu.

[7] In the later epic, the harlot becomes an all-seeing wise-woman who knows that Gilgamesh has already dreamed of Enkidu and reports to him the exchanges that are narrated in column I of Penn (SBV I, especially lines 244–245). As recounted by the harlot, after his mother has finished explaining his second dream, Gilgamesh declares, "My comrade, an advisor, let me acquire; let me acquire my comrade, an advisor" (I 296–297). These changes to the Penn text suggest an attempt to mesh separate ideas from the epic and the Huwawa narrative, as still distinct in Penn and Yale, by moving Enkidu's identity as "advisor" into Gilgamesh's dream.

Moreover, the term "advisor" is never attached to Enkidu in the Penn tablet. Rather, this term is more at home in the Huwawa texts, in which the elders are named Gilgamesh's *mālikū* ("advisors"), and Enkidu consistently functions as Gilgamesh's guide. In fact, the term *mālikum* exemplifies the role of Enkidu in the Huwawa material, a role that is eclipsed by the epic author, who puts Gilgamesh's passion for Enkidu above the latter's position as experienced guide.

Yet it is obv. 3' of Schøyen-1 that offers the best evidence against Gilgamesh speaking in line 2'. In line 3', Enkidu speaks "to her (*ana šâšim*), to the harlot." In all other cases in which *ana šâšim* ("to him, to her") appears in the OB Gilgamesh material, the referent of the pronoun is the last actor.[8] Without the unnecessary reconstruction of the phrase "in dreams" at the end of the line, the harlot is the logical speaker of line 2', the one who saw Enkidu in the steppe and brought him to Gilgamesh, presumably at the king's bidding.[9] With this literal understanding of the verb *amārum* ("to see"), we propose that Schøyen-1 obv. 2' reflects the harlot's original role of introducing Enkidu to Gilgamesh in the Akkadian Huwawa account. By using the iterative form of the verb, Schøyen-1 suggests that the harlot "observed" Enkidu before making contact.[10] Finally, it is worth noting that both Schøyen-1 and Yale (I 43) refer to this woman as "the harlot" (*harimtum*), rather than as Shamkat, a name that seems to be introduced with the epic.[11]

---

[8] This style of introduction to direct speech only occurs otherwise in the Ishchali and Sippar texts. In Ishchali, it appears with every instance of discourse introduction: obv. 6', 10', 14'; rev. 40'. In Sippar, it occurs in I 9'; II 14'; III 16, 25; IV 4, 7, 14, 21 (all instances but I 5'–6', where Shamash initiates a conversation with Gilgamesh that has no prior basis).

[9] The harlot's repeated "seeing" of Enkidu need not assume the wild portrayal of Enkidu, as we see in the Penn tablet and in the SBV. The notion that she must first "see" Enkidu before approaching him is preserved in the SBV (Tablet I 178–179): on the second day, waiting by the water-hole, "Shamhat saw him (*i-mur-šu-m[a]*), the *lullû*-man, the murderous young man from the midst of the steppe."

[10] Unlike the SBV, where the harlot keeps her distance at first because of Enkidu's dangerous nature as a "murderous young man" (*eṭlu šaggāšû*), the OB narrative in Schøyen-1 need assume no such fear. On the contrary, it is as a potential "advisor" that the harlot observes Enkidu, perhaps by reference to his evident skills.

[11] The Penn tablet uses both the name Shamkat (II 50; IV 135, 140; V 176) and the term *harimtum*, "harlot" (II 45, 51; III 94; IV 139, 143). Without more preserved text for the beginning of the Huwawa story in Yale and Schøyen-1, the two uses of the word *harimtum* are suggestive but insufficient to indicate a definite pattern.

B. *The Penn Tablet*

At first glance, Enkidu's response to the harlot in Schøyen-1 obv. 4'–6', in which he thanks the harlot for introducing him to Gilgamesh, seems to recall the events of the Penn tablet. In Penn II 56–60, Shamkat tells Enkidu, "Come, let me lead you to the heart of Uruk-Thoroughfare, to the pure house, the dwelling of Anu. Enkidu, arise, let me take you to Eanna, the dwelling of Anu." The terms echo those of Schøyen-1 obv. 4'–5': both use the verb *redûm* ("to lead") and refer to Uruk-Thoroughfare.[12] When we follow this sequence in Penn, however, we find that Shamkat's invitation to Uruk is not realized in the remainder of the text. In II 73–76, Shamkat "leads" Enkidu (*ireddešu*) not to Uruk but instead to the shepherds' camp, where he is introduced to the trappings of civilization. As the events unfold, the task of bringing Enkidu to meet Gilgamesh belongs to the wedding traveler, whose incendiary description of Gilgamesh spurs Enkidu to confront the king at Uruk. In V 175–176, Shamkat does not in fact "lead" Enkidu to Uruk; rather, he walks in front, with her trailing behind him (*illak Enkidu u Šamkatum warkīšu*).[13] Furthermore, once Enkidu and Shamkat reach Uruk in column V, there is no reference to the temple of Anu, even though it is cited twice as the end destination. On their own, lines II 56–60 indicate that the harlot will lead Enkidu directly to the temple in Uruk, yet neither the temple nor the straight route to the city are documented in the Penn tablet.

These discontinuities suggest that the Penn text has incorporated a narrative segment that was composed to fit a different rendition of Enkidu's invitation to Uruk. The harlot's offer to lead Enkidu to Uruk in Penn II 56–60 represents precisely what Enkidu thanks her for in Schøyen-1. Both texts are most easily understood as remnants of the original introduction to the Huwawa narrative, where the harlot could have accomplished her task in a straightforward manner. This proposal would explain why Shamkat's invitation to lead Enkidu to Eanna is not

---

[12] In Penn II 56–57, the harlot states, "Come (*alkam*), let me lead you (*lurdeka*) to the heart of Uruk-Thoroughfare (*ana libbi Uruk ribītim*) . . ."; cf. Schøyen-1 obv. 4'–5': "Come (*alkīm*), harlot . . . because you led me (*terdîm*) to the heart of Uruk-Thoroughfare-of-the-Land (*ana libbi Uruk ribītu m[ātim]*)."

[13] Enkidu's gratitude to the harlot for showing him "a good partner, a comrade" (Schøyen-1 obv. 6') also does not match Penn, in which neither of these terms (*tappûm* and *ibrum*) is used to describe the relationship between Gilgamesh and Enkidu.

brought to fruition in the Penn tablet. By retaining the harlot's invitation to the Uruk temple, the epic author appears to have preserved a vestige of the original meeting place for Gilgamesh and Enkidu.[14] This earlier meeting would have no need for the anticipatory dreams, the wedding traveler, or the physical contest, all of which are bound to the epic vision that recasts Enkidu as Gilgamesh's ultimate match.[15] Logistically, if the harlot is the one to lead Enkidu directly to Gilgamesh in the original account, as indicated by Schøyen-1, then the wedding traveler and wrestling match automatically would be rendered superfluous to the earlier story. The content of the two dreams, which includes people gathered around Enkidu, anticipates directly the crowds gathered at Enkidu's arrival in Uruk, just prior to the fight scene. Moreover, the dreams set up the passion that Gilgamesh has for Enkidu, a passion that has no part in the simpler Huwawa adventure story. In sum, these three important components of Penn have no place in an earlier narrative that is built around the harlot's introduction of Enkidu to his new partner in adventure, Gilgamesh.

---

[14] The reference in Penn II 56–60 to the temple of Anu, the god of Uruk, may match the religious picture that is preserved in the Yale tablet and Huwawa texts, where gods play a more prominent role than they do in Penn: Gilgamesh prays to Shamash for support, and the elders bless Gilgamesh by Shamash in column VI (see 257 ff.). Huwawa's divine origins are explicated, and he is situated with respect to Adad. References to Adad reappear in Schøyen-2 obv. 34–45 and Harmal-2 obv. 20, and both Lugalbanda and Shamash are tied to Gilgamesh's visions in Nippur and Harmal-1. Enlil is cited twice in IM obv. 27 and 29, and finally, the forest is defined as the "abode of the Anunnaki" in Ishchali rev. 38′ and IM obv. 18. The situation in Penn, however, is starkly different. Besides the reference to Anu's temple, which we identify as a remnant of the original Huwawa material, divine references only occur in descriptions of Gilgamesh and Enkidu (II 53; V 194). Even the final reference to Enlil at the close of column VI is in reference to Gilgamesh's kingship. We must note, however, that the Sippar tablet does involve Shamash (I 5′–15′), though his role as a speaking, active figure again is different from what we find in the Huwawa material, in which numerous gods are simply evoked and referenced. This intimate form of conversation may be rooted in the exchange between Gilgamesh and Utu in the Sumerian tale of Gilgamesh and Huwawa, as discussed above.

[15] The incorporation of the invitation to Eanna into the epic text of Penn illustrates the nature of continuity in reproduction of the Gilgamesh Epic. Although the new vision of the epic stripped Shamkat of her responsibility to lead Enkidu to the Uruk temple, where she could introduce him to Gilgamesh, the invitation of Penn II 56–60 must have survived repeated copying so as to be included in this tablet. Evidently this offer stood at the center of Shamkat's initial address to Enkidu and was not easily dislodged. After all, this was still to be Enkidu's destination. Whatever the explanation, if we are correct in our identification of this block with the Akkadian Huwawa narrative, the appearance of this textual relic in a copy of the epic represents evidence for considerable textual continuity.

It remains to consider why the harlot would go to the steppe to retrieve Enkidu in the original Akkadian Huwawa tale. In the Standard Babylonian version, the wild Enkidu has become a problem for the hunter, as this companion of animals has filled in his pits and torn out his traps (I 130–131). To address the problem, Gilgamesh instructs the hunter to use Shamhat to seduce Enkidu, which will cause Enkidu to lose both his strength and his camaraderie with the wild animals.[16] The solution works, and Enkidu eventually arrives in Uruk, with the story unfolding along lines similar to what we find in the Penn tablet. It is likely that the missing first tablet of the OB epic would have introduced Shamkat to Enkidu in like terms, also involving the hunter. Given the identical format of Penn ("Tablet II") and Yale ("Tablet III"), we know that the first tablet of the OB epic would have had to cover six columns of material. The first three words of the missing Tablet I are quoted in Penn's colophon: *šūtur eli šarrī*, "Surpassing above kings." The phrase opens line 29 of the SB epic, the first tablet of which brings us to Gilgamesh's dreams and the start of the material covered by the Penn text.[17] Jacobsen treated the late text as preserving the OB epic without significant revision.[18] Although the epic must have undergone considerable change through the second millennium, and it would have tolerated some textual variation in the earlier periods, it does appear that we can envision a general continuity of plot.

---

[16] Notice the transition in naming, from just "the harlot" in the Akkadian Huwawa narrative to Shamkat in the OB epic's Penn text, with the name rendered Shamhat in later periods (cf. already MB Ur obv. 11, 20; rev. 48).

[17] Any discussion of Tablet I of the SBV must make reference to the recently discovered prologue to the Gilgamesh Epic from Ugarit, published by Daniel Arnaud in *Corpus des textes de bibliothèque de Ras Shamra-Ougarit (1936–2000) en sumérien, babylonien et assyrien*, Aula Orientalis Supplementa 23 (Sabadell-Barcelona: Editorial Ausa, 2007) 130–133. The first six lines of this text overlap with those of Tablet I of the SBV; then, the two diverge. While lines 7–28 of the SBV proceed to elaborate on Gilgamesh's discovery of "the hidden region" and on his various accomplishments, lines 7–15 of the Ugarit text present a montage of key elements known from the OB epic: Gilgamesh's visit with Uta-napishti, his abuse of the brides, and the people's cry to the heavens of Anu. Its content demonstrates that the precise form of the prologue, along with its linkage to the main text, was still changing. In the Ugarit text, the old opening phrase appears with slight variation in line 16 as *šūtur ana šarrī*. It then seems that a portion of the material that follows has been altered and inserted before this phrase in the SBV (cf., especially, lines 20–28 of the Ugarit text with Tablet I 18–28 of the SBV). In turn, the logic of Gilgamesh's rampart tour is clearer in the Ugarit prologue, which preserves an earlier place for *šūtur eli (ana) šarrī*. For further discussion, see George, "The Gilgamesh Epic at Ugarit," *AuOr* 25 (2007) 237–254.

[18] "The Gilgamesh Epic: Romantic and Tragic Vision," pp. 233–235. Moran shares at least the notion that the SB version has simply taken over the Old Babylonian hymn at this point ("The Epic of Gilgamesh: A Document of Ancient Humanism," 8–10).

It is unlikely, however, that the earlier Akkadian Huwawa narrative was introduced by a scheme that presents Enkidu as a wild man who undergoes a massive transformation to become Gilgamesh's match.[19]

In order to reconstruct the original introduction to the Huwawa narrative, we must work backward from the details of the OB Huwawa material, without assuming the contents of Penn or of the SB epic. In Yale and Schøyen-1, Enkidu's main function is to serve as Gilgamesh's advisor on the expedition to the Cedar Forest, a realm that he knows because he lived in the steppe among herdsmen. It thus follows that Gilgamesh must have found some way to bring Enkidu to Uruk from this distant location. The harlot is mentioned in both Yale and Schøyen-1, so that any other vehicle is unlikely. Gilgamesh himself would have sent her into the steppe to retrieve Enkidu as the ideal partner for his adventure, for we know Gilgamesh has heard of Enkidu's fame as guardian of herdsmen against marauders (IV 151–153). Given the harlot's occupation, the task of luring Enkidu to Uruk surely would have involved sex in the original narrative as well.[20] This proposed scenario would explain why much of Yale is preoccupied with Gilgamesh's attempt to persuade Enkidu to join him on the expedition. Without the wrestling match of the epic, this dialogue would mark the first encounter between Enkidu and Gilgamesh, brought about by the harlot.

Based on the reference to Enkidu's fame as a guardian among herdsmen, it appears that in the Huwawa narrative, Gilgamesh knew Enkidu by name before his arrival in Uruk. In the OB epic, however, Enkidu's arrival in the city is cast as a complete surprise. The two men are destined to meet, but not because of the king's deliberate planning. We know

---

[19] This sense of continuity works well with the larger epic represented by the Penn and Sippar tablets. After the line that defines Gilgamesh as the greatest king, the SB epic continues with a longer praise to Gilgamesh (Tablet I 29–66), which includes reference to his journey to Uta-na'ishtim (lines 41–42), the great epic event after the Huwawa story. In the material that follows, the people complain of their king's oppression (67–91), and the gods create Enkidu as a creature of the wild (92–112) whose first human contact will be a hunter (113–121). The hunter goes to his father, who sends him to Gilgamesh, and Gilgamesh in turn devises the Shamhat scheme (122–187). It is not clear how much of the SB sequence would have originated in the OB epic. Some involvement of the hunter is likely, because it dominates the shape of the long SB introduction, and the OB requires a considerable narrative block.

[20] Abusch ("The Courtesan, the Wild Man, and the Hunter," 428–429) believes that the sexual encounter began as an independent tale of a primitive man and his first encounter with sex, without reference to either the hunter or to Gilgamesh. In a Huwawa account where Enkidu is not presented as wild, we must look for another explanation, and the attractions of the harlot need have nothing to do with specifically primitive desires.

that Gilgamesh could not have sent the harlot specifically to retrieve Enkidu, as seems likely for the Huwawa tale, for Gilgamesh's dreams in Penn reveal that he has never heard of Enkidu. Further, the recounting of Gilgamesh's dreams must take place after Enkidu has already coupled with the harlot, and the wilderness liaison was arranged for other reasons: "While Gilgamesh was relating the dream, Enkidu was settled in the harlot's company; the two of them were making love" (Penn II 44–46).[21]

Such evidence provokes the question, then, as to what incites the harlot to seek out Enkidu in the OB epic. The scenario with the hunter in the SBV, which may have existed in some form in the OB epic, offers a possible explanation. There, the wild Enkidu has filled in the hunter's pits and torn out his traps, prompting the hunter to seek help from the king. Having no prior knowledge of the man, Gilgamesh sends Shamhat out to seduce Enkidu, thus provoking the animals to flee from him, so the hunter would be left to his work. One indirect indication that the hunter already played a role in the OB epic may be the fact that Gilgamesh lives as a hunter in the steppe after Enkidu's death, at the beginning of the Sippar tablet. Gilgamesh would thus return to Enkidu's old terrain, although he could not recreate Enkidu's life among the beasts. We propose that the need to isolate Enkidu from the animals likewise prompted his tryst with Shamkat in the OB epic. After Shamkat has intercourse with Enkidu, she asks, "Why do you roam about the steppe with the beasts?" (Penn II 54–55; cf. SBV I 208), and then shares her clothing with him. From this point, Enkidu begins his identification with humans instead of wild animals.

The fact that Shamkat's proposal to take Enkidu to Uruk is not actually realized in the OB epic prompts us to identify it as a remnant of the Akkadian Huwawa narrative. It is noteworthy that this disjointedness is remedied in the SB epic. In the later rendition, Shamhat again invites Enkidu

---

[21] This indicates that the harlot must have been introduced prior to this scene and therefore in the missing Tablet I. It is worth noting that by coordinating these actions, the narration in Penn splits up the scene in which Enkidu is coupling with the harlot. The same division occurs in the SB epic, where the awkwardness of the intrusion is addressed by having Shamhat report the entire dream scenario; note the parallel of Tablet I 299–300, Tablet II 1, with Penn II 44–46. The fact that the OB epic divides this scene raises the possibility that the prior Akkadian Huwawa narrative included an uninterrupted exchange between Enkidu and the harlot.

to the sacred temple in Uruk, but this time she speaks directly of meeting Gilgamesh: "Come, I will lead you to the heart of Uruk-the-Sheepfold ... where Gilgamesh is perfect in strength, and (where he) establishes his superiority over the young men like a wild bull" (I 209–212). Enkidu then echoes her words, adding that he will challenge Gilgamesh in Uruk. The meeting of Enkidu and Gilgamesh is thus recast as Shamhat's original idea. With this adjustment, the SB epic restores the basic contours of the original introduction to the Huwawa narrative, albeit with a twist. Once again, Gilgamesh sends the harlot to bring Enkidu to Uruk, only this time, he does so unwittingly. The harlot then plants the idea in Enkidu's mind to go fight Gilgamesh at Uruk, so that when the wedding traveler arrives, it is only natural for Enkidu to respond by confronting the king. With this revision, the SB writer smoothes out the wrinkles of the OB epic, reinstating Shamhat as the medium for bringing Enkidu to Gilgamesh. In the final rendition, however, the figure of Shamhat takes on even more importance. Where in the Akkadian Huwawa narrative, she served as the vehicle for getting Enkidu to Uruk, as per royal orders, in the SB epic she functions as the instigator of the entire operation.[22]

II. *Reintroducing Enkidu to Gilgamesh: The Epic Version*

In Gilgamesh and Huwawa B, the king of Uruk undertakes his journey to the highlands because he does not want to die without some heroic effort. The Akkadian Huwawa narrative also presents Gilgamesh as risking death, in this case to gain a lasting name, but death itself does not inspire the expedition. With creation of the epic, death returns to center stage in a role that exacts a terrible personal cost on Gilgamesh. The epic reaches beyond the issue of survival through the establishment of one's name, and instead introduces a darker perspective, occupied simply with the impossibility of escaping death, however urgent the desire to do so. This time, it is the particular death of Enkidu that drives Gilgamesh to risk a dangerous journey—not to confront Huwawa in the Cedar Forest but rather to cross the waters of death to visit Uta-na'ishtim, the man who survived the great flood. For this end, the

---

[22] The role of the gods in creating Enkidu explains his existence and ultimate purpose but not the immediate means of his relocation to Uruk.

partnership between Enkidu and Gilgamesh had to be recast in entirely
new terms. Where the original meeting of the two figures revolved
around the conflict with Huwawa, the new partnership now had to
go beyond the bounds of this single adventure. Gilgamesh thus does
not simply hear of Enkidu's reputation and choose him as the perfect
companion for a dangerous trip to the highlands. When Gilgamesh
dreams of Enkidu in Penn, it is in terms entirely detached from his
role as guide on the Huwawa expedition. Instead, the dreams emphasize
Gilgamesh's passion for his new partner: "When you see him, you will
rejoice ... You will embrace him, and you will lead him to me" (I 20–
23). Quite possibly, the inclusion of anticipatory dreams was inspired by
the sequence of dreams in the original Huwawa narrative, as represented
by Schøyen-2, Schøyen-3, Nippur, and Harmal-1. Where Gilgamesh's
dreams in the Huwawa narrative forecast his victory over Huwawa,
however, the dreams of Penn anticipate not specific events per se but
rather the intense relationship between the two men. Such is exhibited
by Gilgamesh's recollection of the axe in his second dream: "I loved it
like a wife and caressed it. I picked it up and set it by my side" (I 33–36).
Only with this psychological anticipation can Enkidu's death have such
a powerful effect on Gilgamesh.

The need to intensify the partnership between the two men then triggered a thorough revision of their first moment of contact. In the earlier
text, the harlot fulfills a logical narrative function, luring the knowledgeable Enkidu out of the steppe to Uruk so that he can accompany Gilgamesh on his adventure. With the recasting of Enkidu as Gilgamesh's
ultimate match, however, the meeting between the two now had to illu-
minate the pair's physical compatibility. To this end, the harlot's role is
fulfilled by that of the wedding traveler, whose description of Gilgamesh's
first rights to the bride incites Enkidu to confront the king in anger. The
encounter with the wedding traveler sets up a test of strength that will
demonstrate the equivalence in power between the two godlike heroes,
and this match takes over the narrative need of introducing Enkidu to
Gilgamesh. As the wedding traveler replaces the harlot as the one who
brings Enkidu to Gilgamesh, so the unarmed combat becomes the cli-
max of the epic introduction, sealing the bond between the two men.
After experiencing his physical prowess, Enkidu responds to Gilgamesh
with unhesitating praise: "Your head is raised above men, the kingship of
the people Enlil designated for you" (VI 238–240). Such words contrast
noticeably with the protests of Enkidu that launch his relationship with
Gilgamesh in the Yale tablet.

In the extended epic as represented by Penn, the perfect union of Gilgamesh and Enkidu is presented as a marriage of complementary strengths, joining the best of urban society to the marvel of untamed human force, identified only with animals. To this end, Enkidu's origin in the steppe is reinterpreted as total separation from other people. The back country is identified by its isolation from humanity, rather than by the presence of wandering herdsmen. This reinterpretation, however, brought with it an attendant problem. In the Huwawa narrative, Enkidu is a sophisticated guide and dream interpreter, and with the wild origin now attributed to him, he now must be restored to these capacities. As a wild man, Enkidu would need to be socialized, when as a herdsman he faced no such obstacle. This literary difficulty was addressed by revising the role of the harlot.

Where sexual intercourse functioned originally as the bait to bring Enkidu to Uruk, it takes on a new importance in the epic, in which it becomes the first step in Enkidu's process of acculturation. Originally, sex with the harlot was a strictly human matter; in the epic, with its length of seven days and nights, it may take on a ritual aspect as well.[23] Introducing Enkidu to sex is only one part of the harlot's expanded role, in which she also serves as a maternal figure: she provides Enkidu with advice, dresses him in her own clothing, leads him by the hand to the shepherds' camp, and instructs him to eat bread and drink beer. Line 175, in which she follows Enkidu as he enters Uruk, provides the last glimpse of her in the Penn tablet, suggesting that her new role of introducing Enkidu to the customs of society is complete.

III. *Columns I–II of Yale:*
Integration of Older Narrative with Epic Revision

If the Penn tablet represents one part of what becomes the new "introduction" to the Huwawa narrative, then columns I–II of the Yale tablet signal the terrain where the visions of the epic and the older material merge.[24]

---

[23] The possible ritual aspect of their intercourse would be complemented by Sippar II 5'–9', in which Gilgamesh's mourning process, signified by his refusal to bury Enkidu, lasts seven days and nights. Ritual pertains to the society of human communities, and this would mark Enkidu's first participation in society, by his very intercourse with the harlot, even before encountering the shepherds' camp.

[24] By line III 106, it appears that we are securely in Huwawa narrative material. Enkidu

Notwithstanding their broken condition, it is clear that Yale I–II alone could not have constituted the original start of the Huwawa narrative. In sequence with Penn, Gilgamesh and Enkidu have already met, so that the task of bringing Enkidu from the steppe must be addressed prior to the first material in Yale. The first visible statement, "Why do you want to do this?" (I 12–13), is part of Enkidu's response to Gilgamesh's plan, a plan that must have been outlined in the first nine lines of the tablet.[25] In order to graft a new introduction onto the original story, the epic author would have had to incorporate elements of the older material into the new version. Given the lack of references to the Huwawa expedition in the Penn tablet, such integration could only have taken place in material now found at the beginning of the Yale tablet, as the Huwawa story commences. Indeed, several clues in columns I–II indicate the combination of diverse perspectives: the references to dreams and to Gilgamesh's mother, the appearance of the harlot, and the portrayal of Enkidu. It should be noted, however, that any exploration of these elements is severely limited by the fragmentary state of these columns.

Though extremely broken, line 25 of column I does preserve the term *šunātum*, "dreams." In combination with the reference to Gilgamesh's mother in line 60, this would appear to refer back to the anticipatory dreams of the Penn tablet.[26] As noted above, the dreams of the Penn tablet are tied to themes that follow the logic of the epic perspective entirely. Just as the Sumerian tale of Gilgamesh and Huwawa begins without a set of Enkidu-related dreams, there is no reason to assume that the Akkadian Huwawa narrative would have required this backdrop either. Only when Enkidu's death becomes the final thrust of the story does the literary necessity for such dreams arise. In Penn, Gilgamesh's dreams are designed to present Enkidu as Gilgamesh's fated match, the one whom he will embrace and love "like a wife," so that they anticipate the king's overwhelming sorrow at Enkidu's loss. Although

---

states, "I knew (him), my comrade, in the highlands, when I used to roam with the herd," an assertion that combines Enkidu's knowledge with his experience as a herdsman, two themes that are unique to the perspective of the Huwawa narrative.

[25] If the term *ibrī* ("my comrade") is indeed present in line 10, this would seem to indicate the first line of Enkidu's response. Given the format of both Penn and Yale, there would need to be room for the speech formula, which would leave seven or eight lines for Gilgamesh to present his plan to battle Huwawa.

[26] In fact, only *um-mi* ^d[...] is present, though George's reconstruction of GIŠ after this is surely correct.

the broken context of lines 25 and 60 prevents full understanding of these references, both would seem to reflect the later perspective of the epic.

The harlot is also present in column I of Yale, though again in a broken context. In lines 18–19, Gilgamesh and Enkidu form a partnership, and after a considerable break, plural figures, presumably Enkidu and Gilgamesh, "responded to the harlot" (42–43). Although this section is mostly fragmentary, the term harlot (*harimtum*) is certain, which confirms that she is present at this scene in which Enkidu and Gilgamesh are introduced and form a partnership. On its own, I 42 would fit the opening scene of Schøyen-1, in which Enkidu thanks the harlot for showing him a comrade, although there is no direct alignment of preserved text, and we cannot assume a strong match of Schøyen-1 with Yale. In the Huwawa narrative as we have defined it, the harlot's primary role is to introduce Enkidu to Gilgamesh, and as such it is possible that her presence in I 42 of Yale is a holdover from this earlier role. Given that the harlot's task in Penn is complete after Enkidu is transformed, and she is not even present in column VI, the Yale reference may derive from the logic of the Huwawa narrative, in which the harlot is already crucial to the first meeting of Gilgamesh and Enkidu.

It is possible that the partnership formed by Enkidu and Gilgamesh in lines 18–19 also reflects the original circumstances of the Huwawa narrative, in which emphasis is put on the collaboration of the two representatives from city and steppe. Although the phrase *īpušū ru'ūtam* ("they formed a partnership") does not occur elsewhere in any of the OB Gilgamesh texts, the term *ru'ūtum* may reflect the nature of Enkidu and Gilgamesh's relationship in the Huwawa account. In Tablet II of the Late Version of Etana, the serpent and the eagle make a pact before Shamash to watch each other's offspring, with like language: *ru-'ú-a-[u-ta i ni-pu-uš]* ("Let us become partners," line 8).[27] Such terminology reflects a partnership for a targeted purpose. In the context of the Huwawa expedition, Yale I 18–19 would describe Enkidu and Gilgamesh's original partnership in adventure, rather than Gilgamesh's "love" for Enkidu, as depicted in the dreams of Penn. The association begins prior to debate over the merits of confronting Huwawa, as in Schøyen-1 obv. 6', where Enkidu thanks the harlot for showing him "a good partner" (*damqam*

---

[27] The plausibility of the restoration is based in part on the reference to friendship in II 39; see the edition by Jamie R. Novotny, *The Standard Babylonian Etana Epic* (Helsinki: The Neo-Assyrian Text Corpus Project, 2001).

tappâm). Given the largely broken state of Yale I 20–41, however, their alignment with either the epic or the Huwawa narrative perspective must remain uncertain.[28]

Finally, the end of column II preserves a more intact section in which Enkidu tells Gilgamesh, "Wails, my comrade, have entangled my neck muscles. My arms have slackened, and my strength has weakened" (II 85–88).[29] The striking portrait of Enkidu weeping with weakness follows a highly repetitive sequence that first describes Enkidu's tears and then has Gilgamesh echo the same words, either as a statement or a question (II 71–76, 77–82). At first glance, this description of Enkidu's distress would appear to fit the perspective of the Huwawa narrative, as preserved in Yale column IV. In an extended monologue, Gilgamesh tells Enkidu, " 'Here even you fear death. Where is the strength of your heroism? Let me go before you, so that you can cry out to me. Come near, do not fear!' " In line 156, he criticizes Enkidu for speaking like a weakling. If we backtrack to column III, however, we see that Enkidu demonstrates not fear per se, but rather incredulity at Gilgamesh's naiveté: "Why do you want to do this? The dwelling of Huwawa is a battle not to be faced" (113–116). His protests are based on empirical evidence, namely, his firsthand knowledge of Huwawa and his impenetrable defenses. This

---

[28] The confusion is compounded by the preceding section in I 12–17. In line 12, Enkidu questions, "Why do you want to do this?" This statement recurs in columns III and V and appears to reflect the perspective of the Huwawa narrative, in which a knowledgeable and cautious Enkidu questions Gilgamesh's proposal. In line 17, however, Enkidu refers to a "deed that does not exist in the land," a phrase that could reflect his agreement to the plan. Enkidu delivers the same line at the end of Harmal-1, and in this context, he is confident of their success against Huwawa.

[29] Jacobsen viewed this loss of Enkidu's strength within the context of his recent transformation (Jacobsen, *Treasures of Darkness* [New Haven: Yale University Press, 1976] 199–200; "The Gilgamesh Epic," 237). Like Jacobsen, George states that Gilgamesh proposes the expedition to the Cedar Forest in an attempt to brighten Enkidu's spirits after his loss of strength (*Babylonian Gilgamesh Epic*, 192); see also Benjamin Foster, "Gilgamesh: Sex, Love and the Ascent of Knowledge," in J.H. Marks and R.M. Good eds., *Love and Death in the Ancient Near East: Essays in Honor of Marvin H. Pope* (Guilford, CT: Four Quarters, 1987) 32–33. It appears that such interpretations are influenced by the SBV: "Enkidu had become slow; his running was not what it once was" (I 201). Surely this line of thought is foreign to the OB material, both in Penn and in the narrative that follows. The Penn tablet never implies that Enkidu loses strength because of his social adaptation to life with humans, and the Huwawa narrative is not based on that social transformation at all. One way or the other, the weakness has to do with fear of Huwawa. Such fear is out of place in the freestanding Huwawa narrative, in which Enkidu will encourage Gilgamesh that they will be successful, when his nightmares expose him to the terror of Huwawa.

certainty that Huwawa cannot be defeated derives from the Sumerian, where Gilgamesh declares in version B, "Against the warrior, there is no strength" (89), a despair transferred to Enkidu in version A:95–102. In order to persuade Enkidu in the Yale text, Gilgamesh purposely misrepresents his protests as fear, a psychological tactic that proves successful. Gilgamesh will learn to share this response once he has been exposed to Huwawa in dreams. During their journey from Uruk, Enkidu is portrayed as a reliable interpreter, reassuring Gilgamesh that each terrifying vision incorporates the promise of divine deliverance.

The exchange over Enkidu's tears follows a highly damaged section that nevertheless may permit us to make some sense of its structure. "The mother of [Gilgamesh]" appears at the start of line 60, evidently to introduce speech. In the SB epic, which is also broken, she addresses Gilgamesh with words that seem meant to discourage, though no line is complete (II 168–177). Enkidu responds with tears, in roughly the same language found in Yale (SB II 178–181), and the same sequence would fit the traces of Yale. The question is whether the mother's role originates with her function as dream interpreter in the epic. Gilgamesh and Huwawa A raises the specter of the grieving mother, first obliquely with the call for men without mothers (A:50–52) and then with regard to Gilgamesh's own mother when Enkidu intends to return home (A:104–105). She has no speaking role, however, to compare to her verbal participation in Penn and Yale. If Yale II 60 ff. indeed have Gilgamesh's mother cast doubt on her son's plan to take on Huwawa, then this would represent another expression of her role in Penn as wise advisor. She, not Enkidu, would now be the one with special knowledge of their antagonist. In turn, Enkidu's tearful reaction would be explained by what he learned from the mother rather than by what he knows himself from his life in the steppe. All of this would follow the logic of the epic's revision.

In some ways, Enkidu's tearful reaction resembles his distress in the anomalous section at the end of Schøyen-2 (rev. 61–81). Both sections involve iterations of the same intense feelings on the part of Enkidu, with Gilgamesh in the role of comforter. In each case, the sequence begins with a narrative description of Enkidu's woe, Gilgamesh repeats the words as a sympathetic response, and Enkidu elaborates.[30] Although

---

[30] Compare Yale II 71–76 and Schøyen-2 rev. 61–64 (narrator); Yale II 77–82 and Schøyen-2 rev. 65–67 (Gilgamesh); and Yale II 83–88 and Schøyen-2 rev. 68–76 (Enkidu). Both texts include A:B::A':B' repetition, though in different sections: Yale II 71–76 (the narrator) and Schøyen-2 rev. 71–74 (Enkidu).

the affiliation of the Yale section remains uncertain, these details suggest the voice of the epic. Both the Yale and the Schøyen-2 sections present Enkidu as grieving and needy, with Gilgamesh offering confident consolation. This turning of the tables resists the portrayal of Gilgamesh as dependent on his companion, whereas the Akkadian Huwawa narrative treats Enkidu's experience as central to a successful collaboration. Altogether, Enkidu's tearful response in Yale column II suggests a reduction in his capacity as expert guide to suit the perspective of the epic author.

IV. *Role Revision in the Epic Version*

In the process of expanding the Huwawa narrative into an extended epic, each of the key characters of the tale underwent major transformations, as exhibited in the material created to front the earlier story. Where the harlot's original role was to lure the herdsman from the steppe to Uruk, her function in the epic is tied chiefly to her transformation of Enkidu prior to his encounter with Gilgamesh. Traces of her earlier role, however, are present in Penn II 56–60, Schøyen-1, and possibly Yale I 42, notwithstanding the fragmented context. In particular, the assumption in Schøyen-1 that the harlot introduced Enkidu directly to Gilgamesh is neglected in Penn, where no one provides such an introduction and the wedding traveler instigates the meeting by describing the king's objectionable practices.[31]

Without further evidence, it is difficult to determine precisely how Enkidu would have been introduced in the earlier narrative. We know that the harlot must have been sent to entice the legendary Enkidu to leave the steppe, and little else would have been necessary in order to launch the partnership between the two men. In the epic version, however, Enkidu's death and Gilgamesh's reaction to it prompt a massive expansion of the introduction, in which Enkidu is recast as Gilgamesh's ultimate match.[32] Here, Enkidu's origins are set deeper in the

---

[31] Notice that the harlot's role as the one who brings Enkidu to Gilgamesh is then restored in the SB epic, where in an expanded version of the Penn exchange, she tells Enkidu explicitly, "Come, let me lead you to the heart of Uruk-the-Sheepfold, to the pure house, the dwelling of Anu and Ishtar, where Gilgamesh is perfect in strength and (where he) establishes his superiority over the young men like a wild bull" (I 208–212).

[32] On its own, there is no reason to imagine Enkidu's demise in the Huwawa narrative. So far as we can tell, the only one who dies at the end of the Sumerian version is Huwawa,

wild, so that his formidable reputation as a herdsman is all but lost in the expanded story. The epic author must account for Enkidu's association with shepherds, but he recasts it as a transitional stage in his development, no longer attributable to his legendary upbringing in the steppe. In the process of increasing his importance within the tale, however, Enkidu becomes objectified, significant mainly for his role as the target of Gilgamesh's passion. As such, Enkidu is anticipated in Gilgamesh's dreams in the form of objects. Where the Huwawa narrative presents Enkidu as an experienced and knowledgeable herdsman, the epic as reflected in Penn emphasizes his physical strength alone. In turn, the encounter between the two men evolves from a meeting of the minds into a physical contest, concluding with Enkidu's praise of the king. Gilgamesh has become the dominant figure, in spite of the equal stature that attracts him to Enkidu. In making Enkidu a man of the wild, the epic contributes to this focus on Gilgamesh. Even so far as Enkidu's physical character as godlike also derives from the steppe as a world apart from humanity, it leaves him without the independent spirit of free partnership that marked his role in the Huwawa narrative.

Due to the tendency of the epic author to preserve and expand the original components of the Huwawa narrative, the dichotomy between the perspective of the core story and that of the new introduction is often obscured. Rather than eliminate certain details of the original exposition—e.g., sex with the harlot, Enkidu's associations with the steppe and with herding communities, Enkidu and Gilgamesh's first encounter—the epic author took them up, reworking them into a new scheme in which Gilgamesh and Enkidu are cast as a perfect match. The bridge between the new and old material, as represented in columns I and II of Yale, further concealed the process, rendering it impossible to determine where the epic ends and where the older material begins. This is a mark of the epic author's success and skill. Key contrasts in content between the Huwawa material and the Penn tablet, however, indicate that the core Huwawa narrative remained largely untouched in the process

---

at least as we have it in version A (178–179). Tigay (*Evolution of the Gilgamesh Epic*, 48) surmises that the cause of Enkidu's death in the OB epic may have derived from the killing of Huwawa, not the Bull of Heaven. In the Sumerian tale, Enlil is angered by this act, but the god's anger inspires ritual appeasement, and there is no question of direct divine intervention to take the life of either hero.

of expansion. Rather than revise the entire composition, the epic author provided an entirely new framework for introducing the main characters, a framework that alone had the power to transform the reception of the original content.

CHAPTER SIX

CONCLUSION

In the foregoing analysis, we have proposed a new hypothesis for examining the literary history of the Old Babylonian Gilgamesh Epic. Behind the extended Akkadian epic and its tangle of sources, Sumerian and otherwise, we identify a more substantial antecedent and a more specific process. The Gilgamesh Epic grew above all out of the Huwawa adventure at its center, and this tale took an intermediate literary form when the Sumerian account of Huwawa was first rendered in Akkadian. This composition, which we call the Akkadian Huwawa narrative, displays a perspective that is independent from both the earlier Sumerian story and the epic material that surrounds it. In the Akkadian Huwawa narrative, Enkidu hails not from Uruk but from the steppe. This background makes him the ideal partner and guide to Gilgamesh on his expedition to the perilous Cedar Forest. Enkidu himself is not wild, but he knows the wild and its inhabitants intimately. As in the Sumerian, the expedition and confrontation with Huwawa constitute a freestanding story, with no sense that anyone but Huwawa perishes at the end. Such an adventure lent itself to massive outward expansion in a revised narrative that focused ultimately on Gilgamesh alone. The man who embodies vigorous life confronts the obstacle of death, especially in the greatest possible personal loss, the loss of Enkidu, his perfect match. In revision, the first Akkadian Gilgamesh story was recast as the heart of a much longer composition, still shaped by the shared adventure that celebrates the heroes' potential as a pair. Although the Akkadian Huwawa narrative was integrated adroitly into the surrounding material, its independent origins are betrayed by contrasts both with its Sumerian counterpart and with the radically new vision of the epic writer, especially as seen in the Penn tablet.

Up to this point, there has been nothing to compel scholars to isolate the creation of the Akkadian Huwawa story from the rest of the OB Epic of Gilgamesh. Yet with the recent publication of George's magnum opus, *The Babylonian Gilgamesh Epic*, along with his full edition of the Schøyen texts, the prevalence of the Huwawa story among the OB evidence now prompts a closer look. Although several of the Huwawa texts had been published earlier, this is the first time that all of the OB evidence has been presented together in a single up-to-date edition. The UM and Nippur texts, though translated respectively in 1992 and 2000, now appear in print next to the newly published Schøyen-1 and Schøyen-2, finally supplemented by the fragments of Schøyen-3. Both the recent dates of the publications and the chronological layout of George's edition highlight compellingly the importance of Huwawa to the OB Akkadian Gilgamesh tradition. When this evidence is viewed together with the widespread copying of Gilgamesh and Huwawa version A, it becomes necessary to reexamine the process by which the Sumerian Huwawa tale was re-imagined in the Akkadian. Because our analysis of the earliest Gilgamesh Epic depends on copies with roughly the same date, the relative priority of different compositions must be determined primarily by comparing their contents. Unlike the Sumerian stories, the Akkadian Huwawa narrative cannot be identified definitively by tablets that preserve it as a separate entity. Nevertheless, the fact that all eight of the extracted tablets come from the Huwawa tale supplies indirect evidence for its existence as a separate text before the epic became the sole repository of Akkadian Gilgamesh literature.

Even when the epic became the single vehicle for preserving the Huwawa tradition, it seems that scribes still would have understood themselves to have been preserving this tradition in the longer Akkadian composition. Unlike the Sumerian Huwawa texts, which have no parallel wording with the Akkadian, the very method of composition by expansion would have reproduced the Akkadian text from which the epic was created. Positive evidence for the centrality of Huwawa to the process of the epic's formation is provided by the concentration of Sumerian and Akkadian Gilgamesh texts that treat the Huwawa narrative, along with the fact that this narrative offers the one clear incorporation of a Sumerian tale in the OB storyline.

Although none has proposed the existence of a freestanding Akkadian Huwawa narrative, the independent origins of the Huwawa episode have been obvious. It has long been recognized that the OB Huwawa episode has a narrative antecedent in Sumerian, and it thus represents the creative revision of its predecessor. Internally, the OB Huwawa story shows no sign of preoccupation with themes or language that advance the epic's narrative arc, with the one proposed exception in Schøyen-2. The Sumerian Huwawa texts prove that a narrative built around this one adventure could stand on its own. Given the question of whether the Akkadian Huwawa narrative could have persisted as an independent text for some time after creation of the epic, it is interesting to see that the Sumerian story was preserved in two versions. While the much-copied version A seems to have represented the standard text, reflecting the most up-to-date notions of the tale, the contemporaneous version B offers a simpler text as a relic of its earlier recounting. The survival in Sumerian of a parallel text that maintained the basic form of a more archaic predecessor permits the possibility that such could have occurred with the Akkadian Huwawa narrative as well.

It is generally imagined that the reworking of the older Huwawa Sumerian story took place with the creation of the epic, so that all of the OB Gilgamesh material more or less represents the product of one inventive mind, notwithstanding variations. If this were the case, one would expect all of the major differences between the Sumerian tale and the Akkadian rendition to reflect the same perspective as that of the epic, particularly as introduced in the Penn tablet. Given that Penn and Yale are known to have been copied by the same scribe, these texts provide the perfect place to test the continuity of creative vision. If the Sumerian Huwawa tale had been revised only for inclusion in the OB epic, we should find links across Yale and Penn with regard to language, perspective, themes, and their depiction of the protagonists. What we discover, however, is that Yale does not share the same logic as Penn. In particular, Penn's depiction of Enkidu as one who must forget his wild origins does not align with the Enkidu of Yale, whose expert knowledge of Huwawa renders him Gilgamesh's perfect guide in the steppe. Such differences in perspective extend across the rest of the Gilgamesh material, so that Yale aligns with the Huwawa texts and Penn aligns with Sippar. We conclude, then, that the changes from the Sumerian Huwawa story to the Akkadian reflect an independent logic, one that is different from both the Sumerian on the one hand and the epic on the other.

In this light, certain logical tensions between the Penn tablet and the Huwawa material become clear. On the one hand, the new theme of Gilgamesh's passionate partnership with and subsequent loss of Enkidu prompted the radical recasting of both men. In the expanded story, Gilgamesh is an aggressive king who needs a match in physical beauty and power, and who will be undone by the death of this perfect counterpart. Enkidu's origin in the steppe, where he communed with the beasts, is the very thing that makes him the perfect complement to the king. On the other hand, with the Huwawa narrative before him, the epic writer was forced to mesh his new portrait of Enkidu with the older model. For the "original" Enkidu, the steppe is the source not of physical strength but of knowledge essential to the defeat of Huwawa, and he must remember what he acquired there. To serve the vision of the epic, Enkidu must undergo some sort of transformation, so that his wild strength is retained yet restrained, allowing for continuity with his character in the preserved material. Above all, the Enkidu of the received Huwawa narrative is associated with herdsmen as a guardian of their flocks. As a figure who was raised without human contact, he must become that shepherd guardian. At the most basic level of plot development, the entire episode of Enkidu's socialization among herdsmen serves to prepare him for the role he already played in the Huwawa tale, as expressed in Yale. In the logic of the epic, then, Gilgamesh's perfect match can only join the king on the campaign against Huwawa after he has been transformed for human company. Enkidu must be remade into the *awīlum* ("gentleman") who is already depicted in the Huwawa episode. To this end, the seasoned harlot is brilliantly put to good use, acculturating Enkidu so that he can still play his original role as Gilgamesh's guide to the Cedar Forest. After he is fit for human company, Enkidu must naturally acquire the role that is recalled in Yale, as one who defends the shepherds' flocks from predators. In the epic telling of the story, Enkidu's reputation as a protector appears to reflect his role after having left the steppe rather than beforehand.

The complex process by which the epic writer recast the prior Huwawa tale involved principles that may help evaluate the literary history of other Mesopotamian texts. First, it is significant that the later author expanded outward from the center, so that new material was affixed both to the front and to the end of the original composition. Second, expansion and revision were not performed at the expense of the received material. Unlike the first Akkadian Gilgamesh author, who created a new Huwawa story without any direct reliance on the wording of his Sumerian starting point, it seems that the epic author preserved as much of the older story as was logically possible. This approach to both the received narrative and the revision process may explain why the Akkadian Huwawa narrative may not have been copied long after the creation of the epic. Eventually the first OB "epic" would have been viewed as an elaboration of the Huwawa composition, which still survived inside the larger work. It appears, however, that the introduction to the original tale had to be rewritten, so that the new material could flow into the older text. This process all but obscured the origins of the Akkadian Huwawa narrative as a freestanding composition. Although copyists of Huwawa extracts who knew the epic may have added small changes to the received text, as with the elaboration at the end of Schøyen-2, the contrasts between the Akkadian Huwawa story and the surrounding epic remain strong enough to suggest that the majority of the original story was indeed preserved. Even in portraying Enkidu as prostrate with fear and Gilgamesh as his comforter, the scenes in Yale column II and Schøyen-2 make no reference to events outside the Huwawa episode or to themes that characterize the extended epic.

The block in Schøyen-2 rev. 61–81 that suggests the epic's perspective may also reflect the variability of textual reproduction in the OB period, as observed in Chapter 1. These lines do not affect the structure of the Huwawa narrative; moreover, they do not even belong to the scheme of dream and interpretation on the way to Huwawa's abode that occupies lines 1–60. The placement of this elaboration at the end of Schøyen-2 suggests that it was created specially for this extract, whether or not in this particular copy, and this would show one way in which epic perspective could influence Huwawa material. Such textual fluidity is to be expected; notions from the revised narrative could creep into older material and remain visible by their contrast with the larger logic of the Huwawa story. What is significant is the relative rarity (and awkward fit) of such sections in Akkadian evidence for the Huwawa episode.

In the process of recasting the Akkadian Huwawa narrative as the center of a longer Gilgamesh composition, the epic author puts the elements of the original story to radically new ends. Enkidu's origins in the steppe, for example, are not discarded but are instead heightened, so that Enkidu is presented as a wild man, suckled by beasts. The two men's partnership is likewise elevated to a new level of intensity in order to shoulder the burden of Gilgamesh's sorrow at Enkidu's death. The harlot, whose role in the original story was to introduce Enkidu to Gilgamesh, acquires even more importance as the one who must civilize Enkidu before he encounters Gilgamesh in Uruk. As such, sexual intercourse with Enkidu is no longer used to lure him to the king; now it serves as the first step in Enkidu's entry into Uruk society. Further, the fact that Gilgamesh sees the future in dreams on the way to the Cedar Forest provides the model for his anticipation of Enkidu through two more dreams in the epic. In this later version, Gilgamesh's mother—as opposed to Enkidu—functions as Gilgamesh's dream interpreter. By reworking elements from the received narrative, the epic writer integrated his new vision with the older material, masking both the self-sufficiency and the independent perspective of the earlier tale.

Although the nature of the contemporaneous evidence for Gilgamesh in Akkadian during the Old Babylonian period does not permit easy isolation of an independent Huwawa narrative, such a narrative can be reasoned to have existed from the variety of available data. We have two important bodies of evidence: a preponderance of Huwawa texts in both Akkadian and Sumerian, including the limitation of Akkadian extract tablets to Huwawa alone; and significant contrasts in content and logic across the OB Akkadian Gilgamesh texts. Arguments from content and logic have already been invoked for understanding other relationships between early second-millennium Gilgamesh compositions. The chronological priority of the Sumerian Gilgamesh and Huwawa over its Akkadian counterpart is based solely on such contrasts in content and logic, not the dates of texts. Likewise, the notion that version B is the older of the two Sumerian Huwawa tales must rely on issues of narrative logic, not tablet dates. This method can be integrated carefully with attention to patterns and dates of textual finds to produce the greatest interpretive yield for a complex body of literary remains such as that surrounding Gilgamesh, king of Uruk. The independent logic of the Akkadian Huwawa "episode" compels us to explain its relationship both to what preceded it and what followed it. We conclude that the immediate predecessor to the Epic of Gilgamesh was a freestanding Huwawa narrative in Akkadian.

To date, discussion of the development of Mesopotamian literature has rested largely on comparisons between works from the first millennium and their earlier renditions. These comparisons are based on actual texts, concrete copies deriving from different dates. For Akkadian texts, the first versions do not generally precede the OB period, which also bequeaths to us a wealth of Sumerian literature. While older material does exist in both Sumerian and Akkadian, the early second-millennium represents a particular barrier to understanding the compositional background of Mesopotamian literature. Enormous expanses of text make their first appearance in this period, without clear indication of their heritage. Where specialists work carefully with known copies for comparisons with later ages, they may refer only to Sumerian parallels and vague oral sources in an unknowable process for the writing of early Babylonia. In general, literature from the OB period is not probed for its own evidence of written expansion, where the texts themselves may preserve indications of how they were revised. Especially for a long work like the Gilgamesh Epic, it is hard to imagine that such a narrative did not undergo multiple written stages of development in the OB period, a time when textual fluidity was the norm and scribal creativity was at a peak. With such an abundance of evidence from the OB period, the Gilgamesh Epic not only invites a further look but also offers the possibility for coming to some substantial conclusions about its history of formation. While the cluster of evidence available for Gilgamesh in this period is admittedly unique, it is not out of the question that other long works from the OB period would also lend themselves to probing beneath the surface. Embedded in such texts there may be yet older voices, still lying dormant beneath their surfaces, waiting to be discovered.

SELECTED BIBLIOGRAPHY

Abusch, Tzvi. "Gilgamesh's Request and Siduri's Denial, Part I," in Mark Cohen et al. eds., *The Tablet and the Scroll: Near Eastern Studies in Honor of William W. Hallo* (Bethesda, MD: CDL, 1993) 1–14.

———. "Gilgamesh's Request and Siduri's Denial, Part II: An Analysis and Interpretation of an Old Babylonian Fragment about Mourning and Celebration," *JANES* 22 (1993) 3–17.

———. "The Courtesan, the Wild Man, and the Hunter: Studies in the Literary History of the Epic of Gilgamesh," in Yitschak Sefati et al. eds., *"An Experienced Scribe Who Neglects Nothing": Ancient Near Eastern Studies in Honor of Jacob Klein* (Bethesda, MD: CDL, 2005) 413–433.

———. "Hunting in the Epic of Gilgamesh: Speculations on the Education of a Prince," in M. Cogan and D. Kahn eds., *Treasures on Camels' Humps: Historical and Literary Studies from the Ancient Near East Presented to Israel Eph'al* (Jerusalem: Magnes, 2008) 11–20.

Alster, Bendt. "Interaction of Oral and Written Poetry in Early Mesopotamian Literature," in M.E. Vogelzang and H.L.J. Vanstiphout eds., *Mesopotamian Epic Literature: Oral or Aural?* (Lampeter, U.K.: Edwin Mellen, 1992) 23–69.

Arnaud, Daniel. In *Corpus des textes de bibliothèque de Ras Shamra-Ougarit (1936–2000) en sumérien, babylonien et assyrien*, Aula Orientalis Supplementa 23 (Sabadell-Barcelona: Editorial AUSA, 2007).

Bonechi, Marco. "Relations amicales syro-palestiniennes: Mari et Haṣor au XVIIIᵉ siècle av. J.C.," *FM* I (1992) 9–22.

Cavigneaux, A. and F.N.H. Al-Rawi, "Gilgameš et Taureau de Ciel (Šul.mè.kam). Textes de Tell Haddad IV," *RA* 87 (1993) 97–129.

———. "La fin de Gilgameš, Enkidu et les Enfers d'après les manuscrits d'Ur et de Meturan," *Iraq* 62 (2000) 1–19.

———. *Gilgameš et la Mort. Textes de Tell Haddad VI* (Groningen: Styx, 2000).

Charpin, Dominique. "Histoire politique du Proche-Orient amorrite (2002–1595)," in Pascal Attinger, Walther Sallaberger, and Markus Wäfler eds., *Mesopotamien: Die altbabylonische Zeit* (OBO 160/4; Göttingen: Vandenhoeck und Ruprecht, 2004) 25–480.

Charpin, Dominique and Martin Sauvage. "Sippar," in Francis Joannès ed., *Dictionnaire de la Civilisation Mésopotamienne* (Paris: Robert Laffont, 2001) 782–784.

Charpin, Dominique and Nele Ziegler. *Mari et le Proche-Orient à l'époque amorrite: essai d'histoire politique* (FM V; Paris: SEPOA, 2003).

Cooper, Jerrold S. *The Curse of Agade* (Baltimore: The Johns Hopkins University Press, 1983).

Dalley, Stephanie. *Myths from Mesopotamia: Creation, the Flood, Gilgamesh, and Others* (Oxford: Oxford University Press, 1989).

———. "Old Babylonian Tablets from Nineveh, and Possible Pieces of Early Gilgamesh Epic," *Iraq* 63 (2001) 155–169.

Delnero, Paul. *Variation in Sumerian Literary Compositions: A Case Study Based on the Decad*, University of Pennsylvania Ph.D., 2006.

——. "Sumerian Literary Catalogues and the Scribal Curriculum," *ZA* forthcoming in 2010.

——. "Sumerian Extract Tablets and Scribal Education," under review for *JCS* (2009–2010).

Durand, Jean-Marie. "'Hittite' *tišanuš* = mariote *tišânum*," *N.A.B.U.* 1988/15, pp. 10–11.

Edzard, D.O. "Gilgameš und Huwawa A," *ZA* 80 (1990) 165–203; 81 (1991) 165–233.

——. *"Gilgameš und Huwawa": Zwei Versionen der sumerischen Zedernwaldepisode nebst einer Edition von Version "B"* (Munich: Bayerischen Akademie der Wissenschaften, 1993).

Fleming, Daniel. "Mari and the Possibilities of Biblical Memory," *RA* 92 (1998) 41–78.

——. *Democracy's Ancient Ancestors: Mari and Early Collective Governance* (Cambridge: Cambridge University Press, 2004).

Foster, Benjamin. "Gilgamesh: Sex, Love and the Ascent of Knowledge," in J.H. Marks and R.M. Good eds., *Love and Death in the Ancient Near East: Essays in Honor of Marvin H. Pope* (Guilford, CT: Four Quarters, 1987) 21–42.

——. *Before the Muses* (Bethesda, MD: CDL, 1996).

Frayne, Douglas. "The Birth of Gilgameš in Ancient Mesopotamian Art," *BCSMS* 34 (1999) 39–49.

George, Andrew. *The Epic of Gilgamesh* (London: Penguin, 1999).

——. *The Babylonian Gilgamesh Epic: Introduction, Critical Edition and Cuneiform Texts* (Oxford: Oxford University Press, 2003).

——. "The Gilgamesh Epic at Ugarit," *AuOr* 25 (2007) 237–254.

——. *Babylonian Literary Texts in the Schøyen Collection* (Bethesda, MD: CDL, 2009).

Hamori, Esther J. "A Note on *ki-ma* LI-*i-im* (Gilgamesh P 218, 224)," *JAOS* 127 (2007) 67–71.

Harris, Rivkah. "Images of Women in the Gilgamesh Epic," in Tzvi Abusch et al. eds, *Lingering Over Words: Studies in Ancient Near Eastern Literature in Honor of William L. Moran* (Atlanta: Scholars Press, 1990) 219–230.

Hecker, Karl. *Untersuchungen zur akkadischen Epik* (AOAT 8; Neukirchen-Vluyn: Neukirchener, 1974).

Huehnergard, John. *A Grammar of Akkadian* (Atlanta: Scholars Press, 1997).

Jacobsen, Thorkild. *Treasures of Darkness* (New Haven: Yale University Press, 1976).

——. "The Gilgamesh Epic: Romantic and Tragic Vision," in Abusch et al. eds, *Lingering Over Words* (1990) 231–249.

Katz, Dina. *Gilgamesh and Akka* (Groningen: Styx, 1993).

Khait, I. and R. Nurullin. "Observations on an Old Babylonian Gilgamesh Tablet from the Schøyen Collection," *Babel und Bibel. Annual of Ancient Near Eastern, Old Testament, and Semitic Studies* 3 (2006) 529–534.

Kilmer, Anne Draffkorn. "The First Tablet of *malku* = *šarru* Together with Its Explicit Version," *JAOS* 83 (1963) 421–446.

Klein, Jacob. "The God Martu in Sumerian Literature," in I.L. Finkel and Mark J. Geller eds., *The Sumerian Gods and Their Representations* (Groningen: Styx, 1997) 99–116.

Klein, Jacob and Kathleen Abraham, "Problems of Geography in the Gilgameš Epics: The Journey to the 'Cedar Forest,'" in L. Milano et al. eds., *Landscapes: Territories, Frontiers and Horizons in the Ancient Near East* (CRRAI 44; Padua: Sargon srl, 2000) 63–73.

Kramer, S.N. "The Epic of Gilgameš and its Sumerian Sources: A Study in Literary Evolution," *JAOS* 64 (1944) 7–23.

Lafont, Bertrand. "L'admonestation des Anciens de Kurdâ à leur roi," *FM* II (1994) 209–220.

Matouš, Lubor. "Les rapports entre la version sumérienne et la version akkadienne de l'épopée de Gilgameš," in Paul Garelli ed., *Gilgameš et sa légende* (CRRAI 7; Paris: C. Klincksieck, 1960) 83–94.

Meissner, Bruno. *Ein altbabylonisches Fragment des Gilgamos Epos. MVAG* 7/I (Berlin, 1902).

Michalowski, Piotr. "Épopées, hymnes et lettres," in "Sumer," *Supplément au Dictionnaire de la Bible* XIII (Paris: Letouzey & Ané, 1999–2002) 248–269.

Millard, A.R. "Gilgamesh X: A New Fragment," *Iraq* 26 (1964) 99–105.

Milstein, Sara J. "Expanding Ancient Narratives: Revision through Introduction in Biblical and Mesopotamian Texts," New York University Ph.D., projected 2010.

Moran, William L. "The Epic of Gilgamesh: A Document of Ancient Humanism," in *The Most Magic Word* (Washington, DC: CBA, 2002) 5–20.

Novotny, Jamie R. *The Standard Babylonian Etana Epic* (Helsinki: The Neo-Assyrian Text Corpus Project, 2001).

Oppenheim, A. Leo. *The Interpretation of Dreams in the Ancient Near East, with a Translation of an Assyrian Dream-Book* (Philadelphia: American Philosophical Society) 1956.

Pettinato, Giovanni. *La saga di Gilgamesh* (Milan: Rusconi, 1992).

Porter, Anne. "You Say Potato, I Say …: Typology, Chronology and the Origin of the Amorites," in C. Marro and C. Kuzucuoglu eds., *Sociétés humaines et changement climatique à la fin du Troisième Millénaire: une crise a-t-elle eu lieu en Haute-Mésopotamie?* (Varia Anatolica XVIII; Paris: De Boccard, 2007) 69–115.

Robson, Eleanor. "The Tablet House: A Scribal School in Old Babylonian Nippur," *RA* 95 (2001) 39–66.

Römer, W.H.Ph. *Das sumerische Kurzepos 'Bilgameš und Akka'* (AOAT 209/I; Neukirchen-Vluyn: Neukirchener, 1980).

Rubio, Gonzalo. "Excursus: The Reading of the Name of Gilgamesh," in *Sumerian Literary Texts from the Ur III Period* (Mesopotamian Civilizations; Winona Lake, IN: Eisenbrauns, forthcoming).

Sallaberger, Walther. "Ur III-Zeit," in Pascal Attinger and Markus Wäfler eds., *Mesopotamien: Akkade-Zeit und Ur III-Zeit* (OBO 160/3; Göttingen: Vandenhoeck und Ruprecht, 1999) 121–414.

Schwemer, Daniel. *Die Wettergottgestalten Mesopotamiens und Nordsyriens im Zeitalter der Keilschriftkulturen* (Wiesbaden: Harrassowitz, 2001).

Shaffer, Aaron. "Sumerian Sources of Tablet XII of the Epic of Gilgameš" (University of Pennsylvania Ph.D., 1963).

Steiner, Gerd. "Huwawa und sein 'Bergland' in der sumerischen Tradition," *ASJ* 18 (1996) 187–215.

Stol, Marten. *Studies in Old Babylonian History* (Te Istanbul: Nederlands Historisch-Archaeologisch Instituut, 1976).

Tigay, Jeffrey. *The Evolution of the Gilgamesh Epic* (Philadelphia: University of Pennsylvania Press, 1982).

Tinney, Steve. "On the Curricular Setting of Sumerian Literature," *Iraq* 61 (1999) 159–172.

Tournay, R.J. and Aaron Shaffer. *L'épopée de Gilgamesh* (LAPO 15; Paris: Éditions du Cerf, 1998).

Vanstiphout, Herman. *Epics of Sumerian Kings* (WAW; Atlanta: Society of Biblical Literature, 2003).

Veldhuis, Niek. "The Solution of the Dream: A New Interpretation of Bilgames' Death," *JCS* 53 (2001) 133–148.

Wasserman, Nathan. "Offspring of Silence, Spawn of a Fish, Son of a Gazelle ...: Enkidu's Different Origins in the Epic of Gilgameš," in Sefati et al. eds., *"An Experienced Scribe Who Neglects Nothing"* (2005) 593–599.

Westenholz, Aage and Ulla Koch-Westenholz. "Enkidu—The Noble Savage?" in A.R. George and I.L. Finkel eds., *Wisdom, Gods and Literature: Studies in Assyriology in Honour of W.G. Lambert* (Winona Lake, IN: Eisenbrauns, 2000) 437–451.

Wilcke, Claus. "'Gilgameš und Akka': Überlegungen zur Zeit von Entstehung und Niederschrift wie auch zum Text des Epos mit einem Exkurs zur Überlieferung von 'Šulgi A' und von 'Lugalbanda II'," in M. Dietrich and O. Loretz eds., *Dubsar anta-men. Studien zur Altorientalistik. Festschrift für W.H.Ph. Römer zur Vollendung seines 70. Lebensjahres* (AOAT 240; Neukirchener: Neukirchen-Vluyn, 1998) 457–485.

Wolff, Hope Nash. "Gilgamesh, Enkidu, and the Heroic Life," *JAOS* 89 (1969) 392–398.

TRANSLATIONS:
THE EARLY SECOND-MILLENNIUM EVIDENCE

In order to follow our analysis of how the first Old Babylonian Gilgamesh Epic was created from an earlier Huwawa narrative, it is essential to have the relevant texts at hand. Translations of Gilgamesh literature abound, with a range of styles and tones. In presenting our own, we incorporate systematically both the general perspective of this study and interpretations of specific texts, especially where the Penn tablet has influenced common understanding of the Huwawa material. Having undertaken to read the Old Babylonian Gilgamesh afresh, a complete translation allows readers to know how we approach every contributing part. We include all twelve OB tablets, along with the two Sumerian texts for Gilgamesh and Huwawa, which also form a critical backdrop for the hypothesis of a freestanding Akkadian Huwawa narrative. Beyond translation itself, we provide selected notes that explain essential reading choices and offer interpretive observations. For the Akkadian texts, we work from George's foundational editions, which include cuneiform copy either by George himself or by W.G. Lambert with collations by George. George's text editions are accompanied by exhaustive notes providing attributions for alternative readings and interpretations, and we do not duplicate this discussion. For the fullest possible engagement with our work, readers would do best to keep George's indispensable volumes nearby. The Sumerian translations work from the editions of D.O. Edzard (see below). Along with Edzard's translation, see especially George's translations in his *Epic of Gilgamesh* (1999), and the texts and translations based on the work of M. Civil and J.A. Black in the Electronic Text Corpus of Sumerian Literature (www.etcsl.orient.ox.ac.uk).

Several elements of the Huwawa material call for translation that is free from the influence of Penn's interpretive framework, and we highlight the most important ones here:

- Yale I 18–19: The heroes form a partnership for adventure, not the bond of passion anticipated in Gilgamesh's dreams from Penn.
- Yale II 85, and throughout the Huwawa material: The repeated address as *ibrī* is best derived from the Huwawa adventure and does not reflect the bond of Penn. We therefore translate, "my comrade,"

as between equal partners in an enterprise, rather than "my friend." Our goal is to distance the phrase from the context offered by Penn.

- Yale III 106–107: Enkidu used to roam with the "herd," in the sense of domestic livestock, not wild grazing animals.
- Yale IV 151–153: Enkidu defends against the assaults of a lion and of human bandits during the period when he lived in the steppe, before contact with the harlot and progress toward Uruk.
- Schøyen-1 obv. 2′: In his reading of Gilgamesh as the one who refers to the advisor whom he "kept seeing [in dreams]," George assumes the backdrop of the Penn tablet. Examined on its own terms, it appears more likely that the harlot is the speaker.

Column I

1   Gilgamesh arose and related a dream.
2   He spoke to his mother:
3   "Mother, this very night,
4   I was feeling my best and roaming about
5   among the young men.
6   The stars stole across the sky,
7   and a ... of Anu fell toward me.
8   I lifted it, but it became too heavy for me.
9   I got it moving, but I could not keep it moving.
10   The land of Uruk was gathered over it,
11   the young men were kissing its feet.
12   I pressed my forehead on it, and
13   they pushed me.
14   I lifted it and carried it to you."
15   The mother of Gilgamesh, the one who knows all,
16   spoke to Gilgamesh:
17   "Indeed, Gilgamesh, one like you
18   was born in the steppe, and
19   the highlands raised him.
20   When you see him, you will rejoice.
21   The young men will kiss his feet.
22   You will embrace him, and
23   you will lead him to me."
24   He lay down and saw a second one.
25   When he arose, he talked to his mother:
26   "Mother, I saw a second one.
27   ... in the street
28   of Uruk-Thoroughfare.
29   An axe was lying there, and
30   they were gathered over it.
31   As for the axe, its form was strange.
32   When I saw it, I rejoiced.
33   I loved it like a wife and

34	caressed it.
35	I picked it up and set it
36	by my side."
37	The mother of Gilgamesh, the one who knows all,
38	spoke to Gilgamesh:

(lines 39–42 broken)

Column II

43	"... so that he will be your rival."
44	While Gilgamesh was relating the dream,
45	Enkidu was settled in the harlot's company;
46	the two of them were making love.
47	He forgot the steppe where he was born.
48	For seven days and seven nights,
49	Enkidu was aroused and
50	seeded Shamkat.
51	The harlot opened her mouth and
52	spoke to Enkidu:
53	"When I look at you, Enkidu, you are like a god.
54–55	Why do you roam about the steppe with the beasts?
56	Come, let me lead you
57	to the heart of Uruk-Thoroughfare,
58	to the pure house, the dwelling of Anu.
59	Enkidu, arise, let me take you
60	to Eanna, the dwelling of Anu,
61	where they have undertaken rituals.
62	You also, ...
63	you will ... yourself.
64	Come, set out into the territory
65	of the shepherd ..."
66	He heard her instruction, he agreed to her proposal.
67	The woman's counsel
68	penetrated his heart.
69	She took off her clothing,
70	with one part she clothed him,
71	with the other part
72	she clothed herself.
73	Grasping his hand,
74	she was leading him like a god

75	to a shepherd's hut,
76	the place of the sheepfold.
77	The shepherds gathered around him.

(lines 78–84 broken)

Column III

85	"... the milk of the beasts
86	he used to suck."
87	They set bread before him.
88	He scrutinized (it), staring
89	and studying.
90	Enkidu did not know
91	that bread was for eating,
92	that beer was for drinking
93	he had not been taught.
94	The harlot opened her mouth and
95	spoke to Enkidu:
96	"Eat the bread, Enkidu,
97	what is essential for life.
98	Drink the beer, the custom of the land."
99	Enkidu ate bread
100	until he was full.
101	He drank beer,
102	seven goblets.
103	Relaxed, he began to sing.
104	His heart swelled,
105	and his face glowed.
106	He touched ...,
107	his unshorn torso.
108	He anointed himself with oil
109	and so turned into a gentleman.
110	He put on clothing,
111	he became like a man.
112	He took his weapon,
113	he fought off lions.
114	When the shepherds lay down at night,
115	he struck down the wolves,
116	he defeated the lions.
117	While the herding leaders slept,

118	Enkidu was their guardian,
119	a man alert.
120	A certain young man ...

(lines 121–127 broken)

Column IV

(lines 128–134 broken)

135	With Shamkat
136	he was enjoying himself.
137	He raised his eyes and
138	saw the man.
139	He spoke to the harlot:
140	"Shamkat, drive away the man.
141	Why has he come?
142	I want to hear his explanation."
143	The harlot called out to the man,
144	she went to him and talked to him:
145	"Young man, where are you rushing?
146	What is this burden of yours as you travel?"
147	The young man opened his mouth and
148	spoke to Enkidu:
149	"They invited me to the wedding house.
150	The customary gifts of the family
151	at the choosing of a bride
152	I shall heap upon the ritual table,
153	delightful wedding provisions.
154	For the king of Uruk-Thoroughfare,
155	the family net is open for the one who chooses.
156	For Gilgamesh, the king of Uruk-Thoroughfare,
157	the family net is open
158	for the one who chooses.
159	He will seed the designated wife,
160	he first,
161	the husband afterward.
162	By the counsel of the god it was declared, and
163	at the cutting of his navel-cord,
164	she was designated for him."
165	At the words of the young man,
166	his face turned pale.

Column V

(lines 167–174 broken)

175	Enkidu was walking along,
176	and Shamkat was behind him.
177	He went into the heart of Uruk-Thoroughfare, and
178	a crowd gathered around him.
179	He stationed himself in the street
180	of Uruk-Thoroughfare.
181	The people were gathered, and
182	they chattered on about him.
183	"He is a match to Gilgamesh in build:
184	he is shorter in height,
185	but in bone he is more massive.
186	Surely he is one born
187	in the highlands,
188	the milk of the beasts
189	he used to suck."
190	Sacrifices were repeated in Uruk.
191	The young men staged a performance,
192	a leader was appointed.
193	For the young man whose face was fair,
194	for Gilgamesh, like a god,
195	an equal was appointed for him.
196	For Ishhara, the bed
197	was laid, so
198-199	Gilgamesh could join at night with the girl.
200	When he came and
201	stationed himself in the street,
202	he blocked the progress
203	of Gilgamesh.

(line 204 broken, uncertain text at end)

Column VI

(lines 205–208 broken)

209	Gilgamesh ...
210	about him ...
211	He ...

212   Enkidu rose
213   in his presence.
214   They faced off in the Thoroughfare-of-the-Land.
215   Enkidu blocked the door
216   with his foot.
217   He did not let Gilgamesh enter.
218–219 They grappled and leaned in to make a throw.
220   They shattered the door-frame,
221   the wall shuddered.
222   Gilgamesh and Enkidu,
223–224 they grappled and leaned in to make a throw.
225   They shattered the door-frame,
226   the wall shuddered.
227   Gilgamesh knelt,
228   his foot on the ground.
229   His rage calmed,
230   he turned away.
231   Once he had turned away,
232   Enkidu spoke to him,
233   to Gilgamesh:
234   "As one alone, your mother
235   bore you,
236   the wild cow of the fold,
237   Ninsunna.
238   Your head is raised above men,
239   the kingship of the people
240   Enlil designated for you."

(double-line horizontal divider)

(Colophon): Tablet 2, "Surpassing above kings."

Upper edge: 240 lines.

Line 6: The reading of the verb is uncertain. George's *ip-zi?-ru-nim-ma* offers a viable form with OB attestation. According to the *CAD* s.v. *pazāru* 1b, the examples in the G stem from the OB period refer to hidden movement, "to steal through." By this reading, *ša-ma-i* ("sky") could be understood as accusative rather than genitive ("the stars of the sky").

Line 11: The Penn tablet exhibits a recurring pattern of initial predicative forms that set the scene, followed by durative verbs that describe continuing action. See also *šamhākuma attanallak* (line 4); *Enkidu wašib mahar harimtim urta'amū killālūn* (lines 45–46); *ṣabtat qāssu kīma ilim ireddešu* (lines 73–74); *peti pūg nišī ana hayyāri aššat šīmatim irahhi* (lines 157–159); *pahrāma nišū ītawwâ ina ṣērīšu* (lines 181–182); *ana Išhara mayyālum nadima Gilgameš itti wardatim ina mūši innemmid* (lines 196–199). This syntax is associated particularly with the narration of unfolding action in eyewitness mode, a perspective that particularly characterizes the Penn text. Most of the remaining OB Gilgamesh material has a heavier concentration of dialogue, including Sippar, for all its conceptual continuity with Penn. Two more instances of this pattern occur in Yale: *wašbū uštaddanū ummiānū* (line 164); *kamisma Gilgameš [ina mahar(?) Šam]šim awāt iqabb[û]* (lines 216–217).

Line 46: The usage of the verb *râmum* ("to love") in the Dt stem is obscure. Context suggests sex, which is explicit in lines 49–50. Whatever happens in line 46 is mutual, cast as reciprocal "love," whereas in lines 49–50, Enkidu inseminates Shamkat, with the harlot simply the object of his sexual act. Some distinction seems to be intended.

Line 57: The compound preposition *ana libbi* is used as more than an extension of *ana*, "to." It is Eanna, the temple of Anu, that lies at the center of Uruk, and this is the specific destination.

Lines 61–65: This section is badly damaged, and George offers a new rendition, carefully argued. In his notes, George distinguishes what is most secure from the rest. In line 61, the last word is definitely *nēpešētim*, a term that often describes performances of extispicy. He notes, "The restorations of ll. 62–63 remain provisional, however, not least because they produce text that does not yield a satisfactory quatrain" (p. 184). The first sign in line 64 is clearly AL, and in line 65, *ma-a*-AK is unavoidable, though the meaning is obscure. For discussion of line 65, see p. 26 n. 18 in Chapter 2.

Line 61: We tentatively follow George's restoration of *šitkunū* in the middle of the line. "Where" (*ašar*) should refer back to the residence of Anu, specifically.

Line 64: George acknowledges the possibility of both BA and MA for the fourth sign in the line. Aside from the question of whether the 2fs predicative form *alkāti* should be regarded as 2ms in this setting, the more serious difficulty with this reading is the conjunction *-ma* that would follow the verb. Some further verb is expected and is lacking. The noun *alkatī* ("my conduct"), for *alaktī, makes little sense in address to Enkidu. We therefore prefer to read BA, for *ti-ba* (*tibâ*, imperative with ventive).

Lines 80–84: George restores these lines from lines 183–189, where the people of Uruk conclude their admiration of Enkidu with the same words found in lines 85–86.

Line 103: The phrase describes a release of tension that suggests a general suspicion in Enkidu's approach to the shepherds. It is possible that the obscure *ip-te-eq-ma* in line 88 expresses this tension and suspicion, in the context of watching their unfamiliar behavior.

Line 104: The verb *elēṣu* is usually rendered "to rejoice," although it can refer to swelling of body parts. In this context, a physical rendition can still capture the notion of joy.

Lines 106: The line reads *ul-tap-pi-it x*-I. Based on space and traces, George judges that the two most plausible alternatives are [Š]U.I (*gallābu*, barber) and [*m*]*a-i* (water). Although the second may be attractive, the first sign cannot be MA but could be ŠU. The presence of a *gallābu* in the shepherds' settlement is unlikely, however. Hair-cutting (*gullubu*) is attested for formal legal punishment, for marking slaves, for medical or ritual treatment (SB only), and for preparing people for sacred service. All of these occur in urban and institutional settings.

Lines 109 and 111: The particular nuances of *awīlum* and *mutum* are not entirely clear. Enkidu is already human, and the effect of anointing and clothing has more to do with socialization. The higher class of the *awīlum* need not be in view, nor must the *mutum* refer to a warrior's role. Although George reads lines 110–111 in combination with the next lines on Enkidu's armed exploits, it is more natural to pair the two statements about transformation into a "man" (108–111). The two statements about fighting wild animals then go together (112–116).

Line 120: George is persuasive in treating this as the beginning of a new section, so that *ištēn eṭlum* introduces a new character and does not describe Enkidu. He understands this as the man who will be traveling to the wedding in column IV.

Line 140: The D of *akāšu* usually means "to drive away." George translates "to bring over" from context, because the man does in fact come to speak with Enkidu. We keep the common meaning, which would reflect Enkidu's irritation at the interruption of his pleasure (lines 135–136).

Line 142: The last word is uncertain. See the discussion in George, with whom we concur. He argues persuasively for *zikru/siqru* as "reason" (explanation), rather than "name," based in part on comparison with Atrahasis I 113–115.

Line 146: We take the "burden" as literal rather than emotional, because the traveler then refers to the provisions he has with him.

Lines 150–153: Although the noun *nišū* is commonly rendered as "people" in the broad sense of an undifferentiated population, or even an ethnicity, it most immediately refers to a circle of dependents in a household or family. Here, no larger "people" has been defined, and interpretation as "family" would explain the involvement of the traveler.

Line 155: George discusses at length the possibilities for the term translated here as "net." Whether this refers to a veil or a screen, it is most likely defined by reference to the family (*nišū*), which we treat as the same category both here and in line 150.

Lines 191–195: We follow George's readings of ZU (*-ṣú*) in the verb of line 191 and of LU in the last word of line 192, which are supported by his copy. Based on these readings, the text takes on a ritual aspect, suggesting that the fight between Gilgamesh and Enkidu is planned as part of larger festivities. If we read lines 190–199 as having this ritual focus, Enkidu may still know nothing about such a ritual occasion and may appear with his own agenda. The wedding traveler provokes Enkidu to anger or distress at Gilgamesh's conduct with the bride, and Enkidu presumably reaches Uruk with intent to confront its king. These lines present Enkidu as enlisted to join Gilgamesh for some unstated purpose, as part of some performance.

Line 200: This line picks up the description of Enkidu when he first enters Uruk, with Shamkat behind him. Lines 190–199 then appear to represent a parenthesis, providing background for the scene that develops into the unarmed combat between Gilgamesh and Enkidu. Read on its own, the section does not define the ritual performance, and its placement in the larger narrative is somewhat jarring, almost as a gloss to the primary conflict presented. The possible references to Gilgamesh's anger in lines 208 and 211, both broken, could require a genuine confrontation rather than simply a ritual one. Otherwise, we would have to envision a ritualized reaction of anger, with combat typically defined in these terms (see line 229).

Line 212: George proposes to read "Enkidu" at the end of line 212, which does make sense in context.

Line 215: As with the combat itself, the setting offered in lines 190–199 must be kept in mind. The two men stand at city center, and there is no hint of a city gate. Rather, if we follow the lead of lines 190–199, line 215 refers to the entrance to the structure that encloses the bed where Gilgamesh will join with the ritual bride. In a ritualized encounter, Enkidu would block the way to that structure, in a prearranged confrontation that appears to be set up so that Gilgamesh will prevail and proceed to his nocturnal encounter. With Enkidu, the combat is particularly strenuous.

Line 218: This translation follows the proposal of Esther J. Hamori, "A Note on *ki-ma* LI-*i-im* (Gilgamesh P 218, 224)," *JAOS* 127 (2007) 67–71. Alternatively, one may read "They grappled like bull(s)." In the Penn scene, the singular form *le-i-im* does not fit the logic of two men wrestling, and this is the basis for Hamori's reading. A second reference in Nippur obv. 5 would be more amenable to reading as a "bull," in that Gilgamesh is going to "keep butting" (*nakāpum*) Huwawa, and he will "flash against him" *ki-ma le-i-im*—either "to prevail," or "like a bull."

The Yale Tablet ("Yale")

Column I

(lines 1–10 broken)

11	... the body ...
12	"Why do you want
13	to do this?
14–15	... something ... you want so much.
16	...
17	a deed that does not exist in the land."
18	They kissed one another,
19	they formed a partnership.
20	... they discussed,

(lines 21–23 broken)

24	...
25	... dreams.

(lines 26–40 broken)

41	... they alerted ...
42	They responded
43	to the harlot:
44	"... to the house ..."

Column II

(lines 45–56 broken)

57	"... a rival ...
58	Appoint for him ...
59	mourners ..."
60	The mother of G[ilgamesh spoke to(?) ...]
61	"In ...
62	which ...
63	in ... (")

(lines 64–69 broken)

70 [... Enki]du.
71 [His] eyes [filled] with tears,
72 his heart became [sore],
73 he was dejected (from) ...
74 Enkidu's eyes filled with tears,
75 his heart became sore,
76 he was dejected (from) ...
77 [Gilgamesh] ... his face,
78 [he spoke] to Enkidu:
79 [My comrade, why] did your eyes
80 [fill] with tears,
81 did your heart [become sore],
82 were you dejected [...]?
83 Enkidu opened [his mouth] and
84 spoke to Gilgamesh:
85 "Wails, my comrade,
86 have entangled my neck muscles.
87 My arms have slackened, and
88 my strength has weakened."
89 Gilgamesh opened his mouth and
90 spoke to Enkidu:

Column III

(lines 91–96 broken)

97 "... martial Huwawa,

(lines 98–99 broken)

100 [In] the Cedar Forest,
101 [the place where Huwawa] dwells,
102 ...
103 in his dwelling."
104 Enkidu opened his mouth and
105 spoke to Gilgamesh:
106 "I knew (him), my comrade, in the highlands,
107 when I used to roam with the herd.
108 For sixty 'miles' the forest is deserted.
109 Who can penetrate to its heart?
110 Huwawa—his voice is the Deluge,
111 his mouth is fire,

112	his breath is death!
113	Why do you want
114	to do this?
115–116	The abode of Huwawa
	is a battle not to be faced."
117	Gilgamesh opened his mouth
118	and spoke to Enkidu:
119	"... my comrade, I shall scale its highlands,

(lines 120–121 broken)

122	to ...
123	the dwelling of the gods ...
124	an axe ...
125	as for you, ...
126	as for me, I shall ..."
127	Enkidu opened his mouth
128	and spoke to Gilgamesh:
129	"How can we go, my comrade,
130	to the Cedar Forest?
131	Its guard is Wer,
132	he is strong, restless!
133	Huwawa [...] Wer.
134	Adad is first,
135	he is [second].

Column IV

136–137	In order to protect [the Cedar Forest],
	[Enlil] allotted him the seven terrors."
138	Gilgamesh opened his mouth and
139	spoke to Enkidu:
140	"Who, my comrade, can scale the heavens?
141	The gods will always [dwell] with the sun,
142	(but) humanity—its days are numbered.
143	Everything it does is wind!
144	Here, even you fear death.
145	Where is the strength of your heroism?
146	Let me go before you,
147	so that you can cry out to me. Come near, do not fear!
148	If I should fall, my name will stand.

149–150	(People will say,) 'Gilgamesh joined battle with martial Huwawa.'
151	You were born and grew up in the steppe.
152	A lion raided you, and you knew all,
153	young men robbed your ...
154	... you, and
155	... (their) feet.
156	... you speak like a weakling!
157	When [your mouth] went slack, you upset me.
158	Let me begin work and
159	cut down the cedar;
160	let me establish everlasting [fame]!
161	[Come], my comrade, let me head off to the forge—
162	they shall cast [axes] before us."
163	They linked arms and headed off to the forge.
164	Seated, the craftsmen were deliberating.
165	They cast huge axes,
166	they cast battle-axes (weighing) three talents.
167	They cast huge swords,
168	blades (weighing) two talents,
169	the ornaments of their edges (weighing) thirty minas,
170	the mountings on the swords (weighing) thirty minas of gold.
171	Gilgamesh and Enkidu were outfitted with ten talents each.
172	He bolted the seven gates of [Uruk].
173	He called [the young men], the crowd assembled.
174	... in the street of Uruk-Thoroughfare,
175	Gilgamesh ...
176	[... Uruk]-Thoroughfare,
177	... was sitting before him.
178	[Gilgamesh] spoke [as follows]
179	[to the elders of Uruk]-Thoroughfare:
180	"[Hear me, elders of Uruk]-Thoroughfare

(line 181 probably missing)

Column V

182	I, Gilgamesh, shall see the one of whom they speak,
183	he whose name is carried throughout the lands.
184	I shall conquer him in the Cedar Forest,
185–186	to make it heard in the land

that the offshoot of Uruk is strong!
187   I shall begin work and cut down the cedar,
188   to establish everlasting fame!"
189   The elders of Uruk-Thoroughfare
190   returned a word to Gilgamesh:
191   "You are young, Gilgamesh, your heart carries you.
192   You do not know what you are doing.
193   We hear that Huwawa's face is strange.
194   Who can face his weapons?
195   For sixty 'miles' the forest is deserted.
196   Who can penetrate to its heart?
197   Huwawa—his voice is the Deluge,
198   his mouth is fire, his breath is death!
199   Why do you want to do this?
200   The abode of Huwawa is a battle not to be faced."
201   Gilgamesh listened to the word of his advisors,
202   he looked at his comrade and smiled.
203   "Now, my comrade, so ...
204   Shall I fear him ...?
205   ... not ...

(lines 206–212 broken)

213   May your god ...
214   May he ... the road for you,
215   so that you [arrive] safely at the port of Uruk."
216   Gilgamesh was kneeling [before] Shamash, and
217   the words he was saying ...:
218   "I am going, Shamash, to ...
219   Let me arrive safely there, ... my life.
220   Return me to the port at [Uruk].
221   Put protection [over me]."
222   Gilgamesh called ..., and
223   ... his instruction ...

(lines 224–227 broken)

228   in ...

Column VI

229	Tears were trickling down his cheeks.
230	"… my god, on a road that I have not yet traveled,
231	… my god, I have not known.
232	…, let me arrive safely,
233	[let me …] your … with a joyful heart.
234	[Let me …] for you a shrine of luxuries,
235	[let me …] you on thrones."
236	… his equipment,
237	… huge [swords],
238	… bow and quiver,
239	… into their hands.
240	Gilgamesh took the axes,
241	… his quiver
242	and Anshan-style bow.
243	[He placed] his sword in his belt.
244	Outfitted, they were ready to proceed.
245	[The young men(?)] were blessing Gilgamesh.
246	"You will have brought back … to the heart of the city."
247	The elders were blessing him,
248	advising Gilgamesh for the journey:
249	"Do not rely on your strength, Gilgamesh.
250	Keep your eyes bright and guard yourself.
251	Let Enkidu go before you—
252	he has seen the path, he has traveled the road.
253	[He knows] the entrances to the forest
254	(and) all the plots of Huwawa.
255	He who went in front safeguarded his partner,
256	he whose eyes were bright [protected] himself!
257	May Shamash enable you to gain your triumph.
258	May your eyes reflect the utterances of your mouth.
259	May he open for you the blocked path.
260	May he prepare the road for your steps,
261	may he prepare the highlands for your feet.
262–263	May your nights bring you words that you rejoice in, may Lugalbanda stand by you
264	in your triumph.
265	Reach your goal quickly!

266–267 Wash your feet
       in the river of Huwawa, for whom you long.
268   Dig a well in the evening.
269   Always keep pure water in your water-skin—
270   you must pour out cool water for Shamash,
271   you must invoke your [god], Lugalbanda."
272   Enkidu opened his mouth and spoke to Gilgamesh:
273   "Proceed to … that you have established,
274   let your heart not fear, look to me!
275   I know his dwelling [in] the forest,
276   … that Huwawa used to roam.
277   Speak [to the young men] and send them back!"

Left edge.

278   (broken)
279   "… they went with me,
280   … for you."
281   … with a joyful heart,
282   [… they heard] what he said.
283   The young men …
284   "Go, Gilgamesh, may …
285   May your god go …
286   May he allow you to reach …"
287   Gilgamesh and Enkidu …
288   …
289   Between …

   (George estimates six lines lost.)

Lines 12–13: Enkidu's recurring question utilizes the preterite of *hašā-hum*, suggesting that Gilgamesh's desire to embark on such an adventure is located at a fixed point in the past, as opposed to representing a continuous state of mind. Gilgamesh does, however, still desire to undertake this expedition, so that the English present offers a more straightforward translation (see also III 113; V 199). The verb does occur in the durative; see, e.g., *ana etēq huršānīšunu ihaššah libbūšu* ("his heart desires to cross the mountain range") Scheil Tn. II 12 (*CAD* s.v. *hašāhu* 2).

Line 19: The translation "partnership" is intended to capture the sense that this is the moment at which Enkidu agrees to sign on to Gilgamesh's proposition, despite his hesitations. Their embrace in the previous line is then the physical manifestation of such an agreement, on a par with a modern-day handshake. Though frequently translated as "friendship," the term *ru'ūtum* carries the sense of partnership in other literary texts (see p. 105).

Lines 24–25: George proposes that the first two lines on the obverse of Schøyen-1 have a parallel in this text. The only part of Yale I 24–25 that can be read with confidence is *šu-na-tim* at the end of line 25, and this word is not preserved in either of the Schøyen-1 lines (see pp. 104–105).

Line 43: This broken introduction to direct speech represents the one reference to the harlot in Yale. Schøyen-1 confirms that she makes an appearance with Enkidu at Uruk, in some connection with his meeting Gilgamesh, but that short segment cannot match this one. It is not certain whether something like the Schøyen-1 exchange would have occurred in Yale, in some unknown sequence.

Line 44: George has Gilgamesh and Enkidu tell the harlot to "[...] *go into* the house [of the] *elders*," [x (x) x-b]u a-na bi[t (é) šiʔ]-bu-ti. Both the preceding and the following lines are broken, so there is no way to confirm the location. There is no evidence for such a center of operations, and more generally, "elder" language is not connected with the idea of a fixed administrative organization, as represented by a "house." For the OB period, see Andrea Seri, *Local Power in Old Babylonian Mesopotamia* (London: Equinox, 2005) 97–137; Daniel Fleming, *Democracy's Ancient Ancestors: Mari and Early Collective Governance* (Cambridge: Cambridge University Press, 2004) 190–200.

Line 57: In Penn V 195, a *mehrum* is appointed for Gilgamesh at the festival of Ishhara's bed: "for Gilgamesh, like a god, an equal was appointed for him." This figure appears to be Enkidu, though he is not named directly, and it is not clear whether the word assumes the physical confrontation to follow. Whereas the *mehrum* (or *mihrum*) is simply a "match" or "equal," the related noun *māhirum* is associated especially with opposition by a "rival" or "adversary." Here in Yale, after Gilgamesh and Enkidu have met, the word can no longer describe their relationship, and if it does pertain to Enkidu, it is in the sense that he represents an adequate candidate to face Huwawa.

Line 60: This line represents the one appearance of Gilgamesh's mother in Yale or any other Huwawa narrative text. "Gilgamesh" is indicated by the divine determinative, though the name is lost, and no other figure is possible. At the start of a line, this may introduce direct speech. There seems to be some concern about Gilgamesh's possible death, a theme that recalls the mother's indirect role in Gilgamesh and Huwawa A:104–105. In the SBV, in a section that is also damaged, Gilgamesh's mother speaks immediately after her son has introduced Enkidu to her, possibly casting doubt on his ability to help Gilgamesh (II 165–177).

Lines 71–76, 79–82: These lines are badly damaged, but they can be restored based on the full repetition. George reads the verb with "his heart" entirely from the partially visible i[l-] in line 72, from lemēnum, and it is difficult to imagine an alternative. Enkidu's eyes also "fill" in the SBV (II 180, 186), in the same sequence, after Gilgamesh's mother has spoken. There also, breaks hinder reconstruction, but Enkidu's tears follow the reaction from the mother of Gilgamesh.

Lines 83–84: The speech formula "X opened ('used, readied') his mouth and spoke to Y" is also found in the Penn tablet, with identical spelling of the verb is-sà-qar-am ("he spoke"). Penn and Yale have been copied by the same hand, and in spite of striking contrasts of perspective, the work of the copyist is visible in this detail.

Line 108: The word rendered nu-ma-at presents difficulties. George (p. 209) offers a long discussion, concluding that the word must derive ultimately from the verb nawûm ("to surround"), with emphasis more on absence of occupation than ruin of prior occupation. In its application to ruins, the D form (nummû) is generally used for laying waste to a city, sanctuaries, etc., and the verb never indicates general desolation.

Line 133: George translates, "Huwawa [was appointed by] Wer," extrapolating from the context. The role of Wer in Mesopotamian religion remains obscure, considering how often the name occurs in personal names (see Daniel Schwemer, Die Wettergottgestalten Mesopotamiens und Nordsyriens im Zeitalter der Keilschriftkulturen [Wiesbaden: Harrassowitz, 2001] 200–210). This segment of the Yale tablet perhaps offers the clearest identification of Wer (Mer) with the storm god Adad. In the OB Weidner god-list, Wer is not listed in the vicinity of Adad. No outside source illuminates the specific relationship between Wer and Huwawa, and it is worth noting that these explanatory lines are absent from the SBV (II 223–228).

Lines 136–137: The "seven terrors" of Huwawa already appear in both versions of the Sumerian Gilgamesh and Huwawa. Notice that the Yale text follows the tradition of identifying Huwawa's powers in terms of "fear" rather than light.

Lines 140–143: After several previous rounds of dialogue, this section opens the long speech in which Gilgamesh finally convinces Enkidu to accompany him. This successful argument begins with a reflection on human mortality that resembles the rationale of Gilgamesh at the start of the Sumerian story (see A:28–29, to Utu; B:12–13, to Enkidu).

Line 141: In his copy, George identifies most of uš- at the end of this line, and restores [bu], which suits the gap. Nevertheless, we expect dariš to apply to future time, in parallel with humanity's days in line 142. The text may then read u[š-ša-bu], in spite of the limited space.

Line 147: The second part of this line makes sense as part of Gilgamesh's direct speech to Enkidu, without need to separate it as something Enkidu should speak back to Gilgamesh (e.g. George, Dalley). Gilgamesh has just criticized Enkidu's fear of death (line 144), with the same verb. Together with the elders' response and advice, these lines underscore Gilgamesh's overconfidence; in line 146, he boasts that he will go in front, but the elders recommend that Enkidu take this position, based on his experience (lines 251–252).

Lines 149–150: In an extensive note, George elaborates the support for accepting the evident notion of "weaving battle."

Lines 152–153: These two lines have not previously been understood as a pair, with both the lion and the young men representing marauders that Enkidu had to fend off during his life in the steppe. The verbs are synonyms, both commonly applied to raiding. See CAD s.v. šaḫāṭu A3b, "to attack, raid; said of animals," including attacks by lions; e.g. YOS 10 25 r. 70, nēšum ana tarbaṣ awīlim išaḫḫiṭ, "a lion will raid the man's fold" (OB omen literature, Šumma izbu). For the theft of sheep, see *CAD* s.v. *habātu* A1b, "to rob, take away by force; said of cattle," including de Genouillac Kich 2 D 32 r. 4 (OB) and YOS 10 26 ii 14 (Šumma izbu). The target of the lion's raiding is Enkidu himself ("you"), evidently in the form of whatever herds represent his responsibility. In line 153, the same basic situation must be envisioned, though the final word in the line is damaged: George reads *ma-[ha]r(?)-ka*. Again, there must be some relationship to Enkidu, based on the pronominal *-ka* ("you/your"). George translates, "Grown men fled from your presence," translating *habātu* as "to flee," but in OB writing, the verb only occurs in the N stem (*CAD* s.v. *abātu* B 2a). If George's reading of the last word is correct, the prepositional use of *mahar* without *ina* or *ana* compares to *mahar harimtim* in Penn II 45, "before the harlot." It is also possible that *-ma* is the conjunction, and the sign before *-ka* is uncertain. In the SBV, the first two words in the line are confirmed, and the difficult final word is also missing (II 239).

Line 155: The end of this line offers three clear signs without clear meaning. We read *ši-pi-ti* ("feet"), with similar spelling found in line VI 267, *mi-si ši-pi-ka* ("Wash your feet ..."); cf. G. Pettinato, *La saga di Gilgamesh* (Milan: Rusconi, 1992) 254–255. George's reading as *ši-wi-ti* ("in the evening," "evening star") does not fit the context of Enkidu's reputation in the steppe. If feasible, the "feet" would contribute to a description of Enkidu's success over the young men.

Lines 161 and 163: Even the root is uncertain for the forms *lu-mu-ha* and *i-mu-hu*. Both the *CAD* and *AHw* list this text under *mâhu* (meaning unknown), with no other examples.

Lines 167–170: Preparation with swords as well as axes indicates the expectation of battle, unlike the expedition portrayed in the Sumerian version B, where the group from Uruk goes specifically to cut down trees.

Lines 172–173: The bolting of the gates signals an abrupt transition from the prior outfitting of the two men. Gilgamesh bolts the city gates before assembling the people of Uruk, an act that ensures attendance at the meeting. In line 173, we reconstruct *eṭlūtum* (guruš^meš, "young men") as the object of the summons, in anticipation of the young men present at Gilgamesh's departure in line 283, where "the crowd" (*ummānum*) also appears (line 281). This curious reference to the "young men" of Uruk contrasts with the Sumerian story, where Gilgamesh enlists a subset of his city's unattached young men to help him with the labor of lumbering in the distant highlands. Here, the young men stay behind, gathered only to ratify their leader's project. In the Akkadian Huwawa narrative, the absence of the accompanying work crew both reflects the focus on confronting Huwawa more than acquiring timber and emphasizes the partnership of Gilgamesh and Enkidu alone.

Line 175: One peculiarity of the Yale text that is not shared by Penn is the occasional placement of a named participant at the end of a line, outside the introductions to direct speech. Here, we find ᵈGIŠ preceded by -HA/ZA-šu, which George reads as "his throne" ([g]u.za-šu). The appearance of a throne is unexpected, both because Gilgamesh is never named a "king" in Yale and because the setting envisions an open meeting of a crowd in a public place, without reference to a palace.

Lines 178–180: It is almost certain that Gilgamesh is speaking to the elders, given the elders' response to him in line 190. George reconstructs line 180 by comparison with SBV II 260, which also begins with the call, "Hear me."

Line 182: The name ᵈGIŠ can be retained at the start of this line. This would be the only time in the tablet when Gilgamesh's name is used in addition to a first-person precative verb, with an emphasis that may complement his desire to gain an everlasting name, at the end of the statement (189). George translates, "I will see the god of whom they speak." Our reading would remove the one possible reference to Huwawa as a "god" in Yale.

Line 183: Literally, "the one whose name the lands constantly bring/carry."

Line 192: Literally, "You do not know anything that you are doing." The line parallels Gilgamesh's statement in IV 143, where he states that all that humanity does is wind. With our translation, we indicate that Gilgamesh's lack of knowledge is global, not simply a matter of natural human limitation.

Lines 193–194: These two lines belong particularly to the elders and are not found in Enkidu's description of Huwawa in III 106–116. Only the elders speak of his "strange" appearance and the notion that he has "weapons." From this section alone, it is not clear whether the "weapons" are his terrors (137); they give Huwawa a more human-like quality.

Line 202: This combination of the verbs *naplusu* and *ṣâhu* also appears in the tale of Adapa (EA 356:46). After Adapa delivers a joke designed to charm Dumuzi and Gizzida, the gatekeepers of heaven, (Dumuzi and Gizzida) "looked at each other and smiled (*ahāmiš ippalsūma iṣṣenihhū*)." The *CAD* (s.v. *ṣâhu* v. a, "to laugh or smile") translates Yale V 202, "When Gilgamesh heard the speech of his councilors, he stole a mocking glance at his friend." Such a reading does not take into account the surrounding context of this line, however, and there is no indication that Gilgamesh's smile is meant to mock or dismiss the elders' advice. The terminology switches here: the elders are called Gilgamesh's "advisors," and Gilgamesh is said to listen to their counsel. In the next scene, a tearful Gilgamesh beseeches his god Shamash for help on the journey, indicating that the elders' warnings have provoked fear within him, even though he is still determined to proceed. The remainder of the tablet is occupied almost entirely by extensive advice from the elders and then from Enkidu, with Gilgamesh apparently accepting the words of his more experienced counselors. Gilgamesh's statement in line 204, "Shall I fear him …?," should then be read not as boastful indifference but rather within the greater context of his response to the elders' words. From here on there are no more confident monologues on Gilgamesh's part, and the theme of fear is taken up with Gilgamesh's dreams during their journey.

Lines 206–212: At the beginning of this break, Gilgamesh is speaking to Enkidu, refusing to let the elders' warning dissuade him from his goal. At the end, someone is offering Gilgamesh a blessing, and we have missed the introduction to the new speaker(s).

Line 213: George reconstructs *il-ka l[i-ši-ši-ra-am ši-p]i-ka*, translating, "May your god [straighten (the path for)] your feet."

Line 215: Compare SB III 215, as in George's restoration.

Line 218: The final word may simply be *a-[na …]*, "to," rather than *a-š[ar]*, "where."

Line 220: Compare line 215; the last visible sign appears to be *i-*, rather than *ša*, and we may have a variation on the identification of the port with Uruk, as *i-*[*na*].

Line 224: With hesitation, George reconstructs *ekallum* (é.gal), "the palace." Such a reading would imply that the palace to which Gilgamesh refers in this line is his own, an inference that has no precedent in the remaining material from the Yale tablet. Even in Penn, where Gilgamesh is portrayed as an aggressive king, there is no reference to a palace as administrative or ritual center. In Shamkat's invitation to Enkidu, which we consider a remnant of the prior introduction from the Akkadian Huwawa narrative, she names the temple Eanna as their destination, not a royal palace.

Line 235: As part of his promise to Shamash of gratitude for a safe return, Gilgamesh uses the term "thrones" for divine seats in their shrines, a context distinct from the possibility of a seat of office for Gilgamesh himself (line 175). According to the Yale tablet, Uruk is an impressive city with seven gates and a temple for Shamash, who is not the principal god of the city. Even so, Gilgamesh is not honored for his palace in this vision.

Line 242: Anshan is an Elamite city, contributing an eastern orientation that balances somewhat the location of Huwawa in the western mountains, according to Schøyen-2 obv. 26 (Ebla), rev. 55–56 (Amorites?), and Ishchali rev. 31' (Sirion and Lebanon). The Sumerian tale appears to assume an eastward journey, with "the road to Aratta" (B:47). In Yale, the Elamite bow represents the east by this center of military expertise and craftsmanship, rather than by the remote highlands where the Sumerian tale located the dwelling of Huwawa.

Lines 245–246: With parallel "blessings" in lines 245 and 247, the second bestowed by the elders, the most plausible reading of the first is [guruš[me]]š, "young men" (so, George). Using a future perfect verb, these anticipate that Gilgamesh will bring back some sign of his victory over Huwawa.

Line 252: In describing Enkidu's previous experience, the writer chooses two predicative forms, rather than preterites or duratives. According to John Huehnergard's interpretation of the "transitive *parsāku* construction," this usage would indicate "a condition or state rather than a process" (*A Grammar of Akkadian* [Atlanta: Scholars Press, 1997] 394). The text does not recall particular events; instead, Enkidu is characterized by the experience gained from having "seen" and "traveled."

Lines 255–256: These two lines are rendered in simple past (preterite), in repeating form, as if a saying.

Line 266: Huwawa is surely the target of Gilgamesh's longing, not the river.

Line 277: When Enkidu has Gilgamesh send back some group that might otherwise hope to accompany them, this most likely refers to the "young men" who go with Gilgamesh in the Sumerian story. The group that "went" with Gilgamesh in line 279 would also be the young men, an identification that would suit George's reading of a vetitive, "they should not go ...."

Lines 279–280: The last word in line 280 refers to a second-person plural object, which must address the gathering directly. It seems more likely that Gilgamesh would do this, after Enkidu told him to send them back. There is little room for a new introductory formula, and the traces at the end of line 278 do not suggest the typical language.

Obverse

Column I

0′	"[... Why]
1′	[did your] eyes [fill with tears,]
2′	[did your heart] become sore?
3′	Let ..."
4′-5′	Enkidu spoke to him, to [Gilgamesh]:
6′	"Wails, [my comrade, have ...]
7′	In the heart, ...
8′	my strength [has weakened.]
9′	My eyes filled [with tears,]
10′	my heart became [sore ...]
11′	...

Reverse

(too broken to translate)

Lines 0′-3′: These lines clearly echo the language that appears in Yale II 71–82 in three repetitions. The one basis for aligning them with the last repetition is the fact that they are followed by Enkidu's speech, which begins in Yale II 83. Nothing in the lines themselves prevents a different orientation, such as a third-person description, though the formula in line 4′ does indicate that Gilgamesh was speaking previously, as in Yale II 79–82. Line 3′ introduces some element not present in Yale.

Lines 4′-5′: The speech formula is different, reflecting a different copyist than that of Penn and Yale.

Lines 9′-11′: These three lines continue Enkidu's speech beyond what is offered in Yale II 85–88. George expects lines 12′-13′ finally to introduce a response from Gilgamesh, but the minimal traces allow no certainty about whether or not Enkidu continues.

Reverse: George suggests that the barely intelligible lines on the reverse belong to a conversation that would match Yale column V. The one compelling word would be *šu-pa-at* in line 5′, in that "the abode of Huwawa" is part of the repeated description in Yale III 116 (108–116) and V 200 (193–200). Matching this section of UM with any part of Yale, unfortunately, is made difficult by the lack of further correspondence in the preceding traces with the repeating material of the Huwawa description. Gilgamesh is to begin speaking after this (lines 6′–7′), so that "the abode of Huwawa" would be the last line in the previous speech, as with both Yale sequences. We have no indication of the address, however, and Yale V 201–202 present a shift from the elders speaking to Gilgamesh to Gilgamesh speaking to Enkidu. The UM formula is standard, without the Yale transition. In the end, the Huwawa description is stereotyped and capable of application to more than one dialogue, so that we can only know that we are still in the period prior to departure from Uruk. The UM text could have preserved a rather different rendition from what is found in Yale.

Obverse

1'	"…
2'	… Enkidu, the advisor whom I observed."
3'	Enkidu spoke to her, to the harlot:
4'	"Come, harlot, let me do something good for you,
5'	because you led me to the heart of Uruk-Thoroughfare-of-the-Land,
6'	because you showed me a good partner, (because you showed) me a comrade.(")
7'	… of Uruk-Thoroughfare,
8'	… entered.

Reverse

1'	"Let me …,
2'	you, alert me … to …
3'	You were born and gr[ew up] in the steppe.
4'	A lion [raided] you and you knew all.
5'	[Young men robbed] your […],

(a few lines remaining)

Obverse

Line 1': George restores the first visible line as if it were in partial parallel with line 2', which he understands to be spoken by Gilgamesh. Instead, line 2' must be spoken by the harlot to Enkidu, as indicated by the address in line 3'. No visible part of Yale corresponds directly to this section of Schøyen-1, and we decline to attempt a reading.

Line 2': The speaker of this line is not Gilgamesh, but instead the harlot. In line 3', Enkidu speaks *ana šâšim*, "to her," suggesting that the object of his speech is understood from the previous line, the consistent pattern of discourse introduction that uses the pronoun (see Ishchali obv. 10',

14′; rev. 40′; Sippar I 9′; II 14′; III 16, 25; IV 4, 7, 14, 21). We know from Tablet I of the SBV that the harlot's first contact with Enkidu is to "see him," (*i-mur-šu-m[a]*, line 178), which would provide a context for her statement here. In the scenario laid out in Schøyen-1, then, the harlot "observed" Enkidu before approaching him (so, the Gtn). There is no overlap between the obverse of Schøyen-1 and any part of Yale, although one expects a location somewhere in column I. We cannot assume the same text, however, even though Schøyen-1 rev. 3′–5′ does offer a match with Yale IV 151–153. George's reconstruction would seem to recall Gilgamesh's pair of dreams in the Penn tablet: "[I] *have acquired a comrade, the counsellor [that I kept] seeing [in dreams,]* Enkidu, the counsellor that I kept seeing [in dreams!]." The idiom *šutta amāru* ("to see a dream") is certainly common and is used within the OB Gilgamesh material (see Schøyen-2 obv. 4). At the same time, this instance in Schøyen-1 would stand out from the others for several reasons. The Gtn is not used in Gilgamesh's recollection of dreams. In the other cases, when Gilgamesh "saw a dream," the object of the verb is the dream itself, not the image, and he then proceeds to tell the actual dream. Also, the reference to Enkidu as "advisor" would be curious in this context, for such a description is not a symbol in need of interpretation, but rather a description of Enkidu's role. Gilgamesh refers to Enkidu repeatedly as "my comrade" (*ibrī*), not his advisor, and thus the statement would be more at home in the mouth of the harlot. The SBV attempts to smooth out the distinct perspectives of Penn and the Huwawa narrative by having Gilgamesh anticipate "my comrade the advisor," after his mother has interpreted both dreams (I 296–297).

Reverse: As observed above, lines 3′–4′ compare closely to Yale IV 151–152, with a plausible match for the third line in each sequence. It is clear from the traces at the start of lines 1′ and 2′, however, that Schøyen-1 maintains an independent text that cannot be assumed to match the sequence of Yale. Yale IV 148–150 have Gilgamesh envision the possibility of his failure and the hope of gaining fame even in defeat. Schøyen-1 rev. 1′–2′ seem to pertain to the distinct roles for Gilgamesh and Enkidu, as proposed by Gilgamesh.

Obverse

1	Gilgamesh was settled, lying down. The night ... a dream.
2	In the middle watch, his sleep startled him.
3	He arose (and) addressed his comrade:
4	"My comrade, I saw a dream. Why did you not wake me? It was truly terrifying.
5	With my shoulder, I was pushing on a mountain.
6	The mountain buckled and pinned me down.
7	Shakiness clutched my knees,
8	blinding brilliance enveloped my arms.
9	A certain young man ... me like a lion,
10	he was the most radiant in the land, and ... in beauty.
11	He grasped my upper arm, and
12	from the bowels of the mountain he drew me."
13	Enkidu interpreted the dream, he spoke to Gilgamesh:
14	"Now, my comrade, the one to whom we journey,
15	is he not the mountain? Everything is altered.
16	Now, Huwawa, the one to whom we journey, is he not the mountain? Everything is altered.
17	The two of you will meet, and you will do an unprecedented thing,
18	a warrior's office, a man's work.
19	He will unleash his fury upon you,
20	his terror will clutch your knees.
21	But the one you saw was Shamash the king,
22	in days of difficulty he will grasp your hand."
23	It was favorable. Gilgamesh rejoiced at his dream,
24	his heart exulted, his face glowed.
25	A march of one day—a second, and a third—
26	they approached the land of Ebla.
27	Gilgamesh ascended the mountaintop and
28	gazed at all the peaks.
29	He perched his chin on his knees,
30	the sleep that pours over people fell upon him.

31　In the middle watch, his sleep startled him.

32　He arose (and) addressed his comrade:

33　"My comrade, I saw a second one. It was yet more terrifying than
　　the dream I saw before.

34　Adad cried out, the ground was trembling.

35　The day veiled itself, darkness emerged.

36　Lightning flashed, fire flared up.

37　Flames blazed, death was pouring down.

38　At Adad's roar, I was ...

39　The day dimmed, and I did not know where I was going.

40　Finally the blazing fire was quenched.

41　The flames kept falling, they turned to embers.

42　The darkness lifted, the god emerged.

43　... he led me, and ..."

44　[Enkidu] interpreted the dream, he spoke to Gilgamesh.

45　"... Adad will cry out,

Edge

46　[he will ...] and become enraged at you.

47　[You will ...] your ... upon him,

48　... and your eyes will brighten.

Reverse

49　The pure (fire?) ... will be flaring ...

50　... the flames and his weapons

51　you will turn to ashes.

52　Your dreams were favorable. The god is with you.

53　You will reach your goal straightway."

54　They ... day and night,

55　they approached (H)amran, ...

56　... where the Amorite(?) lives.

57　... they kept hearing Huwawa's roar.

58　He ..., the guardian of the cedar,

59　the one who fends off every opponent,

60　[Huwawa], the guardian of the cedar, the one who fends off every
　　opponent.

61　[Enkidu raised] his eyes, he beheld the cedar,

62　its auras covering the peaks.

63　[His] face turned pale ...,

64   fear entered his heart.

65   Gilgamesh attended to him, he spoke to Enkidu:

66   "Why, my comrade, did your face turn pale?

67   (Why) did fear enter your heart?"

68   Enkidu opened his mouth and spoke to Gilgamesh:

69   "I raised my eyes, my comrade, and I beheld the cedar,

70   its auras covering the peaks.

71   Who can wage war with this god,

72   whose weapon is mighty ...?

73   This Huwawa, can we wage war with him,

74   whose weapon is mighty ...?

75   So this is why, my comrade, my face turned pale,

76   (why) fear entered my heart."

77   Gilgamesh opened his mouth, and spoke to Enkidu:

78   "Did not my heart carry me, and ...?

79   [Yet ...] said to me, 'I will go with you'.

80   You must not fear, Enkidu. Guard me!

81   I shall set in motion a battle the like of which you never knew ..."

82   In the evening, they settled, they lay down.

83   His sleep woke him, and he related (a dream) to him.

84   "My comrade, I saw a third one."

Line 1: George (2009) now reads the imperative, "O night, bring me a dream!" Throughout Schøyen-2 and Nippur, Gilgamesh's dreams always come unbidden, and the notion of a request seems unlikely.

Line 4: George (2003) reads *p*[*a*]-*a*[*l*]-*h*[*a*]-[*at*] ("terrifying") at the end of the line, based on comparison with the verb at the end of line 33, but the traces in his copy are highly uncertain.

Line 5: It is not clear how the verb *emēdum* should be understood here. George (2003) has Gilgamesh "propping up" the mountain, but he could equally be trying to push it over. When Gilgamesh dreams of the object from the sky, he pushes against it as a way to move it, in order to bring it to his mother. The objective is not the same in this nightmare, but Gilgamesh may also be trying to move the mountain.

Line 6: Following I. Khait and R. Nurullin (2006), George (2009) now considers the final verb to be *se'û*, "to push down." Neither this word nor his earlier interpretation from *esēhu* ("to gird") offers a clear match of usage in appropriate context, and the translation must remain in doubt.

Line 7: With Khait and Nurullin, George (2009) reads *lu-tum*, against his earlier emendation, which matched this word to the "terror" (*puluhtum*) in line 20.

Line 9: For *ištēn etlum*, see the note for Penn III 120, where the phrase also appears to introduce a new character.

Line 13: It appears that the use of the verb *pašārum* with dreams in Schøyen-2 contrasts with its use in Penn. In Penn, Gilgamesh "relates" (*ipaššar*) his dreams to his mother (lines 1, 44), who then interprets them by simple speech (line 16). In Schøyen-2, Gilgamesh tells his dreams with the verb *atwûm* (lines 3, 32), and Enkidu interprets them by the verb *pašārum* (lines 13, 44). Although the pattern of dreams and interpretation is interrupted on the reverse of the tablet, George (2003) understands the verb *pašārum* to appear in line 83 as part of "relating" a dream, as in Penn. This shift is one detail that raises the possibility that the last part of Schøyen-2 reflects a contribution under influence of the epic.

Lines 15–16: Both lines end with the refrain *nukkur mimma*, which George translates, "He is something very strange!" (cf. *AHw* s.v. *nakā-ru(m)* D 10, St., "ist sehr fremdartig"). Literally, the phrase means, "Everything is changed," and although this describes a reaction to Huwawa himself, it is not clear that Huwawa is the intended subject of the verb. Here and in Harmal-1 rev. 11, the statement occurs in the interpretation of dreams, and it may relate to how difficult it is to grasp the reality of Huwawa's being, even as represented by the images of sleep. "Everything is unintelligible," turned upside down.

Line 26: George (2003) proposes *ma-ti-ib-la*, "the land of Ebla." The reading of *-ib-la* is plausible, and his drawing suggests that there is nothing between the two signs, although there is space for at least one more. The SB text for the corresponding lines, in an expanded version, makes "mount Lebanon" the destination, so some geographical name is expected.

Lines 34 and 38: In Yale, Huwawa is associated with Adad through the name Wēr, as guardian of the Cedar Forest (III 130–134). This dream of Adad's power in the storm seems to make the same connection.

Line 38: Different proposals for the final word are set forth in George (2003 and 2009) and Khait and Nurullin. The last sign does not resemble other examples in this text for either DU (*en-né-ṭù*—"punished"?; *en-ni-iš₇*, "weak") or ŠU (*en-né-šu*, "bewildered").

Line 39: The theme of knowledge reappears with Gilgamesh's declaration that in the darkness, he did not "know" where he was going. This inability to know is a prominent theme in the Yale tablet, contrasted with Enkidu's knowledge of the highland dangers.

Line 51: See the new reading in George (2009).

Line 53: The text may work best with *ši-ib-[q]ì-ka*, "your plan," which we treat as a destination, with the verb *kašādum*, "to reach." In this case, the notion of movement applies literally. William Moran (personal communication, 1986, DF) observed that emphasis on the suddenness of a given occurrence could be understood to indicate divine activity. For example, in Ludlul III 49, Marduk's change of heart toward the sufferer is defined in part by the line, "my illness was ended promptly" (*murṣī arhiš iggamir*). From the sick man's perspective, the rapidity of the healing confirms the god's involvement.

Lines 55–56: In his new rendition of Schøyen-2, George (2009) proposes two names that had not previously been evident: Hamran and Amurrum. Neither name is completely secure. The signs for the first are fairly clear, as *x-am-ra-an*, and the first could be *ha-*, though the name Hamran has no precedent in Gilgamesh and no association with what appears to be a western Syrian setting. The references to travel in lines 25 and 54 suggest a parallel between the two sections, and George concludes that the verbs in lines 26 and 55 should be the same. Some reference to place would then make sense in both of these lines. Amurrum is the eye-catching novelty, and the reading is plausible from the signs. George takes this as a general reference to Syria, but the "land" (*mātum*) of Amurrum was probably between the Orontes River and the Mediterranean coast south of Ugarit, as in the later second millennium period of the Amarna letters (see Dominique Charpin and Nele Ziegler, *Mari et le Proche-Orient à l'époque amorrite: essai d'histoire politique*, FM V [2003] 29). One letter from Samsi-Addu to his son Yasmah-Addu, king of Mari, mentions messengers from Hazor and from four allied Amorite kings who must go home by way of Qaṭna, on the Orontes. Given the later geography, the Amorites would logically inhabit the mountains between the river and the sea (A.2760, in Marco Bonechi, "Relations amicales syro-palestiniennes: Mari et Haṣor au XVIIIe siècle av. J.C.," *FM* I [1992] 10). These high mountains would represent the principal location of the great cedars that were such an attraction to Mesopotamians from lands to the east.

Lines 58–60: Although these lines are severely damaged, the repetition adds confidence to potential restorations. At the start of line 58, however, the first word is not certain. Some verb must be restored, and George has switched his reading from *i-[d]e-šu-[m]a* ("he knew him") to *i-[ṭ]ù-š[u]-[nu]-t[i]* ("he watched them"). The first would render Huwawa as object, where the second regards him as subject. George's new reading requires that the sequence *i-ṭù-* be understood as the verb *eṭû* ("to become dark") in line 39 but as *natālu*, with final *-l-* assimilated to the following suffix in line 58.

Lines 61–62: Although these lines are badly damaged, they can be restored by comparison with lines 69–70.

Lines 69–76: Enkidu's question about who can enter combat with Huwawa recalls the responses of Enkidu and Gilgamesh after they are struck down by Huwawa's terrors in the Sumerian story (A:97–105, Enkidu; B:81–89, Gilgamesh). Only B:89 poses a question: "Against the warrior there is no strength. Who has it?" In the Sumerian version B, it is Gilgamesh who cannot imagine how to face Huwawa, and Enkidu provides a solution.

Lines 72, 74: George (2009) now proposes "among the Igigi" (*ina Igigi*) for the end of line 72 and "in the world" (*ina kibrātim*) for the end of line 74. The traces are uncertain for both readings, and the notion of a parallel of two different names, neither with precedent in this text or the OB Gilgamesh evidence, suggests caution.

Lines 78–79: George's restoration in line 78 (2009) is supported by the elders' response to Gilgamesh in Yale V 191. In this case, Gilgamesh seems to accept their conclusion that he was carried away without knowledge, even as he trusts that a protecting god has promised victory anyway. Only the verb of speech is completely clear in line 79, but this sense is plausible.

Lines 82–84: The pattern for introducing the third dream changes strikingly from the repeated format of the first two. Both of the first two dreams include the statement, "in the middle watch, his sleep startled him" (lines 2, 31), which is omitted for the third dream. Moreover, the introduction of the third dream switches to the Penn text's use of *pašārum* for "relating" a dream rather than interpreting one. See Penn I 1 and II 44, along with line 83 here; in contrast to Enkidu interpreting Gilgamesh's dreams in lines 13 and 44 of Schøyen-2. Line 83 is awkward, without designating a singular reference for the pronouns and verb, after the plurals in line 82.

Fragment 1

1′   … [its] cry …
2′   …
3′   … awesome radiance …
4′   … in [its] body
5′   … with …
6′   A certain young man, strange in form,
7′   … approached me to …
8′   … came out …
9′   … after him …
10′–12′ (traces)

In line 1′, George restores the feminine singular suffix *-ša*, by comparison with the Anzû bird in the "fourth" dream described in the Nippur text (obv. 11). As a whole, fragment 1 includes two details that could suggest overlap with the fourth dream of Nippur: the "awesome radiance" (*šalummatum*) of line 3′ (cf. Nippur rev. 4′); and in line 6′, the young man, strange in form (cf. Nippur obv. 15). Fragment 2 offers explicit reference to a dream, evidently in context of Enkidu's interpretation, so that the notion of a dream text for the heroes' journey is plausible. No part of this material parallels directly the contents of Nippur, however, and the relationship of the Schøyen-3 material to the Nippur text and the dream sequence in general must be considered uncertain. We cannot even be sure that a numbered dream is intended; Harmal-1 recounts a dream and its interpretation without the counted pattern.

Fragment 2

1′–2′   (traces)
3′   Enkidu [interpreted] the dream, [he spoke to Gilgamesh]:
4′   "The seven auras …
5′   He will see you …
6′   On high, the god …
7′   and the one …
8′   in …

The pattern of Enkidu serving as dream interpreter for Gilgamesh is indicated by the two preserved words at the start of line 3′; the fragment belongs to the left edge of the tablet. Nothing in the "fourth" dream of the Nippur text refers to the seven auras of Huwawa, which appear as "terrors" in Yale IV 137.

The narrative placement of Schøyen-3 in the heroes' journey is supported by two apparent references to "favorable" dreams in other miniscule fragments (3:2′ and 5:3′).

Nippur

Obverse

1   "My comrade, we have approached the forest.
2   The dream is approaching us, battle is rushing near.
3   You will behold the dazzling beams,
4   Huwawa, whom your mind constantly fears.
5   You will gore and flash down on him like a bull.
6   You will bring his head low by your strength.
7   The old man whom you saw is your mighty god,
8   the one who engendered you, Lugalbanda."
9   "My comrade, I have seen a fourth.
10   It was beyond my three dreams.
11   I was gazing at Anzu in the sky.
12   It rose up and like a cloud it soared above us!
13   ..., its face was strange.
14   Its mouth was fire, its breath was death.
15   A young man, strange in form,
16   ... was present in (the vision of) my night.
17   ... its wings, he grasped my arm.
18   ... and threw it down before me.
19   ... on it.

     (several lines missing)

Reverse

     (several lines missing)

1'   It rose up and like a cloud it soared above us!
2'   ... and its face was strange.
3'   Its mouth was fire; its breath was death.
4'   You fear its awesome radiance, (but)
5'   I will ... its foot, I will raise you up.
6'   The young man whom you saw was strong Shamash.

Line 1: This excerpt appears to begin with Enkidu's interpretation of a "third" dream, judging by the "fourth" introduced in line 9. The text

portrays the third dream as occurring at the verge of confronting Huwawa, which follows appropriately the notion that they were hearing
Huwawa's voice after the second dream and at the time of the third,
according to Schøyen-2 rev. 57.

Lines 3–4: In their form of light (*namrīrū*), as opposed to "terror," the
powers of Huwawa are visible to the eye. "Huwawa" is also the object
seen, parallel to "brilliance," which is "of the god." This "god" need not be
Huwawa, but could rather be the source of powers granted to the forest
guardian.

Line 5: The verbs *nakāpum* ("to gore") and *barāqum* ("to flash" like
lightning) are singular and refer to Gilgamesh's attack rather than an
ongoing test of strength. Although at first glance one may expect the
modifying phrase *kīma le'îm* to have the same meaning as in Penn VI 218
and 224, the uses are strikingly different. In Nippur obv. 5, the singular
form is appropriate to Gilgamesh as the sole subject, and the first verb
introduces the bull image. Esther Hamori observes the grammatical
impossibility of two men fighting like one bull in the Penn scene (see
comment to Penn translation). The awkwardness of that usage suggests
that the epic writer may have reused this phrase from the Huwawa
narrative without changing the form. Either that author took over the
"bull" simile intact and ignored the awkwardness, or more elegantly, he
reread the phrase as a verb.

Line 7: The characterization of Lugalbanda as an "old man" fits his role
as Gilgamesh's father. Interestingly, the god Shamash is a "young man"
in full vigor (Schøyen-2 obv. 9; Nippur obv. 15; rev. 6'). While the term
puršumum was current in the OB period, it may have had particular currency in Nippur, where the noun was abstracted as *puršumūtum*, "office
of the elder" (*CAD* s.v. *puršu* 1, with the Sumerian spelling nam.bur.šu.-
ma). The specific Nippur connection highlights the likelihood of local
variation in renditions of widely copied literature. In this case, the wording cannot be assumed to occur in copies produced elsewhere.

Harmal-1

Obverse

1	"Climb to the mountain cliff, so as to see …"
2	"I am deprived of god-given sleep.
3	My comrade, I saw a dream—how cloven, how …, how cloudy!
4	I had seized a wild bull of the steppe,
5	by its bellow it was cleaving the earth, its dust dotted the sky.
6	In front of it, …
7	He was grasping … was encircling my arms.
8	…
9	My cheek …; he offered me water from his water-skin."

Reverse

10	"The god(?), my comrade, the one to whom we go,
11	is he not the wild bull? Everything is altered.
12	The apparition that you saw was shining Shamash.
13	In hardship he will grasp our hand.
14	The one who offered you water from his water-skin
15	was your god who honors you,
16	Lugalbanda. The two of us will meet and
17	perform an unprecedented thing, a deed that does not exist in the land.

Nippur and Harmal-1 are rather different from the two Schøyen tablets, although all of these are single-column school texts. Both of the Schøyen tablets would have been long to the point of physical awkwardness. In contrast, Nippur and Harmal-1 are of modest proportions, with Harmal-1 being particularly small. The Nippur text is somewhat longer, with the reverse only partially inscribed. Whereas Nippur treats parts of two dream accounts and ends abruptly, with further space available but unused, Harmal-1 fills its small tablet with the rendition of one unnumbered dream on the obverse and its interpretation on the reverse. Neither text mentions Gilgamesh or Enkidu by name in speech introductions, unlike Schøyen-1, Schøyen-2, and Ishchali.

Lines 1–2: The introduction to the dream is difficult to follow, with what seems to be an instruction to Gilgamesh from Enkidu, his only companion. It is jarring for Gilgamesh to complain of lost sleep directly after Enkidu has told him to climb a cliff, but the combination of viewing the landscape from an elevated position and then dreaming is also found in the second dream in Schøyen-2 obv. 27–33.

Line 3: The first description reads *la-ta-at*, which George emends to yield *la-⟨ap?⟩-ta-at*. The uncommon verb *letû* occurs two lines later in this very text, however, and the dream may be described in terms that anticipate its contents. See also Ishchali rev. 31', with the cleaving of a single massif into the ranges of Sirion and Lebanon. The second of the three adjectives in Harmal-1 obv. 3 is legible but obscure, as *ne-ma-at* (or, *ne-ba-at*), where *-at* represents the 3fs predicative, describing the dream.

Lines 4–5: By the logic of these two lines together, only one animal is involved, and the plural marker on AM in line 4 is generic.

Lines 6–9: These are severely damaged, but both the last line and the interpretation, along with the parallel dream sequences from Schøyen-2, suggest that this section switches to the hope of divine help, at least in line 9. The subject of line 7 is uncertain; it is not obvious that a bull would "grasp" something.

Lines 10–17: The interpretation on the reverse follows closely several elements of the first dream in Schøyen-2 (lines 14–22), but this does not mean that the Harmal-1 dream was also first in an alternative sequence. The dream itself in Harmal-1 is quite different from the first Schøyen-2 dream, with a wild bull as the focus instead of a mountain. Also, help arrives in the form of two figures rather than just one, with Lugalbanda, Gilgamesh's personal god, in addition to Shamash. The Harmal-1 text therefore may simply imitate the format of an earlier interpretation.

Lines 10–11: Compare Schøyen-2 obv. 14–15, which match these lines almost word for word. The first word in the Schøyen-2 section is *inanna* ("now"), as opposed to the proposed [*i-l*]*um* ("the god"), and the initial identification in line 10 here would present quite a different syntax. Nonetheless, the traces on the copy do suggest the LUM-sign. As in Schøyen-2, the question repeats the main figure of the dream, in this case, the wild bull.

Lines 12–16: This text moves directly from the identification of the dream figure as Huwawa to the rescue by the patron gods of Gilgamesh, neglecting any account of the attack (cf. Schøyen-2 obv. 17–20). Lines 12–13 parallel closely Schøyen-2 obv. 21–22, before the contribution of Lugalbanda as a second divine helper in lines 14–16a.

Lines 16–17: The text concludes with a combination of language from two different parts of the Huwawa narrative. "The two of us will meet and perform an unprecedented thing (*ninnemmidma ištiat neppiš*)" recalls Enkidu's words to Gilgamesh in interpretation of his first dream in Schøyen-2 obv. 17, "The two of you will meet, and you will do an unprecedented thing (*tennemmidāma ištiat teppuš*)." After this statement, Harmal-1 extends the "unprecedented thing" with the notion of "a deed that does not exist in the land (*šipram ša lā ibaššû ina mātim*)." These match exactly the language found at the start of Yale (I 17), in a very different context. In Yale, Enkidu speaks this way after asking skeptically, "Why do you want to do this thing?" (Yale I 12–13; cf. III 113–114). In Yale, though the section is damaged, the words seem to emphasize the foolhardiness of Gilgamesh's plan rather than its greatness. Given the combination of language from two different parts of the Huwawa episode, it appears that these lines were plucked from elsewhere to provide a neat ending for this brief excerpted text. The fact that this ending may draw on column I of Yale could demonstrate this particular copyist's awareness of the epic, though it is difficult to be certain.

Obverse

(lines 1–3 broken)

4   "… my comrade …
5   May your voice rumble like a kettle-drum."

(lines 6–13, too damaged to translate)

14   "When, my comrade, we …, and … Huwawa …
15   There are tracks, the path is clear, …
16   We have come to the … not to go; your side …
17   Let us place a … at the doorway of Huwawa …
18   … of the steppe.
19   …
20   … Adad will …

(lines 21–28 too damaged to translate)

Reverse

(lines 29–35 too damaged to translate)

36   In the forests …
37   … they paid homage to him; he turned toward the auras …
38   in order to strike, "We are certain not to live, Gilgamesh …
39   … without Huwawa."
40   …
41   "… life … … Gilgamesh …
42   She bore you, the wild cow of the fold, Ninsumuna(??).
43   …
44   By the mouth of the warrior Shamash, …
45   … Gilgamesh …
46   Let me cultivate for you cedar, cypress, juniper—the tallest trees,
47   woods worthy of the palace." The one born in the steppe was able to advise:
48   "My comrade, the man Huwawa will not …
49   … Sîn …

(lines 50–63 too damaged to translate)

The Harmal-2 text is badly worn and characterized by irregular spelling (George, p. 252). George undertakes a cautious yet ambitious reconstruction, in hope of bringing some sense to partly legible passages. Often, the resulting readings are possible but far from secure. Rather than rest important interpretive choices on proposals that remain uncertain or doubtful, we leave even more material untranslated than does George. As a whole, Harmal-2 must fit where George has placed it, after the heroes' arrival at the Cedar Forest and before the guardian Huwawa is slain. The broken text makes it extremely difficult to follow the exchanges that precede Huwawa's plea for life on the reverse.

Line 5: George observes that this line resembles SB IV 241, where one of the comrades, evidently Gilgamesh, exhorts the other to face Huwawa bravely. In the late version, this sequence occurs after all the dreams.

Lines 6–13: Gilgamesh may be mentioned twice in this badly damaged section, in lines 9 and 13. In line 5, the second-person suffix ("your") is restored, and we cannot be certain that this opening section involves any direct address. The KA-sign appears in lines 6 and 7, without clear associations. If these represent the pronominal suffix, then we do have direct address, and it would seem that Enkidu is talking to Gilgamesh, rather than the reverse.

Line 14: The verb is certainly first-person plural, but the traces are elusive. Huwawa (written *Hu-bi-bi*) is not marked with the divine determinative in Harmal-2, neither here nor in lines 17 and 48. We have no reference to him as a god, and he should perhaps not be assumed one in this version. This detail suggests how variable the OB evidence for Gilgamesh may be, in conception as well as in narrative.

Line 15: Enkidu appears to be speaking to Gilgamesh, in his usual role of advisor. The *kibsu* is the actual track left by footsteps, human or animal, and the two companions follow Huwawa's trail like hunters. This line shows that they have reached his home but have not yet encountered him.

Line 16: George's reconstruction is plausible and interesting, even as it raises difficulties: "We have come to a place where one should not go! ([*n*]*e-ta-al-ka aš-šu-ru la a-la-ki-im*)." This solution attributes two key features to dialectal idiosyncrasy: *ne-* in the opening verb and *aš-šu-ru* as a variant spelling of *ašru*, "place." The second is particularly uncertain, and another possibility would be *ana* plus *šurrû*, "beginning," though the final vowel would be grammatically incorrect.

Line 17: The phrase *ana bāba* suggests a completely different physical locale than the woods of the Cedar Forest alone; the term "doorway" consistently refers to constructed habitations. In the Sumerian version A, Huwawa has a "house in the cedars" (A:121).

Line 18: The visible signs at the start indicate a feminine plural subject, which would have to be understood as collective for the verb *il-qé* to make sense. This is doubtful. With the verb uncertain, George's reading of *aš-ṭú* as a separate word has no compelling basis.

Line 19: George translates from line 18 into line 20, "The *fierce one* of the wild [declared] to his friend, 'The onslaught of a tempest is [Huwawa!]'." Much of line 19 is visible, but the divisions between words are not at all clear. George begins by envisioning a verb of speech, which would make sense with *ib-ri-šu*, although no other conversational exchange has the narrator cast one of the heroes as "his comrade" in introduction to direct discourse. In any case, Harmal-2 has no other possible instance of introduction to direct discourse. Lambert's drawing renders the supposed *-ri-* in a form more like *-sa-*. George interprets the end as a description of Huwawa, but the name is restored, and the tablet shows no evidence for dividing a verbless sentence between lines in this way.

Line 37: If the verb *karābu* is correct, then the subject should be plural (i.e., the two heroes), and the action is more deferential than neutral "greeting" (George). Although the "auras" are clear and must pertain to Huwawa, the subject would switch to singular without warning or identification. It would appear that this line is narrative, without direct speech, yet there is no introductory formula for transitioning into speech in the following line.

Line 38: George renders this as speech by Huwawa to Gilgamesh, as if the guardian would speak in the first-person plural. The switch would be made without signal, and without introductory formula. Accepting the reading of the predicative, it remains unclear who is speaking and whether Gilgamesh is being addressed.

Line 39: At the end of the line, it is preferable to read *i-na ba-li Hu-b*[*i-bi*], as George observes in a note. Given the number of unique forms that George already proposes for this difficult tablet, and the fact that the traces fit perfectly, the form *ba-li* does not prevent reading *bala* ("without"). The sense of the line remains obscure.

Line 40: George reads first an imperative, then a preterite: "Look! ... had he looked at the trees ...." The switch from direct address to third person declarative point of view mid-line is unexpected. Neither verb is clear, and we leave the line untranslated.

Line 41: George reads "my life," though the pronominal suffix is in a section of badly damaged text, and he has no explanation for what seems to be a verb, *pu-tu*. Even the *-ka* for "your" at the end of the line is not secure. We could perhaps read *i-na ba-li-ka*, "without you," parallel to "without Huwawa" in line 39.

Line 42: As George reads the line, it closely resembles Penn VI 235–237. The text is badly damaged, and the proposed reconstruction would have a barely legible ÁB ("cow") for Penn's *ri-im-tum* ("wild cow"). At the end of the line, the name would be read *Ni-in-su-mu-na* instead of ᵈ*Nin-sún-na*. The absence of both the divine determinative and the Sumerian NIN would be surprising. It is possible that George's restoration relies too much on the Penn comparison, and the line should be left untranslated.

Lines 46–47: These two lines confirm at last that Huwawa is speaking (compare SB V 153–155). George's reading depends heavily on his collation and is difficult to evaluate independently, but it is attractive. With enough continuous text to allow a view of the transition from one direct discourse to another, we find that no introductory formula is provided, so we cannot expect to find them elsewhere in the text. Enkidu is not named, even when he is about to speak, although both Gilgamesh and Huwawa appear by name. Notice that the reference to a palace treats Gilgamesh as a king.

Line 48: George separates the category *awīlum* from Huwawa, as if they must be distinct. Combined with the fact that Huwawa is neither marked with the divine determinative nor elsewhere called a god, it is equally possible that this line confirms the alternative treatment of the figure. Here, he is a man, explicitly. It is no wonder, then, that he has a "doorway" in line 17.

Obverse

    (about 10 lines completely missing)

    (five lines too broken to translate)

6'	Enkidu spoke to him, to Gilgamesh:
7'	"Strike Huwawa ... of your gods.
8'	...
9'	... you have shown mercy to him."
10'	Gilgamesh spoke to him, to Enkidu:
11'	"Right now, my comrade, ...
12'	The auras are vanishing into the thicket,
13'	the auras are vanishing, and the dazzling beams are going into the underbrush."
14'	Enkidu spoke to him, to Gilgamesh:
15'	"My comrade, catch a bird, and where will its chicks go?

Edge

16'	Let us find the auras afterward,
17'	(which are) like chicks running around in the thicket.
18'	Strike him again, and so strike down the one who sustains them(?)."

Reverse

19'	Gilgamesh heard what his comrade said.
20'	He took the axe in his hand,
21'	he drew the sword from his belt.
22'	Gilgamesh struck the neck,
23'	His comrade Enkidu did the heart.
24'	... he fell,
25'	... were taking away his blood.
26'	Huwawa the guardian he struck to the ground,
27'	for two 'miles' ... distant.
28'	Along with him, he struck ...

29'   the forests ...
30'   He slew the monster, the guardian of the forest,
31'   at whose roar Sirion and Lebanon were cloven into two.
32'   ... the highlands.
33'   ... all the mountain ranges shook.
34'   He slew the monster, the guardian of the cedar,
35'   ... the broken ... After he slew the seven (auras),
36'   the net of two talents and the sword of eight,
37'   he took a load of ten talents. He went down and decimated the
        forest,
38'   he uncovered the secret seat of the Anunnaki.
39'   While Gilgamesh was chopping down trees, Enkidu ...
40'   Enkidu spoke to him, to Gilgamesh:
41'   "... Gilgamesh, strike the cedar.
42'   ... which is at your side.
43'   ... 30 reeds' length."

(10–12 lines missing, and two lines on the edge, mostly broken)

In form, this tablet resembles Schøyen-1 and -2 more than Nippur, Harmal-1, and Harmal-2. George observes that between a quarter and a third of the tablet is missing, which would make it roughly 60–70 lines long, slightly shorter than the Schøyen texts. Note that George was able to consult the unpublished copy by A. Westenholz, which is evidently not reflected in his own drawing. The style of introducing direct speech is particularly close to Schøyen-1, with the independent pronoun anticipating the named object (see lines 6', 10', 14', 40'; cf. Schøyen-1 obv. 3'), though the orthographies are different. Certain details in Ishchali recollect features already encountered in the Yale text, as noted below.

Line 9': This line could be a question, but the beginning is broken. In any case, Enkidu observes that Gilgamesh has spared Huwawa's life, while he himself advocates taking it. The contrast between the approaches of the two heroes is important. Gilgamesh has not come to the Cedar Forest in order to kill its guardian, even though he must survive Huwawa's assault. According to Yale IV 148–150, Gilgamesh will make a name for himself just by facing Huwawa in battle, whether or not he lives. Enkidu, ever the wise counselor, believes that Huwawa must be slain in order for them to escape safely.

Line 11′: George reads [li]-ta-am ne-ša-ka-ma as lītam nišakkanma, "we must achieve victory." The suggestion is plausible, though the noun is uncertain.

Line 13′: We read the end of the line, nam-ri-ru i-ru-bu a-na ni-bi, as opposed to George's i-ru-pu a-na er?-pí, "the radiant sheens are fading into the mist." The noun nib'u offers an appropriate parallel to qīšum ("thicket"), in the preceding line. See CAD, "(wild) growth, field covered with wild growth," including an OB (Kudur-mabuk) text with the spelling ni-pi.

Line 18′: The reading of muttabbilšu may be possible from the traces, but it is bewildering in context. No part of the OB Gilgamesh material treats Huwawa as having either a servant or any human company in the forest. There appears to be room for one more sign at the end of the line, so that the participle would refer to Huwawa himself, as the one who provides for the auras: mu-t[a-b]i-il-š[u-nu] (Gtn, wabālum).

Line 20′: The weaponry of Gilgamesh recalls the visit to the forge described in the Yale text. There, Gilgamesh and Enkidu cast two types of implements, axes (pāšum and haṣṣinnum) and swords (paṭrum); Yale IV 165–167. Here, the combination of axe and sword indicates a use that suits preparation not for cutting down trees but for combat. Note that the sword is kept in the belt in both Ishchali rev. 21′ and Yale VI 243.

Line 23′: George reads i-pu-uš li-ib-ba, which he translates tentatively as "gave encouragement." This is not a standard idiom. The verb epēšu may appear with the phrase kī or kīma libbi ("according to [his] heart"), in a clause that means, "he does as he pleases." The lack of a pronominal suffix adds to the doubt. With Gilgamesh in parallel with Enkidu, and Gilgamesh striking the neck, the "heart" or "middle" may also have a purely physical point of reference, as the midsection or gut.

Line 24′: We expect to find reference to Huwawa by name, since the subject clearly changes, but the traces do not fit.

Line 25′: George reads "ravines" at the end of the line (ha-ar-ru). Note that in Enuma elish, the wind carries away Tiamat's blood; here, the subject in Huwawa's case is uncertain.

Line 28′: One expects that Gilgamesh also struck down the plural *melem-mū*.

Line 30′: George derives the meaning of *harharum* from context, as "monster, freak," so "ogre." Previously, the word had only been found in later contexts, where it carried overtones of moral or social failures. It is usually translated as "scoundrel, rogue," etc., but George objects that the notion of lawless behavior is probably a later development.

Line 35′: The "seven" auras of Huwawa that must be slain echo the seven terrors attributed to Huwawa in Yale IV 137.

Lines 36′–37′: The logic of ten total talents provides the restoration of two for the net. Compare the total weight of ten talents carried by each traveler, according to Yale IV 171.

Line 39′: The actions of the two companions are continuous and contemporaneous. It is not clear what Enkidu does; choosing special timber and digging up stumps have been suggested.

Obverse

(two lines too broken to translate)

3   ... the forest,

4   ...

5   ...

6   ... and let us sit, alone.

7   ...

8   ... and let us sit, alone.

9   He slew ... of the cedar, the guardian ...

(lines 10–14 broken)

15   ... he struck a blow,

16   ... five times.

17–18 ... he decimated the forest, the cedar.
       He uncovered the secret seat of the Anunnaki gods.

19   The one born in the steppe was able to advise, he spoke to his
       comrade:

20   "By your own strength you slew the guardian.

21   What can put you to shame? The forest of trees is flattened.

22   Find me a lofty cedar, whose crown vies with the sky,

23   I shall build a door, whose width is a reed.

24   It should not have a pivot, it shall slide in the frame.

25   Its edge shall be a cubit, its width a reed.

26   May no outsider approach it, may the god ...

27   Let the Euphrates bring it to the hand of Enlil.

28   Let the host of Nippur celebrate,

29   let Enlil rejoice at it.

(The reverse is too broken for useful translation.)

Line 9: Ishchali rev. 30′ (cf. 34′) reads, "He slew (*i-ne-er*) the monster, the guardian of the forest." Ishchali rev. 39′ then parallels almost exactly IM obv. 18, with reference to the Anunnaki. The traces at the start of IM obv. 9 would allow *i-*, though the first identification of Huwawa must offer a different epithet, defined by his connection with the cedar.

Line 15: At the end of the line, the signs *te-ri-ik* must belong to the root *t-r-k* ("to lash about, to wield a weapon," etc.). The noun *tirku* can mean "blow, hit, stroke," which would work with the verb *nêru*, more than *teriktu* as an "unplanted, uncultivated area."

Line 19: Although the traces for *ṣe-ri-im* do not fit well, the line is parallel to Harmal-2 rev. 47, and George's reading is plausible.

Line 21: "Putting to shame" indicates defeat. George reads the first word in line 22 with this line. The Š-stem of *niālu* may be associated with bodies laid out for burial, which may suit the felled trees.

Line 22: Without certainty regarding the verb, we follow George's choice.

Line 27: George suggests the alternative *qá-ti* for *bi-ti*; we expect É for "house."

Line 28: The reference to Nippur is appropriate for Enlil but is nevertheless striking in a tradition focused on an ancient king of Uruk.

The Sippar Tablet

Column I

1'	… wild bulls, …
2'	He put on their skins, he ate the flesh.
3'	Gilgamesh dug water holes where there had been none,
4'	he drank the water and followed the winds.
5'	Shamash began to worry. He bent down to him,
6'	he spoke to Gilgamesh:
7'	"Gilgamesh, where are you wandering?
8'	The life you are seeking you shall not find."
9'	Gilgamesh spoke to him, to the warrior Shamash:
10'	"After roaming, wandering the steppe,
11'	there will be plenty of rest in the world below!
12'	I will have all the years to sleep, so
13'	let my eyes regard the sun, that I may be sated with light.
14'	The darkness is as far off as the light.
15'	Shall the dead ever see the rays of the sun?"

(about 30 lines missing)

Column II

0'	"[My comrade, whom I love mightily,]
1'	who journeyed with me through every harm,
2'	Enkidu, whom I love mightily,
3'	who journeyed with me through every harm.
4'	He met the fate of humanity, and
5'	day and night I wailed over him.
6'	I would not let him be buried,
7'	in case my comrade might arise at my cry,
8'	for seven days and seven nights,
9'	until the worm fell from his nose.
10'	After his leaving, I have not found life.
11'	I keep roving like a hunter in the midst of the steppe.
12'	Now, lady tavern-keeper, I have seen your face,
13'	let me not see death, which I always fear."
14'	The lady tavern-keeper spoke to him, to Gilgamesh:

Column III

1	"Gilgamesh, where are you wandering?
2	The life you are seeking you shall not find.
3	When the gods created humanity,
4	they imposed death on humanity,
5	they kept life in their own hands.
6	You, Gilgamesh, let your belly be full,
7	day and night, you should always be feasting!
8	Hold a celebration daily,
9	day and night, dance and play.
10	Let your garment be clean,
11	let your head be washed, bathe yourself with water.
12	Bask in the little one who holds your hand,
13	let a partner always take pleasure in your loins.
14	Thus ...,
15	which the living one ..."
16	Gilgamesh spoke to her, to the lady tavern-keeper:
17	"Why, lady tavern-keeper, do you speak ...?
18	My heart aches for my comrade ...
19	Why, lady tavern-keeper, do you speak ...?
20	My heart aches for Enkidu ...
21	You live, lady tavern-keeper, by the flats of the sea,
22	with your heart, you have seen all ...
23	Show me the path ...
24	If it is acceptable, let me cross the sea."
25	The lady tavern-keeper spoke to him, to Gilgamesh:
26	"There has not been, Gilgamesh, one like you ..."

(lines 27–28 too broken to translate)

(about 20 lines missing)

Column IV

1	He smashed them in his rage.
2	He returned and stood over him,
3	Sursunabu fixed his eyes upon him.
4	Sursunabu spoke to him, to Gilgamesh:
5	"What is your name? Talk to me!
6	I am Sursunabu, in the service of Uta-na'ishtim, the Distant One."

7   Gilgamesh spoke to him, to Sursunabu:
8   "Gilgamesh is my name. I am
9   the one who journeyed from Uruk-Eanna,
10   the one who roamed the highlands,
11   the distant road where the sun rises.
12   Now, Sursunabu, I have seen your face.
13   Show me Uta-na'ishtim, the Distant One."
14   Sursunabu spoke to him, to Gilgamesh:
15   " . . .
16   . . . Uta-na'ishtim, the Distant One.
17   . . . you shall board a boat,
18   . . . I will conduct you to him."
19   They sat down and discussed it together,
20   then he made him a proposal.
21   Sursunabu spoke to him, to Gilgamesh:
22   "The Stone Things, Gilgamesh, are what allow me to cross over,
23   because I must not touch the waters of death.
24   In your rage, you smashed them.
25   The Stone Things, they were with me in order to cross over.
26   Take the axe in your hand, Gilgamesh,
27   to cut me three hundred poles, each sixty cubits long.
28   . . . set them with . . ."

(remainder of column missing)

As discussed in Chapter 3, the Sippar text shares important themes and language with the Penn tablet, and we therefore assign its contents to the extended OB epic. At the same time, it displays many distinct features that are associated with the particular episode, and the tablet itself derives from a separate compilation. Aside from the four-column format, the introductions to direct speech resemble those of Schøyen-1 and Ishchali more than those of Penn and Yale. Moreover, Gilgamesh's city is identified as Uruk-Eanna (IV 9), rather than as Uruk-Thoroughfare (Penn I 28; II 57; IV 154, 156; V 177, 180; Yale IV 174, cf. 179, 180; V 189; Schøyen-1 obv. 5', 7'). It is interesting to find that after eschewing association with the city in all his time of wandering, Gilgamesh now defines himself first of all by origin at Uruk, though not as its king.

Line I 1': The bulls are followed by *tišānu*, some kind of wild grazing animal (see George's note to this line).

Line I 3′: Gilgamesh is associated with digging wells or water holes in various contexts (see George, pp. 94–95). Although the first words of lines 3′ and 4′ are in doubt, we offer no alternative to George. The statement about new water holes appears to emphasize the wild terrain traversed by Gilgamesh. No one has frequented these places before.

Line I 11′: George proposes to read DU as -*ṭù*- at the end of the line, although he considers the spelling exceptional in this tablet. In general, the TU-sign dominates, rendering -*dú* in III 7 and -*ṭú* in III 15, 24 (cf. George's reading of I 13′). In one case, DU does take the value -*du*- (III 8). We are faced with a choice between "much" and "little" rest.

Line II 10′: The theme of finding life is picked up from Shamash's challenge in I 8′, which in turn will be picked up by the tavern keeper in III 2. Gilgamesh admits the very thing that these two characters offer as an insurmountable obstacle, evidently to the tavern-keeper herself. By taking up the words of Shamash, the tavern-keeper seems to serve the god's concerns, and even though she cannot persuade Gilgamesh to give up his quest, her contribution to his cause represents proof of the god's assistance. Gilgamesh only finds out about Uta-na'ishtim from the tavern-keeper.

Line II 11′: The word *hābilum* is much better attested as "criminal, wrongdoer," but the first reference to beasts and hides indicates that Gilgamesh has in fact been hunting. This line defines the *ṣērum* as the domain of wild animals, entered especially by hunters, in contrast to the land of herdsmen that is assumed for Enkidu in the Yale tablet.

Lines III 1–5: The object that Gilgamesh seeks is cast in terms of "life" (*balāṭum*), here and in I 8′, and the gods are set apart by their sole possession of life. When Gilgamesh exhorts Enkidu to courage in Yale IV 140–143, the gods are distinguished not by "life" but by their distant residence in the heavens. This limit on humanity's days should lead the bold to make a lasting name for themselves.

Lines III 7–9: We translate the verb *hadû* and the derived noun *hidûtu* with reference to feasting, based on the parallel with eating in line 6 and the combination of the noun with *šakānu* in line 8. The dancing and play also may be associated with ritual and feasting.

The Sumerian Gilgamesh and Huwawa

VERSION A

The Sumerian story that provides the direct point of reference for the Akkadian Huwawa narrative is that of Gilgamesh and Huwawa, and so we offer translation for the two versions of this Sumerian Gilgamesh tale. Version A is longer and is far better attested than version B, with at least 85 texts known for A as opposed to 5 for B. Nevertheless, the shorter B version kept separate currency, with copies from the same period as that of version A. Three of the five known copies for version B come from Nippur, where 59 of the texts for version A were found.[1] Most likely, then, the Nippur scribes who knew the archaic and now rarer B version were also familiar with the ubiquitous version A. One copy of version B comes from Uruk, which produced no exemplars of version A. It appears that the shorter text was not simply an isolated alternative copied by scribes who had never encountered the popular version A. Rather, some scribes seem to have respected version B as a rendition of the Huwawa story that was sufficiently different to warrant preservation as a separate text.

Version A is currently found in 85 tablet fragments, and a full score is provided in Paul Delnero's dissertation, which is still unpublished. We have followed the lineation and text identification found in the current standard edition of Edzard, who designated texts by a combination of the site of origin and letters of the alphabet in sequence. The following abbreviations refer to individual tablets mentioned in the translation and notes that follow:

---

[1] The numbers for version A reflect the calculations of Paul Delnero, in the score for his dissertation, which he kindly provided for our consultation. The count of 85 follows collations and joins that reduce the number of 92, according to Eleanor Robson, "The Tablet House: A Scribal School in Old Babylonian Nippur," *RA* 95 (2001) 39–66. See also the editions of D.O. Edzard, "Gilgameš und Huwawa A," *ZA* 80 (1990) 165–203; 81 (1991) 165–233, especially 80:167; and *"Gilgameš und Huwawa": Zwei Versionen der sumerischen Zederwaldepisode nebst einer Edition von Version "B"* (Munich: Bayerischen Akademie der Wissenschaften, 1993), especially pp. 14–15. Edzard includes 82 copies of version A, with only 59 from Nippur, while Robson attributes at least three more texts to that city than does Edzard. Delnero's count restores Edzard's number.

NiA (from Nippur): lines 1–18, 24–37, 45–69, 75–125, 134–163, 170–182, 193–202

NiC (from Nippur): lines 145–149, 188–199

NiI (from Nippur): lines 11–20, 185–196

NiNa (from Nippur): lines 1–13, 44–47

NiO (from Nippur): lines 1–16, 44–53

NiV (from Nippur): lines 20–25, 40–43

NiTT (from Nippur): lines 154–163, 170–182, 185–187, 193–202

NiDDD (from Nippur): lines 198–202

UrA (from Ur): lines 41–58, 93–102, 107–123, 125–127, 152–163, 170–176

UrF (from Ur): lines 54–67

UrG (from Ur): lines 148–151, 153–158, 160–163, 171

IsA (from Isin): lines 1–20, 64–96, 135–142, 144–154

IsC (from Isin): lines 148–157

IsD (from Isin): lines 186–191, 194–198

KiA (from Kish): lines 26–51, 77–128, 156–181, 187–189

SiA (from Sippar): lines 1–18, 62–66, 137–140, 143–162, 201–202

SiB (from Sippar): lines 4–10, 199–202

UnB (unknown origin): lines 99–162, 173, 175–202

UnC (unknown origin): text to fit between lines 148 and 149

UnD (unknown origin): text to fit between lines 148 and 149

1   The lord indeed set his mind toward the highlands of the living one,

2   the lord Gilgamesh indeed set his mind toward the highlands of the living one.

3   He spoke to his servant Enkidu:

4   "Enkidu, since no young man can elude life's end,

5   I shall enter the highlands, I shall set up my name.

6   Where a name can be set up, I shall set up my name,

7   where no name can be set up, I shall set up the names of the gods."

8   His servant Enkidu replied:

9   "My king, if you want to enter the highlands, we should inform Utu,

10   we should inform Utu, valiant Utu.

11   Any scheme in the highlands is Utu's affair,

12   any scheme in the highlands for felling cedar is valiant Utu's affair, and we should inform Utu."

13   Gilgamesh prepared a white kid,

14   he clasped to his chest a brown kid, a kid for offering,

15   the pure staff was in his hand, in front of his nose.

16   He spoke to Utu-of-the-Sky:

17 "Utu, I want to enter the highlands. May you be my ally!

18 I want to enter the highlands for felling cedar. May you be my ally!"

19 Utu replied from the sky:

20 "Young man, in your own right, you are indeed a native son, but what would you be in the highlands?"

21 "Utu, I want to speak to you, to my word, your ear!

22 I have visited you, may you give heed.

23 In my city, a man dies, the heart is stricken,

24 a man is lost, my heart recoils.

25 I craned my neck over the rampart,

26 a corpse was floating on the water in a canal, and it caught my eye.

27 I myself will do the same, I indeed will come to this.

28 However tall the man, he cannot reach the sky,

29 however broad the man, he cannot span the highlands.

30 Since no young man can elude life's end,

31 I shall enter the highlands, I shall set up my name.

32 Where a name can be set up, I shall set up my name,

33 where no name can be set up, I shall set up the names of the gods."

34 Utu received his tears as if a gift,

35 as if a man of compassion, he showed him compassion.

36 Warriors, sons of one mother—they were seven.

37 The first, their eldest brother, had a lion's paws, an eagle's claws.

38 The second, a ... -serpent, had a mouth ...

39 The third, a dragon-serpent, a serpent ...

40 The fourth would roast with fire ...

41 The fifth, a prime serpent, ... in the hill country.

42 The sixth would lash the chest like a raging flood.

43 The seventh would blaze like lightning (that) no man could turn back.

44 These seven the warrior, valiant Utu, gave to Gilgamesh.

45 They would lead him through the hill-country ravines.

46 He gladdened the one who would fell cedars,

47 he filled the lord Gilgamesh with joy.

48 In his city he blew the horn like a man alone,

49 like two men together he blew it in harmony:

50 "He who has a house—to his house! He who has a mother—to his mother!

51 Let single grown men, like me, fifty in number, set themselves at my side."

52 He who had a house (was) to his house, he who had a mother (was) to his mother.

53 Single grown men, like him, fifty in number, set themselves at his side.

54 He set his foot to the forge,

55 he had them cast a mace(?) and a battle-axe, his warrior arms.

56 He set his foot to the dark grove in the steppe,

57 he had them fell ebony, willow, apricot, and box.

58 The sons of his city who were accompanying him—(tools were) in their hands.

59 The first, their eldest brother, had a lion's paws, an eagle's claws.

60 They did indeed lead him through the hill-country ravines.

61 He crossed the first range, his heart did not show him the cedar.

62 As he was crossing the seventh range, his heart showed him the cedar.

63 He made no more inquiries, he sought no further.

64 Gilgamesh started felling the cedars.

65 Enkidu cut the wood for him, and the widows' sons who accompanied him

66 stacked it.

66a Gilgamesh had spooked Huwawa in his lair,

67 so (Huwawa) unleashed his terrors.

68 Gilgamesh was overcome as by sleep ...

69 [Enkidu(?) ...] was struck as by a flash flood.

69a The sons of the city who accompanied him

70 trembled like puppies at his feet.

71 Enkidu arose, he had been dreaming. He shuddered, it was only sleep.

72 He rubbed his eyes, there was empty silence.

73 He shook (Gilgamesh), but he could not rouse him,

74 he spoke to him, but he would not reply:

75 "You who sleep, you who sleep,

76 Gilgamesh, lord, son of Kulaba, how long will you sleep?

77 The highlands have dimmed, a shadow has stretched (over them),

78 the last beams of twilight are passing.

79 Head raised, Utu is going to the lap of his mother Ningal.

80 Gilgamesh, how long will you sleep?

81   The sons of your city who accompanied you
82   should not stand waiting at the foot of the hill country.
83   Their mothers should not be forced to twine rope in the main square of your city."
84   He put (this) in his right ear,
85   his warrior's word cloaked (Gilgamesh) like a robe.
86   (Gilgamesh) picked up thirty shekels of oil and coated his chest,
87   he then stood on the great earth like an ox,
88   he lowered his neck toward the ground and bellowed:
89   "By the life of my mother Ninsun, of my father, the pure Lugal-banda,
90   should I be (back) on the lap of my mother Ninsun, so as to sleep?"
91   And (Gilgamesh) spoke to him a second time:
92   "By the life of my mother Ninsun, of my father, the pure Lugal-banda,
93   until I have found out whether that man is human or divine,
94   the foot that I have set toward the highlands I shall not set back toward the city."
95   The servant wheedled and cajoled,
96   he replied to his king:
97   "My king, you yourself have not seen that man, so you are not distressed.
98   I am the one who laid eyes on that man, so I am distressed.
99   A warrior—his mouth is a dragon's maw,
100   his eye is a lion's glare,
101   his chest is a raging flood.
102   None can approach his head, which consumes the canebrake.
103   My king, while you head into the highlands, I shall head back to the city.
104   I will tell your mother you are alive, so she will laugh.
105   But afterward, when I tell her you are dead, she will surely shed tears for you."
106   "Onward, Enkidu. Two men together will not die, a reed bundle will not founder.
107   None can cut through triple-folded cloth.
108   Water can drag no one from a rampart.
109   In a reed hut, fire cannot be put out.
110   You help me, so I shall help you. What then can anyone do to us?
111   When it sank, when it sank,

112   at the time the Magan-boat sank,
113   when the barge sank,
114   at least the boat's life-saving reed bundle was rescued.
115   Onward, then, let us go to him, let us lay eyes on him.
116   If we go to him,
117   (where) there is fear, there will be fear in return,
118   (where) there is knowledge, there will be knowledge in return.
119   Whatever you think, onward still, let us go to him."
120   When anyone comes as close as sixty rods,
121   Huwawa has already reached his house in the cedars.
122   He gives him the eye, and it is the eye of death,
123   he shakes his head at him, and it is the nod of condemnation,
124   when he speaks to him, he wastes not a word:
125   "Though you are a young man, you will not go back to the city of your mother who bore you."
126   Into his muscles, into his feet, fear poured in, (Huwawa's) terror poured in.
127   He could not budge his foot from the ground,
128   the foot—his big toe dragged the foot,
129   into his side, into his …, it poured.
130   "Supple with oil, lasting offshoot,
131   native son, splendor of the gods,
132   stout ox, in fighting stance—
133   your mother knew just how to form a child,
134   your wet nurse knew just how to feed a child on her lap.
135   Do not be afraid, place your hands on the ground."
136   He placed his hands on the ground, he spoke to him:
137   "By the life of my mother Ninsun, of my father, the pure Lugalbanda,
138   no one knows your home in the highlands, your home in the highlands should be known.
139   Let me bring you my older sister Enmebaragesi as a senior wife in the highlands."
140   And again he spoke to him:
141   "By the life of my mother Ninsun, of my father, the pure Lugalbanda,
142   no one knows your home in the highlands, your home in the highlands should be known.
143   Let me bring you my younger sister Ma-tur as a junior wife in the highlands.

144   Exchange with me one of your fears, so I may enter among your kin."

145   He exchanged with him his first terror.

146   The sons of his city who accompanied him

147   clipped its growth, tied it up,

148   and stacked it at the base of the hill country.

149   After the seventh terror was gone, (Gilgamesh) attacked his abode.

150   He followed him like a snake on the wine- ...

151   and feigning a kiss, he struck him on the cheek with open hand.

152   Huwawa bared his teeth.

Text UrG:

a Huwawa spoke to Gilgamesh:
b "Warrior, you have acted treacherously ..."
c The two of them ...
d [He took(?)] the warrior from his abode, and he told him, "Sit down."
e [He took(?)] Huwawa from his abode, and he told him, "Sit down."
f The warrior took a seat, began to weep, turning pale.
g Huwawa took a seat, began to weep, turning pale.
h His eye began to weep ...

Text UrA: lines d–g from UrG, plus the following:

h Huwawa begged Gilgamesh:

Text SiA:

a Like a captive wild bull, he tied a halter on him,
b like a captive young man, he bound his arms.

Text UnB: lines a–b from SiA, plus the following:

c Huwawa began to weep ...

153   He took Gilgamesh by the hand:

154   "Let me say a word to Utu:

155   Utu, I knew neither mother who bore me nor father who raised me.

156   I was born in the highlands, and you yourself raised me.

157   Gilgamesh swore by the sky, he swore by the earth, he swore by the highlands."

158	He clutched at (Gilgamesh's) hand and prostrated himself.
159	At that moment, Gilgamesh, native son—he pitied him.
160	Gilgamesh spoke to Enkidu:
161	"Enkidu, let the captive bird go home,
162	let the captive young man return to his mother's lap."
163	Enkidu replied to Gilgamesh:
164	"Supple with oil, lasting offshoot,
165	native son, splendor of the gods,
166	stout ox, in fighting stance,
167	young lord Gilgamesh, exalted in Uruk—
168	your mother knew just how to form a child,
169	the wet nurse knew just how to feed a child on her lap.
170	One who is tall, yet has no forethought,
171	fate will consume, and he will know nothing of his fate.
172	When the captive bird goes home,
173	when the captive young man returns to his mother's lap,
174	you yourself will never return to the city of the mother who bore you."
175	Huwawa spoke to Enkidu:
176	"Against me, Enkidu, you speak malicious words to him.
177	Hired man—he hired you for your keep, for you to follow after him. (Now) you speak malicious words to him."
178	While he was speaking this way,
179	Enkidu, enraged and in fury, sliced through his neck.
180	They placed (the head) in a leather sack
181	and brought it to Enlil and Ninlil.
182	After they kissed the ground before Enlil,
183	they threw down the leather sack and brought out his head.
184	They placed it before Enlil.
185	When Enlil saw Huwawa's head,
186	he grew angry at Gilgamesh's story:
187	"Why have you acted this way?
188	Was it declared that his name be wiped from the earth?
189	He should have sat before you,
190	he should have eaten the bread that you ate,
191	he should have drunk the water that you drank."

The texts diverge:

192	NiC and NiI: "There should have been provided the proper adornment."

UnB: From his seat, Enlil gave out his auras.

193   His first aura he gave to the field,

194   his second aura he gave to the river (or, to the field),

195   his third aura he gave to the canebrake (or, to the river),

196   his fourth aura he gave to the lion (or, to the canebrake),

197   his fifth aura he gave to the palace (or, to the lion),

198   his sixth aura he gave to the forests (or, to the palace, to the hill country, to the lion),

199   his seventh aura he gave to Nungal (or, to the forests).

200   (SiB, UnB): The rest of the auras, Gilgamesh ...

200   (NiA, NiTT): ... he kept ... his terror(s).

201–202   (NiA, NiTT, NiDDD, SiA): Mighty Gilgamesh, who is praised, (to) Nisaba, a hymn.

201–202   (SiB): Huwawa ..., who is praised, (to) Enkidu, a hymn.

201–202   (UnB): (To) mighty [Gilgamesh], a hymn, (to) Enkidu, [a hymn], (to) [Huwawa(?)], a hymn.

Lines 1 and 2: Throughout both versions, Sumerian kur is translated as "highlands" rather than as a single "mountain." In lines 1 and 2, this term refers to the entire region inhabited by Huwawa rather than to a specific peak. Likewise, as "highlands for felling cedar" (line 12, etc.), they represent a region that is attractive for its timber. The directional phrase identifies the highlands with a "living man" or a "man who lives (dwells)" there, in either case referring to Huwawa. Possibly this heading, which does not occur in version B, plays off the opening words of Gilgamesh in line 4.

Line 4: Throughout, our translation maintains distinctions of social categories where possible. Here, the ĝuruš is a "young man," fully active, whether as soldier, workman, or adventurer. The lu_2 of lines 1 and 2 is more generally a "man" or individual.

Lines 8 and 9: Although the leadership terms en and lugal have origins in distinct third-millennium settings and political conceptions, in these early second-millennium texts, they may be separated as "lord" and "king." In version A, the title lugal is used only to identify Gilgamesh as "master," the complement to Enkidu as "servant" (IR_3/$arad_2$), a pattern not evident in version B. Version B represents Gilgamesh directly as a lugal, when he departs Uruk in line 57.

Line 20: The word dumu-ĝir$_{15}$ occurs also in lines 131 and 159. So far as it distinguishes a proper citizen of a Sumerian center from outsiders, it does not separate a "noble" from his peers but rather a "native" from foreigners.

Line 28: The focus is on sheer physical size, with particular attention to the highlands, which are identified with the underworld (see version B:10–14). Evidently, either to reach the gods' immortality in their heavenly dwelling or to avoid entry into the underworld, it would take physical size that is impossible for humans. A similar sentiment appears in Yale IV 140, where Gilgamesh acknowledges that humans are not gods, so no one can reach the sky.

Lines 37–43: A majority of the texts omits all but the first in the list that describes the individual warriors. The others show some variation as well, with NiV in line 42 the most striking: "The sixth was a shackle, (which) the rebellious land, the hill country …," followed by a second line that continues like the others.

Line 44: Two Nippur texts (NiNa and NiO) offer several lines not found in the others, severely damaged in both cases. In NiO, the goddess Nisaba makes some contribution. These texts then make the statement found here in line 44.

Line 45: Some variants make the verb precative, with second person reference: "let them lead you …" In these, the statement concludes an address begun in the broken lines of NiNa and NiO.

Lines 48–49: The parallel statements about one man and then two together may indicate either the way in which the horn is sounded or the nature of those summoned.

Line 52: The words repeat exactly those of line 50, where they represent instructions.

Line 55: The specific implements are not certain. Version B does not include this visit to the forge to make weapons, a theme that is familiar to the Akkadian Huwawa narrative in Yale IV 161–170. Later in version A, Huwawa is overcome not by weapons but by verbal trickery. Once he has given up all the "terrors" that carry his power, Gilgamesh can lead him away like an ox, with a rope. No weapons are needed. It is possible then that this sequence in version A reflects the influence of the Akkadian story.

Line 56: In this case, the steppe cannot be far from the city, though it perhaps represents the outside world.

Lines 59–61: There is some variation in how the texts render the second reference to the warriors and then the seven ranges, though a majority abbreviate as presented here.

Line 65: This rendition comes from text UrF, which provides the most legible evidence for this and the next few lines. We therefore follow the lineation of UrF in 66 and 66a.

Line 69: We expect kur-ku to represent another image of sleep, though the literal meaning has to do with overwhelming water.

Line 90: Gilgamesh envisions a babe asleep, not "awestruck" (George 1999) or "astonished" (Edzard).

Line 93: This line occurs only in version A, and its challenge is irrelevant to version B, where Huwawa is never identified with deity. Here, "that man" (lu_2) must be identified as either "human" (lu_2-u_{18}) or "divine" (diĝir). A being that appears generically to be a "man" could turn out to be a variety of "god."

Lines 111–114: The raft float is a life preserver, the one object sure to remain on the surface when all else is submerged.

Lines 130–134: These lines appear in similar form three other times in the Sumerian Gilgamesh texts, Gilgamesh and Huwawa A:164–169; B:1–4; and Gilgamesh and the Bull of Heaven 91–96. Translations vary widely, especially for the opening line, which is usually understood to begin with an exclamation, as in George ("Ho, hurrah!") and Edzard ("Heho, Heldenhafter ..."). The second phrase in line 130 combines terms for duration and the offshoot of a plant, to suit the ideal of lasting rule from a continuous line, not necessarily as a "scepter." Note that Gilgamesh is called "the offshoot of Uruk" in Yale V 185, with the word *perhum*, an Akkadian synonym of u_3-luh-ha. Because the combination lum-lum stands in parallel with su$_3$-su$_3$ ("lasting"), it should have some adjectival aspect that derives from the verb "to be fruitful, to be satisfied, to shine." If anointing is in view, the opening word may simply be read, "in oil." Earlier in version A, when Gilgamesh prepares to reproach Enkidu for his cowardice, he anoints himself with oil and stands like an ox (A:86–87). Our translation echoes this combination. For similar renderings of the opening lines, see Bendt Alster, "Interaction of Oral and Written Poetry in Early Mesopotamian Literature," in M.E. Vogelzang and H.L.J. Vanstiphout eds., *Mesopotamian Epic Literature: Oral or Aural?* (Lampeter, U.K.: Edwin Mellen, 1992) 66, "Oh (you who are) anointed with fine oil"; A. Cavigneaux and F.N.H. Al-Rawi, "Gilgameš et Taureau de Ciel (Šul.mè.kam). Textes de Tell Haddad IV," *RA* 87 (1993) 107, "florissant de graisse." Douglas Frayne appears to adopt Alster's translation ("The Birth of Gilgameš in Ancient Mesopotamian Art," *BCSMS* 34 [1999] 46). He includes "plant-shoots" with the material for anointing, which is unlikely. George argues that the variability of spellings for the first words argues against interpretation of these literally, but phonetic equivalents and orthographic variability are common in these texts. In Edzard's edition, see for example, murgu/murgu$_2$/mur$_8$-gu$_2$/mur$_7$-gu$_{10}$ (A:4, 30); usan/u$_2$-sa$_{11}$-an (A:78); ku$_4$.r/ku$_7$.d (A:95); ušumgal/ušum-gal (A:99); du$_{11}$/du (A:104, 105); eš$_5$/eš (A:107).

Line 148: At this point, the various texts handle the sequence of taking away Huwawa's terrors in different ways. UrG and IsA simply count the terrors, to indicate repetition, and SiA repeats line 145, with its statement of allotment. IsC and UnB repeat lines 145–148 for the second through sixth terrors, in somewhat longer format. UnC introduces a completely distinct text, repeating lines 140–148, with a variety of gifts:

- third: "finest flour, foodstuffs of the great gods, and a skin of cold water";
- fourth: "large sandals for large feet";
- fifth: "small sandals for your small feet";
- sixth: "rock crystal, chalcedony, and lapis lazuli."

Text UnD then diverges entirely from the others, without counting.

Line 151: Translators generally understand the hand or palm as a "fist," but this is not required by the context, and it is not clear that the blow is intended to do serious injury.

Line 152: UrG adds, "he furrowed his brow." In line 152f, UrG concludes with an action that could refer to prostration in submission, if we read the verb sig … gar.

Line 157: The translation refers to the literal points of reference, though the sky is the abode of the gods and the highlands are associated with the underworld.

Lines 161–162: Here, Gilgamesh simply proposes to let the "captive" Huwawa go free. In version B, he offers a more elaborate scenario. Huwawa will not just go free; he will join Gilgamesh and Enkidu as mountain guide for their further adventures (138–138a). The rendition in version A suits the greater attention to Huwawa, whose dangerous character is elaborated much more fully than in B. In version A, the only issue is whether or not to kill Huwawa, because the confrontation itself has become the journey's objective.

Lines 164–169: Here, Enkidu repeats exactly the speech with which Huwawa had addressed Gilgamesh earlier, with all the same praise. Only line 167 is added, from text KiA alone, with specific reference to Uruk. Uruk is not otherwise named explicitly in the tale, which typically refers simply to "the city."

Line 170: There are two variants for the lacking trait, both of which reflect Akkadian loans: dim$_2$-ma reflects ṭēmum, with its range of meaning from information to planning; and ĝalga (or, malga) reflects milkum, a term for advice.

Line 174: The text UnB adds five lines after line 174, none of which derives from another part of the narrative: a) A captive warrior, released, or a captive ruling priest, [restored] to the temple residence; b) a captive anointed priest, restored to luster, from days gone by, …; c and d are too broken to translate, and e has some reference to giving attention. The en as priest may be either male or female. The gudu$_4$ is "anointed," and the term hi-li ("beauty, luxuriance," etc.) seems to be the gleaming condition of being oiled.

Line 177: Edzard takes the opening reference to a "hired man" as parallel to the address to "Enkidu" in the previous line. Alternatively, George translates, "A hired man is hired for his keep, following behind his leader."

Line 181: UnB reads, "they entered before Enlil," and only KiA refers to both deities.

Line 192: As with Enkidu in Penn, the sequence in NiC and NiI includes food, drink, and attention to the body. The "honor" (Edzard) or "proper" treatment (George) would have concrete expression in some "adornment." All of this concludes Enlil's speech. UnB introduces the distribution of auras that ends the narrative.

Lines 193–199: In general, the texts repeat in full the distribution of Huwawa's seven powers to various destinations. Most of the texts that do attest the conclusion of the narrative are nevertheless damaged, with the list obscured and incomplete.

Line 200: In version A, the term me-lam$_2$ ("aura") only occurs in this list, as opposed to the word "terror" (ni$_2$ or ni$_2$-te). The word "aura" appears in texts NiDDD, SiB, UnB, with indirect restoration possible in IsD (line 195, [me-lam$_2$]-ma-ni). Texts NiA and NiTT use the word "terror" (ni$_2$-te) in their concluding statements, and me-lam$_2$ is only restored for the list, so perhaps we should expect ni$_2$-te there as well.

Lines 201–202: In UnB, Edzard restores Nisaba, but it could equally be Huwawa, since this is one of the texts that marks both Huwawa and Enkidu with the divine determinative. Along with SiB, this line could offer Huwawa a hymn, which gives him some cultic status.

Gilgamesh and Huwawa B is only known from five copies, only one of which (Text B) preserves substantial sections of the narrative beyond the opening lines. The lines represented in each copy are as follows:

Text A: 1–18, 49–60, and 123a–133
Text B: 9–15, 24–33, 42–51, 60–66, 73–82, 84–97, 102–109, 123–131, 135–146, 151–156
Text C: 1–14, 45–48
Text MM: 19–26, 61–69
Text W: 132–141

Comparison with parallel lines in version A helps with restoration, although even in these sections, variation may be significant.

1	Supple with oil, lasting offshoot,	B:1–4 // A:130–132, 164–167
2	native son, splendor of the gods,	
3	stout ox, in fighting stance,	
4	young lord Gilgamesh, exalted in Uruk.	
5	"In Uruk, the mind is stricken,	B:5–8 // A:23–26
6	a man is lost, heartache …	
7	I craned my neck over the rampart,	
8	a man was floating on the water, and it caught my eye.	
9	The mind perishes, the heart is stricken.	B:9 cf. A:23
10	Because the limit of life is blocked,	
11	because the grave, the highlands that hold power, spare no one,	
12	because however tall, none can bar the highlands,	
13	because however broad, none can span the highlands,	
		B:13 // A:29
14	because no young man can elude life's end, the limit,	
		B:14 // A:4, 30
15	—by the life of my mother Ninsun, of my father, the pure Lugalbanda,	B:15 // A:89, 92, 137, 141
16	my god Enki, the lord Nudimmud, [inspires my plans].	

(lines 17–19 broken)

20	… to its … I shall complete.
21	… what is felled, I shall bring back."

22	[His servant Enkidu] spoke to him:	B:22–28 // A:8–12
23	"[My king, if] you want to enter [the highlands],	
24	you should inform [Utu],	
25	if you want to enter the [highlands] for felling cedar,	
26	you should inform Utu.	
27	Any scheme in the highlands is Utu's affair,	
28	any scheme in the highlands for felling cedar is valiant Utu's affair."	
29	Utu-of-the-Sky donned his lapis diadem	
30	and came with head held high.	
31	Gilgamesh, lord of Kulaba, grasped the pure staff in his hand, in front of his nose.	B:31 // A:15
32	"Utu, I want to enter the highlands. May you be my ally!	
		B:32–33 // A:17–18
33	I want to enter the highlands for felling cedar. May you be my ally!"	
34	[Utu replied …]:	B:34–37 // A:19–20, 34–36?

(lines 35–41 are broken, begin Utu's words; restore 37–41 from sequence)

37	"[Seven (guides) …]	
38	[The first …]	B:38–44 // A:37–43
39	[the second …]	
40	[the third …]	
41	[the fourth …]	
42	[the fifth …] … could seize …,	
43	[the sixth] would lash the chest like a raging flood.	
44	The seventh would blaze like lightning (that) no man could turn back.	
45	These (beings) shine in the sky, they know the route on earth.	
46	In the sky they shine …, they give light,	
47	on earth, [they know] the road to Aratta,	
48	they know the trails like merchants,	
49	they know the mountain niches like (carrier-)pigeons.	
50	They shall lead you through the hill-country ravines."	
		B:50 // A:45
51	Gilgamesh signaled a muster,	B:51–52 cf. A:48–49
52	in Kulaba he blew the horn.	
53	"(People of the) city: he who has a wife—to your wife! He who has a child—to your child!	B:53–56 cf. A:50–51

54   Seasoned warrior, and unseasoned warrior,
55   he who has no wife, he who has no child,
56   let these ones take their place at my side, in the company of Gilgamesh."
57   The king departed from the city,
58   Gilgamesh departed from Kulaba.
59   Heading in the direction of the highlands for felling cedar,
60   he crossed the first range, his heart did not show him the cedar.

B:60–61 // A:61–62

61   As he was crossing the seventh range, his heart showed him the cedar.
62   Gilgamesh started felling the cedars.   B:62–65 // A:64–66
63   His servant Enkidu made them into logs,
64   and the sons of his city who accompanied him
65   stacked them.
66   At that moment, just as one warrior had drawn close to another,
67   the aura ... assaulted(?) them like a ...
68   ... slept peacefully(?).

(lines 69–73 broken)

74   "You who sleep, you who sleep,   B:74–76 // A:75–77
75   young lord Gilgamesh, how long will you sleep?
76   The highlands have [dimmed], a shadow [has stretched (over them)].
77   ...   B:77 // A:78?
78   Gilgamesh arose, he had been dreaming.   B:78–80 // A: 71–72
79   He shuddered, it was only sleep.
80   He rubbed his eyes, there was empty silence.
81   "By the life of my mother Ninsun, of my father, the pure Lugalbanda,   B:81 // A:89, 92, 137, 141
82   my god [Enki, Nudimmud, inspires my plans.]
83   ...
83a   ...
84   I my[self laid eyes on him(?)], so I am [dist]ressed.

B:84–87 // A:98–102

85   A warrior—his eye is a lion's glare,
86   his chest is a raging flood.
87   None can approach his head, which consumes the canebrake.
88   On his tongue, like that of a man-eating lion, the blood never dries.

89   Against the warrior, there is no strength. Who has it?"

90   His servant Enkidu spoke to him:

91   " . . .

92   . . .

93   By the life of [my mother Ninsun], of my father, [the pure Lugalbanda],

94   your god [Enk]i, [Nudimmud, inspires your plans]:

95   'Warrior, your home in the highlands should be known.

B:95 // A:138

96   For your small feet, let [small] sandals be made,

B:96–97 // A:148 text UnC

97   for [your] large feet, [let large] sandals [be made].(' ")

(lines 98–101 broken)

102   . . . he entered:

103   "By the life of my mother Ninsun, of my father, the pure Lugalbanda,

104   my god Enki, Nudimmud, inspires my plans.

105   Warrior, your home in the highlands should be known.

B:105–106 // A:138, 148 texts UnC, UnD

106   For your small feet, let small sandals be made,

107   for your large [feet], let large sandals be made.

(lines 108–122 broken; see note for 114–122)

122a   stacks in the hill country, they . . .

123   After the seventh aura was gone, (Gilgamesh) attacked (Huwawa's) abode.   B:123–129 cf. A:149–152

124   He struck him on his ear with open hand.

125   (Huwawa) furrowed his brow, he bared his teeth.

126   Like a captive wild bull, he tied a halter on him,

127   like a captive warrior, he bound his elbows.

128   The warrior began to weep, turning pale,

129   Huwawa began to weep, turning pale.

130   "Warrior, you have played me false, you planned to strike me with your hand, even as you swore an oath.

131   By the life of your mother Ninsun, of your father, the pure Lugalbanda,

132   [your] god [Enki], Nudimmud, inspires your plans.

133   [Like a captive wild bull], you have tied a halter on me,

134   [like a captive warrior], you have [bound] my elbows."

135   [At that moment], Gilgamesh, native son—[he] pitied him.

B:135 // A:159

136   He spoke to his servant Enkidu:

137   "Indeed, let us set the warrior free!   B:137–138 cf. A:161–162

138   Let him be our guide, let him be our guide who scouts out the
       lay of the road.

138a Let him be my ..., let him carry my pack."

138b ...

139   His servant Enkidu replied:

139a "[One who is tall], yet has no forethought,   B:139a // A:170

139b ... who has no ...

139c ... who has no ...

140   A captive warrior is set free,   B:140–143 // A:174a–b (UnB)

141   a captive lord is restored to the sacred residence,

142   a captive anointed priest is restored to luster,

143   from days gone by, who has seen such?

144   The highland road he will ...,

145   he will confuse the highland trail.

146   We will not [return to the city] of the mothers who bore us."

B:146 // A:174

(lines 147–150 broken)

151   [Huwawa] replied to ...:

152   "My mother who bore me was a hole in the highlands,

153   my father who begat me was a hole in the hill-country.

154   Utu, you made me live by myself in the highlands."

155   Gilgamesh spoke to Huwawa:

156   "Indeed ..."

Lines 1–4: The opening four lines of version B match exactly lines 164–167 of version A in KiA, the one text with explicit reference to Uruk. The first three lines are repeated twice in version A. Huwawa addresses Gilgamesh in these terms when they finally meet, before Gilgamesh tricks him out of his powers (lines 130–132); and Enkidu begins his recommendation that Gilgamesh kill Huwawa with the same words of praise (164–166). The same hymn occurs in Gilgamesh and the Bull of Heaven 91–96. Here in version B, the lines have no narrative context, and they appear to be plucked from the larger Gilgamesh literature to provide an introduction. So far as version B may preserve an earlier and simpler story line, this opening may not have been part of it originally.

Lines 5–8: After the opening hymn, Gilgamesh speaks without introduction, with words that parallel closely his motivating account to Utu of why he wants to go to the highlands for felling cedar (A:23–26). In line 7, one expects gu₂ ("neck") or saĝ ("head") where Edzard reads su? ("body, flesh") from A. Cavigneaux's copy.

Line 6: The verb is lost and does not match that of A:24.

Lines 10–14: All of the five clauses in these lines are nominalized, so that they are subordinate to the statement that will declare Gilgamesh's intent to undertake his dangerous journey. This declaration is largely lost in the broken lines 17–21, but the relationship between the conditions and the result is causal, so we translate "because."

Lines 15–16: The recurrent reference to Enki is restored from line 132, where it is complete. Generally the pair of lines introduce a plan of action, with the verb "to go out, to bring out." Enkidu proposes to trick Huwawa out of his auras (lines 93–94), and Gilgamesh executes the scheme (103–104); Huwawa complains that Gilgamesh has schemed to capture him (131–132). Only in lines 80–81 does this sequence introduce speech that is not yet bound to action, when Gilgamesh is overwhelmed by Huwawa's power and cannot decide what to do.

Lines 20–21: The speech of Gilgamesh that begins in line 5 appears to continue uninterrupted all the way to line 21, before Enkidu gives advice as in version A:8–12. B:20–21 provide the only possible indication of Gilgamesh's plan, and there is little to go on. In version A:9, as in B:23, "entering" refers to those who go into the highlands, not to anything brought back. Version A describes the cutting of timber by the verbs ku₅ ("to cut," 12, 18, 65, 147) and saĝ₃ ("to chop down, strike," 46, 57, 64), with the latter reserved especially for felling trees. "Cutting" is applied to trimming branches (65; cf. 147, with Huwawa's terrors). In version A, the verb šub (B:21) is not associated with harvesting trees; in A:183, it refers to "throwing down" the sack with Huwawa's head.

Lines 34–37: Version A records Gilgamesh's original request for help before he tells Utu why he wants to set out on this adventure. After Gilgamesh proposes a visit to the highlands, Utu shows compassion and offers seven warriors (A:34–36). Something like these lines would appear to occupy B:34–37, though we cannot be sure that the beings are called "warriors." In version B, if Utu replies with direct speech, and the seven guides are introduced with a line similar to A:36, then Utu's introductory words to Gilgamesh would occupy two lines (B:35–36). Based on the precative in line 50, the description of the guides that follows appears to be cast as part of someone's instruction, evidently that of Utu.

Lines 38–44: The seventh guide is described in line 44, with part of a description visible for the sixth in line 43. It is therefore reasonable to conclude that the five preceding lines are also devoted to the guides offered by Utu, as in A:37–43. Given that the descriptions for the sixth and seventh guides in B:43–44 are close to those in A:42–43, it is possible that the first five also match the renderings in version A (so, George).

Lines 45–50: The celestial companions receive more elaboration in B than in A, with only the closing line 50 matching A:45. They appear to be stars, inhabiting the sky with Utu the sun god, and in spite of the fearsome descriptions, the companions serve especially as guides, not as soldiers or even guardians.

Line 47: The reference to Aratta occurs only in version B, and even here, it is linked only to the extensive geographical knowledge of the celestial guides, not to the location of Huwawa and the highlands.

Line 54: "Knowing" (zu) and "not knowing" (nu-zu) most logically refer to experience, rather than personal fame (George) or acquaintance of others (Edzard).

Line 60: Text B repeats the numbers for each range, "so the first range, so the second range," etc. Text A picks up only with the seventh range in line 61, and text MM is too badly damaged for certainty.

Line 67: The simile is uncertain, with šu-gur somehow derived from the verb šu ... gur, "to roll, wrap." George translates "headcloth"; Edzard, "spear." The Pennsylvania Sumerian Dictionary (ePSD) renders the term as "ring; a rolled up mat," neither of which offers a clear application to this line.

Lines 74–76: Version B parallels closely version A:75–77. In version A, Enkidu is the first to arise, rub his eyes, and try to rouse Gilgamesh

(A:71–74). In version B, however, these actions are attributed to Gilgamesh, in a sequence that occurs after Enkidu's speech (see B:78–80).

Line 77: The one text B for version B is broken; it could still match A:78, "the last beams of twilight are passing."

Line 78: The text has "Enkidu arose," but the oath in lines 81–82 indicates that Gilgamesh is speaking, giving voice to his distress, and Enkidu answers in line 90, with the proposal to trick Huwawa into giving up his powers.

Line 84: The traces of this line suggest a match with A:98, where Enkidu declares that his fear of Huwawa is well founded, based on direct sight of him, and Enkidu launches into a description. Here, it is Gilgamesh who describes Huwawa, reversing the roles.

Line 88: The action of the tongue is uncertain, with relation to "blood" or "the dead."

Line 89: The personal capacities of neither Gilgamesh nor Enkidu are in view. Rather, the auras of Huwawa render him invulnerable to physical strength in any form. This unavoidable fact provides the rationale for Enkidu's solution, which draws the only logical conclusion: Huwawa must be stripped of his auras by other means.

Lines 93–94: The formula for Gilgamesh's oath is fixed so that even when Enkidu repeats it, the first person is still used. With the next formula for Enki's participation, however, the text switches to the second person, confirming that Enkidu is giving directions to Gilgamesh.

Lines 96–97: Version B makes no mention of offering sisters in marriage. The only two gifts that are visible in the text here and in the surviving text of B:106–107 appear also in the longer list of gifts in text UnC of version A.

Line 102: It appears that Gilgamesh has just entered Huwawa's presence and is about to speak. The verb begins with the u_3- prefix, which would mark the first in a sequence that leads into Gilgamesh's statement to Huwawa.

Lines 103–104: The pronouns continue to be jumbled in these lines, with "his mother" in the oath (but "my father"), and "your god" with Enki, where it should now be "my." This repeated confusion, including the replacement of Gilgamesh with the mistaken "Enkidu" after Huwawa's assault (line 78), all occurs in the B text, which is the only copy available from lines 73–122.

Lines 114–122: In Edzard's proposed restorations, the broken text describes only the giving of the first "aura" (me-lam$_2$), which is stacked by the accompanying men. The next lines would then list only the second through sixth auras, until the text arrives at the seventh aura in line 123.

Line 122a: This line represents the first visible contribution of text A, which has no counterpart in text B.

Lines 123–129: The development of Huwawa's capture in version A varies considerably from text to text, and version B, attested in both texts A and B, parallels elements of individual version A copies. In version A, however, Huwawa takes offense at Enkidu's role, whereas in version B, the entire exchange ignores Gilgamesh's companion.

Lines 133–134: In both texts A and W, the verbs are written with the common third-person singular dative -ni- instead of indicating the first person.

Line 138: This translation follows text B, which is more complete. Huwawa is seen as a "knowledgeable man" (lu$_2$ zu), recalling the term for seasoned warriors in line 54. Text W attributes to Huwawa some other service (la$_2$, possibly as "to look after").

Lines 138–139: Lines 138a and b, and 139a–c, all come from text W only, which both elaborates Gilgamesh's optimism and offers a direct critique from Enkidu in language similar to version A:170. By itself, text B moves straight from the proposal that Huwawa be their companion to Enkidu's answer, which begins with the comments in line 140.

Line 141: Or translate, "a captive ruling priest is restored to the temple residence." The title "lord" (en) is applied to Gilgamesh twice in version B, as "young lord" in the introductory hymn (line 4) and then as "lord of Kulaba," his city, in line 31. It would be most natural to identify the en in B:141 by the same ruling role rather than as a separate "en-priest." The ĝi₆-par₃ is a residence that suits both the sacred and the political functions of a ruler. Gilgamesh is called "lord" (en) in version A (lines 1, 2, 47, 76, 167), with "king" (lugal) applied especially to the opposition of king/servant (8–9, 95–96, 103). He is also "lord of Kulaba" in A:76.

Line 154: Edzard renders the line as a question: "Are you leaving me all alone with him in the highlands 'to sit'?"

Lines 157 to the end: At the end of his edition, Edzard observes that there are twelve short lines after line 156. In his rendition of the lines for text B, however, he estimates only six lines (157–* 162). None of the other tablets offer a clear picture of the closing section. In any case, it appears that the text leaves little space for Gilgamesh's statement beginning in line 156. If he kills Huwawa, the deed must take place quickly.

INDEXES

The following indexes have been prepared by hand, not generated electronically, in an attempt to offer practical help for readers in tracking particular ideas and references through the manuscript. In the subject index, because major characters such as Gilgamesh, Enkidu, and Huwawa are ubiquitous, we have isolated only some specific themes. The text index applies only to the early second-millennium Gilgamesh material included in our translations, and other references may appear in association with broader categories, such as "Mari texts" or "Atrahasis." Where ideas or texts occur repeatedly, the indexes focus on the most important uses. References to words in the translation notes are only indexed where these are a particular focus, and references to texts only when beyond the immediate context.

SUBJECTS

AKKADIAN AND SUMERIAN WORDS

Translations are provided in parentheses, to provide a partial glossary.

Akkadian

akāsu (to drive away), 133
alākum (to go), 62
amārum (to see), 95
ana šâšim (to him/her), 95, 152
awīlum (gentleman), 19, 41, 91, 114, 132, 171

balāṭum (life), 181
barāqum (to flash like lightning), 164
bērum (double-hour, "mile"), 86
būlum (herd), 10, 20–25, 29, 31, 62

edûm (to know), 34–35, 37, 39–40
ekallum (palace), 148
elēṣu (to rejoice, swell), 132
emēdum (to push), 156
êš (where?), 49
eṭlum (young man), 22, 49, 95, 145–146

habātum (to rob), 22, 145
hābilum (hunter), 45, 181
hadû (to rejoice), 181
harharum (monster), 175
harimtum (harlot), 95, 105
haṣṣinnum (axe), 174
hašāhum (to desire, want), 141

ibrum (comrade), 33, 60, 96, 104, 123–124, 153
inanna (now), 80, 166
ištu (after), 49

karābu (to bless, beseech), 170
kibsu (track, footsteps), 169

le-i-im (to prevail; a bull), 134, 164
letû (to cleave), 166
lullû (unsocialized man), 95

ma-a-AK (uncertain meaning), 26
māhirum (rival, adversary), 142
mālikum (advisor), 33, 59, 95
marhītum (sexual partner), 49
maṣṣārum (guardian), 56, 80
mātum (land), 24
mehrum (match, equal), 142
melemmū (auras), 57
milkum (counsel), 39
mudeat kalâma (knower of all), 38, 40
mutum (man), 132

nakāpum (to gore), 164
nakārum (to change, become different), 59, 157
nammaštûm (beasts), 10, 20–22, 24, 25, 62
namrirū (dazzling beams), 57, 80, 164
naṣārum (to guard), 56
nawûm (to surround), 143
niālu (to lie down), 177
nib'u (underbrush), 174
nišū (people, family), 133

pašārum (to relate, interpret), 64, 157, 160
pašum (axe), 174
paṭrum (sword), 174
pazāru (to steal through), 130
pulhiātum (terrors), 57
puršumum (old man), 164

Sumerian

AUTHOR INDEX

CITATIONS FROM THE TRANSLATED GILGAMESH TEXTS

Schøyen-3	
Fragment 2:3′	60
Fragment 2:4′	55, 57
Nippur	
obv. 1	60, 61
obv. 1–8	60
obv. 3	57
obv. 3–4	80
obv. 9	60, 63
obv. 9–10	77
obv. 11	161
obv. 13	59
obv. 14	57
obv. 15	161
rev. 1′–6′	60
rev. 3′	57
rev. 4′	57, 161
rev. 6′	58
Harmal-1	
obv. 1	61
obv. 3	60
rev. 10	60, 80
rev. 10–17	60
rev. 11	59, 157
rev. 12–16	58
Harmal-2	
obv. 4	60
obv. 14	60
obv. 20	97
rev. 37	57
rev. 42	36, 63
rev. 43	61
rev. 44	82
rev. 46–47	61
rev. 47	61, 177
rev. 47–48	59
rev. 48	60
Ishchali	
obv. 6′	36, 95
obv. 10′	36, 95, 152
obv. 11′	60
obv. 12′	61
obv. 12′–13′	57, 58

obv. 14′	36, 95, 152
obv. 14′–15′	60
obv. 15′	60
obv./edge 15′–17′	79
edge 16′–18′	60
edge 17′	61
edge 18′	78
rev. 19′	39
rev. 19′–22′	47
rev. 23′	36, 60
rev. 26′	56, 80
rev. 29′	61
rev. 30′	56, 80, 176
rev. 31′	30, 57, 80, 166
rev. 32′	61
rev. 34′	80, 176
rev. 35′	57
rev. 35′–39′	80
rev. 37′	61
rev. 38′	97
rev. 39′	36, 176
rev. 40′	36, 95, 153
rev. 40′–43′	60
IM	
obv. 17	61
obv. 18	97
obv. 19	39, 59, 60, 61
obv. 20	56, 80
obv. 20–21	61
obv. 21	61
obv. 27	97
obv. 29	97
Sippar	
I 1′–2′	45
I 3′–4′	45
I 5′–6′	95
I 5′–15′	97
I 7′	49
I 8′	181
I 9′	95, 153
I 10′–11′	62
II 0′–3′	46
II 2′	36
II 5′–9′	103
II 7′	46

PLATES

www.ingramcontent.com/pod-product-compliance
Lightning Source LLC
Chambersburg PA
CBHW020238290326
41929CB00044B/253